John M. Sellinger
Jan. 1938

POPE PIUS THE ELEVENTH

DON ACHILLES RATTI
1879, The Year of Ordination

POPE PIUS THE ELEVENTH

By

PHILIP HUGHES

Nam in primis ea fuit indole, quam
egregie factam dixeris ut ad
imperandum, ita ad parendum

Letter of Pius XI, *Meditantibus Nobis*,
to the General of the Society of Jesus

NEW YORK
SHEED & WARD
MCMXXXVII

NIHIL OBSTAT : ERNESTUS MESSENGER, M.A.
CENSOR DEPUTATUS
IMPRIMATUR : LEONELLUS CAN. EVANS
VIC. GEN.
WESTMONASTERII, DIE 18 OCTOBRIS 1937
PRINTED IN GREAT BRITAIN

EXCMO ET RMO DNO
DNO ARCHIEPISCOPO
WESTMONASTERIENSI

CONTENTS

BIBLIOGRAPHICAL NOTE

THE chief sources for the study of any pontificate are the official documents that bear the pope's name and those issued under his authority by the various Roman Congregations and Commissions. These are all published in the official gazette called *Acta Apostolicæ Sedis*. There is, however, a smaller collection, much more easily handled, the *Actes de S.S. Pie XI*, published by the Maison de la Bonne Presse, 5 rue Bayard, Paris 8°. So far, for the present reign, seven volumes of this collection have appeared.[1] They contain the Latin text, and a French translation, of practically all the papal letters of one kind and another that are of public interest from 1922 to the end of 1931. It is this collection that has been used down to that date. For the later period I have used the texts in the *Acta Apostolicæ Sedis* (noted as *A.A.S.* with roman figures for the year of the issue, and arabic for the number).

The following is a list of the chief books consulted and quoted in the text :—

BEYENS. *Quatre Ans à Rome*, 1921–1926, by the Baron Beyens. Paris, 1934.

CARR. *International Relations since the Peace Treaties*, by E. H. Carr. London, 1937.

CIVIS ROMANUS. *The Pope is King*, by Civis Romanus. London, 1929.

CLIMBS. *Climbs on Alpine Peaks*, by Abate Achille Ratti. London, 1923.

D'ABERNON. *The Eighteenth Decisive Battle of the World*, by Lord D'Abernon. London, 1931.

[1] Tome I.   1 March, 1922—20 Dec., 1923.
,,   II.   8 Jan.—18 Dec., 1924.
,,   III.   24 Jan., 1925—20 Dec., 1926.
,,   IV.   5 Jan., 1927—20 Dec., 1928.
,,   V.   6 Jan.—24 June, 1929.
,,   VI.   15 Aug., 1929—31 Dec., 1930.
,,   VII.   18 Jan.—25 Dec., 1931.

DUDON. *Saint Ignace de Loyola*, by Paul Dudon, S.J. Paris, 1934.

DYBOSKI. *Poland*, by Roman Dyboski. London, 1933.

FÉLIX. *Notre Dame du Cénacle*, by J. Félix, S.J. Paris, 1885.
Translation (same title), by Miss Deak. New York, 1896.

FONTENELLE. *Sa Sainteté Pie XI*, by Mgr. Réné Fontenelle. Paris, 1937.

GALLARATI-SCOTTI. *La Vita di Antonio Fogazzaro*, by Tommaso Gallarati-Scotti. Milan, 1920.

GIANNINI. *I Concordati Postbellici*, by Amadeo Giannini. Milan, 1920.

LONGHAYE. *La Société de Notre-Dame du Cénacle*, by G. Longhaye, S.J. Paris, 1898.

MALVEZZI. *Pio XI nei suoi scritti*, by S. N. Malvezzi, Senatore del Regno. Milan, 1923.

MOLLAT. *La Question Romaine de Pie VI à Pie XI*, by G. Mollat. Paris, 1932.

MOORE. *Peter's City : An Account of the Origin, Development and Solution of the Roman Question*, by Thomas Ewing Moore. London, 1929.

NOVELLI. *Pio XI*, 1857–1922, by Angelo Novelli. Milan, 1923. (Contains 150 illustrations.)

PERNOT. *Le Saint-Siège, l'Eglise Catholique et la Politique mondiale*, by Maurice Pernot. Second Edition, Paris, 1929.

PERROY. *Une grande humble : Marie-Victoire-Thérèse Couderc, Fondatrice du Cénacle* (1805–1885), by Henry Perroy, S.J. Paris, 1928.

PERTINAX. *Le Partage de Rome*, by Pertinax. Tenth Edition, Paris, 1929.

PRATI. *Papes et Cardinaux dans la Rome moderne*, by Carlo Prati. Paris, 1925.

QUERRE. *Les Accords du Latran et le Conflit entre le Saint-Siège et le Gouvernement Fasciste*, by Daniel Querre. Paris, 1932.

RATTI. *Essays in History*, written between the years 1896–1912, by the Rt. Rev. Mgr. Achille Ratti, now His Holiness Pope Pius XI. London, 1934.

RIVET. *La Question Romaine et le Traité du Latran*, by Louis Rivet. Paris, 1931.

SELDES. *The Vatican : Yesterday, To-Day and To-morrow*, by G. Seldes, with Historical Chapters by Geo. London and Ch. Pichon. London, 1934.

SODERINI. *Leo XIII, Italy and France*, by Count Eduardo Soderini; translated by Barbara Barclay Carter, *Lic-ès-Lettres*. London, 1935.

POPE PIUS THE ELEVENTH

CHAPTER I

DON ACHILLES RATTI, 1857–1918 :
SCHOLAR, LIBRARIAN, WRITER

POPE PIUS XI—Ambrose[1] Damian[2] Achilles Ratti—was
born on 31 May, 1857. Desio, where he came into the
world, is a semi-industrial village some ten miles to the
north of Milan, whence the first foot hills of the Alps can
be seen, as from the edge of the great Lombard plain. He
was the fourth of the five children born to his father and
mother—Francesco Ratti and Teresa Galli—and the
youngest boy. The family from which he came—its
pedigree can be easily traced in the baptismal records as far
back as the seventeenth century—was not native to Desio.
Its origins and quiet history are linked with the district of
the Alta Brianza, and particularly with the little town of
Rogeno that stands roughly midway between Como and
Lecco in the peninsula that separates the two southern arms
of the beautiful Lake of Como—*Quel ramo del lago di
Como, che volge a mezzogiorno, tra due catene non interrotte
di monti*,[3] it is the countryside, immortal now, of Manzoni's
great romance.

Here for centuries the Ratti lived, simple *contadini*, so
the registers describe them, plain, honest peasantry as
sundry photographs of the older generation bear witness.
From the time when, little by little, the silk industry took
root in the district the name Ratti begins to be found con-

---

[1] The name of his paternal grandfather.
[2] The name of his father's eldest brother, Don Damiano Ratti, Provost of Asso
in the Alta Brianza.
[3] *I Promessi Sposi*, ch. i.

nected with it, but still in a simple humble way, different members of the clan being noted in the registers as weavers. Now and again one of them is more successful than his fellows and some act of benevolence to a local charity attests the good use of his modest fortune.

The pope's father was such a one whom the new industry had claimed. He was born in 1823, at Rogeno, and it was not until his marriage, in 1851, that he came to Desio, to take up an appointment as manager of the little silk mill there, owned by the brothers Conti. Ten years later he had moved to Carugate, the Conti having gone out of business.[1]

The association of the Ratti with Desio was then but temporary, and the honour that one of the little town's children should reach to the highest of human distinctions as it were an accident. The pope, whose lot it would be to guide the Church through the most critical years Europe has known for five hundred years, has something appropriately modern in this circumstance of a birth detached from all the natural good fortune that is commonly bound up with the fact of birth and education in circumstances long traditional to the family.

The family in which the pope grew up was not, then, noble nor was it rich. It would be much indeed to say that it was in easy circumstances. We know that to keep his four boys at school at the same time taxed severely all the father's resources and the mother's administrative skill.

The child was baptised, the day after he was born, in the great church which is Desio's one claim to any notice beyond what comes to the score of similar villages in the region. When he was old enough he went, as a little child, to the town's one school, where in these days before governments had begun to think of education as among the duties of a state, a Milanese priest, assisted financially by the local Congregazione di Carita, taught, during forty-three years, for the love of God, the elements of their religion and their

[1] The pope's father died in 1881, the mother lived to see her son Visitor Apostolic to Poland. She died 29 September, 1918.

culture to whatever children he could persuade to come to him. The name of this first instructor of one who was to be himself a teacher of note, and in his supreme office ever the teacher before all else, ought not to be forgotten, Don Giuseppe Volontieri. He lived to see Achilles Ratti ordained and one of the staff of the great theological seminary of Milan, and it was this pupil who, at the old priest's funeral, before a great crowd that filled the town square, spoke the town's gratitude and love for a life spent in its service.

Achilles Ratti showed very early in life something of an inclination towards the service of the Church. His father's eldest brother was a priest, a well-known priest indeed of the great archdiocese, and it was no doubt by his advice and with his assistance that the nephew, in 1867, entered the preparatory seminary of St. Peter Martyr.

Of his life for the next twelve years little remains recorded save the somewhat monotonous tale of an exemplary student, who made all possible use of quite unusual gifts of memory and intelligence. A gravity and practical judgment beyond his years seems always to have distinguished him. Patient, calm, reflective, decided, " my youthful sage," as the Archbishop of Milan of those days said smilingly of him, once he came to know him. " The new pope is not like an Italian at all," a scrittore of the Vatican Library said to me a day or two after the election, " he is more like you serious English." " Wonderfully balanced," said an American cardinal.

It was through his uncle, Don Damiano Ratti, Provost of Asso, that the young ecclesiastic came to be known personally to his archbishop. The diocese of Milan counts to-day almost three million Catholics and well over two thousand secular priests. No bishop could hope to know personally every one of these and in addition every candidate for orders in his different colleges. To be the nephew of the Provost of Asso was a considerable recommendation. For this uncle was one of the best-known priests in the province. He was one of those shrewd kindly men in whom practical judgment seems intuitive, a born director of souls and a skilful administrator of the temporalities. In those difficult years when, throughout Italy, it was not always easy to reconcile love of country and zeal for religion, it fell to Don Damiano Ratti to occupy the delicate post of Royal Administrator of vacant benefices. Here he had to satisfy two masters, the new Italian state and his bishop. It was one of those rare appointments that give general satisfaction, and the government decorated the Provost of Asso with a knighthood.

His home at Asso, in the midst of the lovely sub-alpine scenery of the mountainous mass that divides the two arms of the Lake of Como and ends in the promontory of Bellagio, was open to all the young clerics of the district during the long holidays, and here for years the nephew spent weeks and months at a time. One year, convalescence after a long illness brought to Asso the Archbishop of Milan, Mgr. Nazari di Calabiana, and the young cleric met in his bishop his first—and truly appreciative—patron.

So with all the peaceful uneventfulness of a really happy life the years of boyhood and adolescence went by, and the first signs of an ecclesiastical vocation were succeeded by a more and more serious resolve. After his humanities Achilles Ratti passed to the seminary properly so-called, in 1876, read three years of theology, and then, after some time in the preparatory seminary where he taught Latin and arithmetic, the archbishop decided to send him to the newly reopened College of the Lombards in Rome. It is interesting to know that he showed a marked ability in mathematics, so much so that the first determination had been to send him to Turin to read for a degree in mathematics rather than to Rome for theology and canon law.

It was in October 1879 that he went into residence—just two months after the publication of the ever-memorable letter *Aeterni Patris* by which the newly elected pope, Leo XIII, gave orders for the restoration of the philosophy of the schools to its ancient place in seminaries and universities. It is not without interest thus to recall that the pope whose great encyclical on St. Thomas Aquinas (*Studiorum Ducem* of 4 August, 1923) is in a sense the complement of the *Aeterni Patris* knew by the personal experience of his own early student days in Rome all the enthusiasm of those first tentative steps in the work of restoration, and knew also the mutterings and the deprecating head shakings of the defeated party.

Don Achilles Ratti remained as a student in Rome for three years. Two months after his arrival he was ordained priest, on 20 December, 1879, and the following day he said his first mass in the church of San Carlo in the Corso, the great Lombard centre of Rome where is preserved the heart of St. Charles Borromeo. During these three years he studied canon law at the Gregorian University under such eminent canonists as Father Wernz, S.J.—later to be a famous general of his order.

He took his degree of doctor in 1882, and in the same year gained a doctorate of theology from the University of the Sapienza, and a degree in philosophy from the newly-founded Academy of St. Thomas Aquinas. Among the examiners for this last degree was the Jesuit Liberatore, one of the greatest figures among the pioneers of the movement to restore scholasticism. So brilliant was the young priest's performance before the board of examiners that Liberatore brought it to the notice of Leo XIII, and on the eve of his leaving Rome presented Don Ratti to the pope to receive his personal congratulations and the strongest of all possible motives to persevere in the good work begun.

So the pope of one age meets, without knowing it, blesses, encourages and sets in the appointed way, the pope of the next age. It is a subject that lends itself to a meditation not wholly sentimental this meeting of Leo XIII and Pius XI, popes so different in origin, in personality, in their careers, and yet as popes showing such a resemblance in the tremendous evidence of their moral and intellectual power, in their bold re-examination of the very foundations of the world's life, in the simple means by which they plan to reach their end. *Abyssus abyssum invocat*, the pope of

Aeterni Patris and *Rerum Novarum* to the pope of *Studiorum Ducem* and *Quadragesimo Anno*, the pope formed in the Europe of Chateaubriand, de Maistre and Montalembert to the pope whose business has lain with Mussolini, Hitler, Stalin.

The young priest's stay in Rome was at an end, nor did he see Rome again for seventeen years. He returned to Milan, to teach the young clerics in the seminary the art of preaching—Sacred Eloquence in the official terminology—and a special course of dogmatic theology. He was just twenty-five years of age, and for six years the quiet round of classroom, study, and seminary chapel were all his life. Those whom he taught recall that for the matter of his lectures on preaching he went to the great ecclesiastical writers and orators of the early Church, St. Ambrose, St. John Chrysostom, St. Augustine ; that it was the matter rather than the manner that most concerned him, that the artist in him gave way to the scholar—which, given his years and his inevitable lack of experience in the practice of what he was teaching, shows him, thus early in his career, exercising a practical wisdom in making the best of a difficult post. It shows too how, from the very beginning of his life, nothing short of the sources themselves satisfied the need of his mind. There is no question of manuals or of anthologies. The young, almost youthful, lecturer in his very first task bases his work on the primary sources.

All through these six years he continued to read steadily and to perfect his acquaintance with the chief modern languages. Then, in 1888, his opportunity came. One of the doctors of the Ambrosian Library died, and, invited by the prefect himself, no less a person than Antonio Ceriani, Don Ratti applied for the vacant position. He was accepted.

The great libraries of the world, the Vatican, the Bibliothèque Nationale, the Bodleian, the British Museum, are to the world of scholarship what the great laboratories are to the world of science. Here are to be found all the relevant printed books in which are stored the known conclusions of past ages, and those manuscripts of whose contents, despite the labours of centuries, we are yet very imperfectly instructed, and also there are to be found some of the inhabitants of that world of learning who only live to increase the store of human knowledge. A lifetime's labour, in daily attendance at the holy place, has given to each of these his own special competence. Each knows, as from a well-thumbed map and hours and weeks of tramping every road and every bypath, every hill and hedge and stream, every peculiar specimen of fauna and flora his own province holds. The different works and their relative importance; the various editions; the critical value of their editor's work; the ancient handwriting; the materials which carry it; the inks used and the significance of all these in establishing the authenticity of the text; the places where exactly ascertained knowledge ceases and where instructed conjecture takes its place; the likely sources of future knowledge; the cul-de-sacs in whose exploration time, as regards a particular problem, has been wasted, and will be wasted yet again and again; such is the lore that makes up the competence of the *érudit*. And for the understanding of texts, for their preliminary reconstruction and correction, what a world of scientific general knowledge is called into play, something of history, something of law, something of philosophy, of theology, a mastery of the classical languages, a working acquaintance with the chief of the modern tongues, a familiarity with all the great works of both, Homer, Thucydides, Cicero, Vergil, St. Augustine, St. Cyril, Dante, Shakespeare, Descartes, Cervantes, Goethe, at any moment it is the chance reminiscence of something once scientifically absorbed that flashes the needed illumination.

To the life of the library then the student goes, his preparatory studies and university apprenticeship at an end. Here from the professionals of the world of scholarship he will receive his final formation, from their conversation, their example, their correction, from the encouraging spectacle of the survival of their zeal, despite the difficulty of the work, the general ignorance of its importance, the habitual neglect from those who should support it and for whom it is ultimately done.   Nowhere in this world is there seen a greater charity, longanimity, mildness and faith than in the welcome these veterans of learning give to the newest recruit, in their interest in his work, in the generosity with which time and again their own is put aside to save him the mistakes that have once cost them so much.   They are indeed a great company " which no man can number, of all nations, and tribes, and peoples, and tongues," thanks to whom the dim and dusty airless halls which are their haunt become, very truly, " a permanent congress of learning, which offers to the scholar the inestimable opportunity, that no congress properly so called can give, of the greatest possible facility of mutual knowledge, of exchange of ideas, and of mutual aid."   The quotation is from Achilles Ratti himself, describing, years before he came to rule it, that Vatican Library which is one of the greatest of them all.[1]

This conception of the functions of a library is modern and in origin is Italian.   The first library of this kind was in fact that Ambrosian Library of Milan to a post in which, at the age of thirty-one, Don Achilles Ratti had been appointed, and it was so by the express intention of the great archbishop who was its founder, Cardinal Federigo Borromeo.   " We have now to meet a personage," says the author of *I Promessi Sposi*—as his narrative approaches the moment where the cardinal appears—" whose name and whose memory, in whatsoever time they come before a man's mind, be that man who he may, refresh and recreate it with a moment of peace and reverence, with a happy feeling of sympathy.   For so rare a personage we must at all costs spare a few words."

There follows that description of the library and its founder which, better than any other, conveys not only the

---

[1] *Di una edizione critica dei diplomi pontifici fino ad Innocenzo III*, Milano, Cogliati, 1903.

letter of what Cardinal Federigo accomplished but its very spirit. No description certainly would be more suitable— but that it is so full—for any sketch of the career of the particular librarian of the Ambrosian who is the subject of this book. For while Achilles Ratti is not the least among its many doctors, and this by reason of what he achieved in his twenty-five years there, no writer after Dante has, self-confessedly, had a greater influence on his thought and his very style than Alessandro Manzoni.

The cardinal was a young cousin of St. Charles Borromeo. His youth was formed by his uncle and then by St. Philip Neri, St. Robert Bellarmine and Baronius. Sixtus V created him cardinal at the age of twenty-three and Clement VIII, when he was barely thirty, forced on to his reluctant shoulders the see of Milan. For nearly forty years he showed himself the model bishop, as preacher, writer, founder of schools, ecclesiastical reformer, and defender of the Church against the continual encroachment of the Spanish kings' viceroys, in a saintly personal life, and in a charity to the poor that knew no limits. The plague of 1627–1628 found him, like his cousin fifty years earlier, at the personal service of its wretched victims, and more than two thousand of the poor were fed daily in his palace. In Manzoni's pages he lives immortally, those wonderful chapters in which the robber nobleman, the mysterious *Innominato* comes to the cardinal to relieve his soul, and where the cardinal infuses something of his own serene courage into the fear-stricken soul of the hapless Don Abbondio.

" The cardinal," says Manzoni,[1] " was one of those men, rare in any age, who bring to the great works they under- take a truly superior mind, the resources of vast wealth, the advantages of privileged rank, and an unchangeable purpose in the search and pursuit of the better things." To the library he founded he made over his own valuable collec- tion. He housed it well and endowed it liberally. More, he despatched eight chosen scholars to scour the world in a

[1] *I Promessi Sposi*, ch. xxii.

search for further books and manuscripts. Not Italy alone, nor France, Spain and Germany but Greece, too, the Levant, and as far as Jerusalem saw and welcomed this learned expedition. "Real conquerors' voyages they were," says the future pope,[1] "the signs and trophies of which were the bales of printed books and manuscripts sent home from time to time." To the wonder, almost to the scandal, of contemporaries the new library was open to all. There was paper provided for the student to write his notes on, ink too and pens. "The room is not blocked with desks to which the books are tied after the fashion of the libraries common in monasteries," wrote another admiring visitor,[2] "but is surrounded with lofty shelves on which the books are sorted according to size." Such were the origins of the first public library to be opened to all without distinction.

To the college of administrators the cardinal added a college of doctors, and for their *rôle* in his foundation we cannot do better than quote Don Achilles Ratti himself.[3] "The Doctors, under the direction of their Prefect, are charged with the care of the books and the manuscripts and the duty of waiting on the learned clientèle who make use of them. They keep in close contact with the world of savants. They apply themselves to the study of the treasures committed to their care, each one making some subject his speciality as the founder's device bids them *Singuli Singula*. The Doctors should also, from time to time, publish the results of their study, and to assist them the library was equipped from the beginning with a polyglot press." This was indeed one of the most striking features of Cardinal Federigo's foundation, the establishment of a printing press, with types for the different oriental languages.

In 1910 the Ambrosian Library, it was reckoned, contained some 8,600 manuscripts and over 200,000 printed books. There was also the picture gallery, the Settala

---

[1] MGR. ACHILLE RATTI in *Mélanges offerts à M. Emile Chatelain par ses élèves et ses amis*, Paris, 1910.

[2] Quoted in *Catholic Encyclopædia*, I, 393.

[3] In his *Guide to the Ambrosian Library*, Milan, 1907.

Museum, the collection of medals and the prints. The whole foundation forms one of the most imposing and important centres of European culture.

The success of these great centres of study is largely bound up with the personality of those who direct them. It is, very often, the character of the librarian that makes all the difference, whether to the novice who is making his first difficult steps in this business of erudition or to the more experienced scholar faced with problems of a practical order. Hundreds of scholars, from all over the world, came to know Don Achilles Ratti in the course of the thirty years he spent at the Ambrosiana and the Vatican. Since his elevation to the papal throne many of them have in books, magazine articles, and letters to the press, revived their memories of the librarian. Here again, as in the records of his one-time pupils of the Milan seminary, the first and most lasting impression is of his habitual kindness, his patience and an unusually courteous manner.

The librarian's special virtue of putting his own intellectual interests second and those of his visitors first he had, one would say, to perfection. One-time colleagues have noted this self-denial as the secret of his equal success, whether in the long years when he was no more than a subordinate or in those fifteen years when he rose, so very rapidly, through one place of authority after another, to the very highest place of all.[1] "If one had occasion to consult him, whether in the days when he was just one of the doctors of the Ambrosian, or when later he was that great library's prefect, or when he ruled in that same office the Vatican Library itself, the experience was always the same. With charm and courtesy he gave exactly the information one desired, concisely, in a few words, but always it was complete and reliable : and this no matter

----

[1] *Cf.* the pope's own words on St. Ignatius Loyola quoted on the title-page of this book.

how complex and varied the details of what one put before him. If one wrote he always found time to reply, and with such a wealth of careful annotation, even in matters that were somewhat recondite, as to excite one's surprise and one's admiration. There was always, about his activity, an innate modesty, the modesty natural to the man of really great learning, who knows how much he knows and therefore how much there is yet to be known." [1]

This is the testimony of a fellow librarian of great distinction, the prefect of the Laurenziana Library which is to Florence what the Vatican is to Rome and the Ambrosian to Milan. Side by side with it we may set the picture of the scholar-librarian as he appeared to one of the learned clientèle who used the Ambrosiana. The citation, if long, is useful as a practical illustration of the kind of work that filled thirty of the forty-two years that lay between Achilles Ratti's ordination and his election as pope, of the kind of work and the varied learning and qualities of mind and will that it called for and developed. Here again it is from Dr. Novelli's admirable volume [2] that the quotation is borrowed.

"It is now some years ago," writes Dr. Giorgio Barini, "since I began the laborious work of those minute researches, palæographical and bibliographical, which should furnish me with the material I needed for the production of the critical edition of *Cantari cavallareschi dei secoli XV e XVI* with which Giosue Carducci had charged me. . . . It is in these little poems that there appear in verse for the first time the feats of the Paladins of France and the stories of Charlemagne's court which were later to be the matter of Briardo's noble and more finished work, and to feed the powerful genius of Ariosto. The work entailed the collation of an incredible number of ancient popular printed books and old manuscripts, the collection of endless series of variants, if the text was ever to be published with any real approach to its original, authentic form."

[1] ENRICO ROSTAGNO, *Dall'Ambrosiana al Vaticano* in *Marzocco*, 12 February, 1922, quoted Novelli, p. 57.
[2] Novelli, pp. 58-59.

The writer then describes his introduction to the great libraries in Milan, and speaks of " la piu lusinghiera cortesia " with which Mgr. Ratti welcomed him. He explains how the number of books and manuscripts he had to consult was too vast for the time at his disposal. It seemed as though, after all, he would have to return to Rome without accomplishing one of the main objects of his journey, namely, the comparison of a codex in the Ambrosian with two fragments, the one of an Oxford MS. the other of a manuscript in the Riccardian Library at Florence. The authorship of a certain poem, *Vanto dei paladini*, had been attributed by Quadro to a certain Giovanni dei Cignardi, and Dr. Barini was relying on the comparison of the Ambrosian MS. with these two others to test the value of this earlier judgment of Quadro.

" Monsignor Achilles Ratti," he continues, " had followed my work with the greatest interest. His knowledge, sure and complete, of the great library where he presided, his wide and really profound literary scholarship, his ability as a palæographer, his unique gift of sympathy, removed more than one embarrassment from my path. He declared himself willing to continue and, to finish for me, any further research. All I need do was to furnish the text to be compared, and an exact statement of what it was I desired to know from the examination of the particular manuscript.

" So, from Rome, I wrote to him. I sent a copy of the verses which had to be compared and a note of the question of date and authorship which had to be settled. Mgr. Ratti's reply, which I guard very jealously, brought the manuscript before my eyes in all its detail. The letter is eloquent testimony to an unusual degree of courtesy and to a degree of interest on the part of one scholar in the work of another that goes far beyond what is usual. The mind of the writer judges with great exactitude, there is certainty and a real depth of palæographical and literary knowledge in the writer. With a few brief words, incisively, but with remarkable completeness, and very rapidly, Mgr. Achilles Ratti gave a minute description of the codex as a whole, marking decisively the places where parts were missing. He picked out every reference that could have any value in determining the date, he noted all such data actually to be met with in the poems, explained their meaning and assessed their value ; he remarked every single feature that might contain a hint as to the author, he drew my attention to critiques and illustrations of medieval writings that had appeared in recent publications ; on other questions he expressed himself with judicious reserve."

Such is the scholar at his best, generosity of disposition equal to the capacity of the intelligence. Such a scholar was Achilles Ratti.

Perhaps no one who has not, at some time, had before him the task of initiating a piece of research in one of these vast depositories can form any real idea of the sudden sense of being stranded in the midst of chaos, of the futility of one's own petty information, confronted now with the vast mass from some as yet unknown part of which the required information is to be digged, the discouragement and even despair which a week of untutored labour there can rouse in the soul. It is here that the generosity the librarian shows is at its greatest, in the patient instruction of ignorance, and, since the ignorant of this class are, inevitably, timid (for to no man is his own ignorance and lack of skill more strikingly evident), it is here that matters supremely the exterior which this benevolence presents to the world. For there are scholars, simple, willing men (as the event proves) whose generosity is hidden behind such a façade of splendid natural impatience with fools, that it would be a hardy man indeed (or one in really desperate need) who would approach them.[1]

We are given another glimpse of Mgr. Ratti at work as a

[1] It was never this writer's fortune to know *in minoribus* Pope Pius XI, the kindness of whose disposition is evident in every line of his strong, resolute face, as it is in all these varied testimonies, but from both his predecessor at the Vaticana, Fr. Franciscus Ehrle, S.J., and his successor Mgr. Giovanni Mercati—both of them since that time created cardinals by this librarian who filled the space between them—he received, during two years of daily attendance, all that a beginner could wish to receive from such distinguished scholars. This would seem an opportune place to mention and to acknowledge it.

doctor of the Ambrosian in the letters he wrote to the prefect when, part of the duties of his office, he was engaged in research work in libraries abroad. Thus in 1891 he was at work in Vienna (where he inspected some of those manuscripts from Bobbio the story of whose dispersal he was one day to tell in a very charming brochure [1]) and at Budapest. Two years later his friendship with an old schoolfellow, who had entered the papal diplomatic service about the same time that Milan had reclaimed Achilles Ratti, resulted in an official visit to Paris. This schoolfellow —Mgr. Radini-Tedeschi—had been named as *ablegate* with the duty of conveying to Paris the cardinal's hat conferred at the recent consistory on Mgr. Bourret, Bishop of Rodez. Don Ratti figured in this diplomatic mission as his friend's secretary. There were the state functions at the Elysée, when the President of the Republic, the unfortunate Sadi Carnot, imposed the hat on the new cardinal and a presentation to the Minister for Education and Worship, Raymond Poincaré. There was also, on Don Ratti's part, a snatched pilgrimage to Lourdes. But at Paris the librarian did not lose his opportunity. His post at Milan, and the letters of introduction he carried, opened to him the most sacred places of the Bibliothèque Nationale, the Mazarin, the Bibliothèque de l'Arsénal and the Bibliothèque Ste. Geneviève.

In 1899 he was in Rome—the first visit since his student days ended seventeen years earlier—and for the best part of two months he was hard at work in the different libraries. He had broken the journey at Florence " where in the Riccardiana, the Laurenziana, and the National Library I did a good deal of useful work." As for the Vatican Library, from the care of which fifteen years still separated him, " The collation of the [Liber] Diurnus is finished, and I have also finished my survey of the inventories and catalogues of the Secret Archives. In the Library I have done even better. I have seen something like a hundred

---

[1] *Le ultime vicende della Biblioteca e dell'Archivio di S. Colombano di Bobbio*, Milan, 1901. HOEPLI, pp. 43 *con una tavola.*

codices. At the moment I am working through the very important correspondence of Cardinal Sirleto. I have also examined, in its entirety, the catalogue of the Vittorio Emmanuele [library]. There they brought me some sixty codices and I have been through about twenty of them. There are some from Milan, from Como, from Pavia, from Aquafredda, thanks to the, well to the raids, of Rancati and Besozzi. The further I go the more I get to like it all."

This was written on 19 November. Nearly three weeks later he was still deep in the work and writes that " The tough bit here is the Secret Archives at the Vatican. For many days now I have had in my hands all the data furnished by whatever inventories and catalogues they possess here. But for some sections there are no catalogues, and, for the most important at least, I have had to lay my hands on the bundles of documents themselves. There are something like sixty boxes full of parchments of every shape and every colour and deriving from every part of the world, a very orgy for the palæographer, a real babel of history. I was very keen to see everything, because, although as far as the *Acta* as such are concerned there is not very much (as in the rest of the Archives), for Milan—both for its civil and its ecclesiastical history—there is very much indeed, and I have already had several of the parchments copied or photographed. For example, I have found, partly here, partly there, six lists that are a little treasure, for all that they are incomplete. There should be twenty-five, with the *names* of all the citizens of Milan qualified to take an oath and who in fact did in 1266 take an oath of fidelity to the Roman Church and to the pope in the presence of the papal legate, the names arranged according to the different parishes. It is really a great pity that, as I hinted, there is only a fragment of it. Even so, there are nearly five metres of parchment with the names, now in three columns, now in four. Whether one's interest is in the names or in the statistics, it is something, and, given the nature of the matter, a good deal more than something. It is true that

Giulini gives a hint of the business, and Il Fiamma also seems to speak of a census made in 1266."

Besides visits to other countries—most of all to Germany, which he came to know really well—Mgr. Ratti twice came to England, thus adding a name to the slender list of popes who, in other times, have known London. His first visit, commemorated now in the Cenacle Convent at Manchester where he stayed, was in 1900. Here he would find himself in a little world that recalled the great city he had left—a convent of the same order of nuns whom, in Milan, he served as chaplain and across the road a Catholic grammar school whose rector, Louis Charles Casartelli,[1] was the child of parents born in that same countryside whence sprang his own family. Alas for the writers who in later days must seek picturesque and personal detail about the early careers of great men ! No one knew that the genial and learned Italian priest would, twenty years later, be Pope Pius XI. No one observed him so carefully that any very distinct recollections remain. He visited, of course, the newly-opened Rylands Library and he visited, thoroughly, in the continental sense, all the city had to show. He saw the poor of the Italian quarter, and preached to them, and, rising well before daybreak, he saw the bustle of the city markets, the then chairman of the Markets Committee of the City Council being a prominent Catholic of the town.[2]

His next visit to England was in 1914, just before the outbreak of the war. This time he came to represent the Vatican Library at the Royal Society's celebration of the seventh centenary of the birth of Roger Bacon. It was at Oxford that the commemoration was held and at the ceremonial dinner at Merton Mgr. Ratti sat at the right hand of the Chancellor, Lord Curzon—one of those chance *rencontres* of personality that tempt comment—and in a Latin speech he described the recent discovery in the Vatican Library of two new manuscripts of the great Franciscan's writings.

[1] Afterwards Bishop of Salford (1903–1925).
[2] The late Sir Daniel McCabe, D.L., K.S.S.

One last special feature of these long years at the Ambrosian Library must at least be mentioned, for it not only shows, yet once again, the wide range of Mgr. Ratti's intellectual interests, but is at the same time an early evidence of his gifts as an administrator, proof, if such were needed, that his genius was ultimately practical rather than speculative. This evidence and proof is the reorganisation of the great library, its picture galleries and museums, a vast task carried to completion in the years 1905–1907. A memorial inscription rightly commemorates this great work and the three artists who were responsible for so much of it. But it was Mgr. Ratti who composed the inscription, as he had planned and directed the work, and his name has no place in it. Nor did he set his name to the admirable *Guide* to the reorganised collection which appeared that same year, 1907, and which is a model of its kind, full of learned information simply conveyed. It is pleasant, however, to remember that the Italian Government, even in those far-off unhappy days of chronic strife between Vatican and Quirinal, did not overlook the great achievement and the doctor of the Ambrosian was honoured with the knight's cross of the Order of St. Maurice.

Mgr. Antonio Ceriani, the prefect of the Ambrosian Library, died in 1907, and it was no surprise [1] when Don Ratti, the pupil, disciple and friend of half a lifetime and the most variously gifted doctor of the whole Ambrosian college, was named to succeed him. Five years later Mgr. Ratti—he had been named Domestic Prelate to Pius X in 1907—received a still more notable promotion when Pope Pius X appointed him vice-prefect of the Vatican Library, an office very largely consultative which did not, for the moment, entail a continuous residence in Rome. Two years later with the outbreak of war, it was thought that the fact of the direction of the great library

---

[1] " With the unanimous consent and the general applause of the world of learning, as at the news of a fortune come to the family." *Archivio Storico Lombardo*, quoted in MALVEZZI, p. 67.

being in the hands of a subject of one of the contending powers might be an embarrassment to the international work of learning, and Fr. Ehrle, S.J., who had governed the Vaticana since 1891, retired. On 1 September, 1914, Mgr. Achilles Ratti took up the succession. He was, at the same time, made a canon of St. Peter's and a protonotary apostolic.

In the three and a half years that was all that his reign at the Vaticana lasted, the new librarian saw to the development of all the works inaugurated by Fr. Ehrle, particularly the great task of cataloguing the manuscripts. Mgr. Ratti's own particular contribution was to begin the preparation of a similar catalogue of the printed matter, of which so far there had never been a catalogue, and he made a great bid to secure for the library the unique collection of Prince Chigi. Here he was not successful and it was some ten years before this finally came to the Vatican, a gift to Mgr. Ratti, now Pope Pius XI, from the new Italian Government.[1] The statistical detail of the work at the Vatican of these years is as follows : Manuscripts ; Catalogues of the codices Vaticana 9852–10300 and 10301–10700, together with the third volume of the collection Urbinati, and volumes 26 to 31 of the series called *Studi e testi*.

The various archbishops who governed the see of Milan during these long years of the pope's " hidden life " were not, by any means, unmindful of his abilities and they made all possible use of Don Ratti in the diocesan administration. Particularly was this the case with Cardinal Andrea Ferrari, whose successor he was himself, for a brief space, one day to be. In the first year after his appointment to Milan, Cardinal Ferrari, in 1895, charged Don Ratti with the important task of negotiating with the municipal authorities the reorganisation of religious teaching in the public schools, after a long period of neglect due to anti-Catholic prejudice. The librarian's prestige as a scholar and his friendship with the personalities of the world of education, no doubt assisted all that his enthusiasm and his tact could

[1] *Cf.* p. 208 *inf.*

effect. In the end he succeeded in obtaining authorisation for the entry into the schools of something like a hundred priests as instructors in religion.

The next year there was new trouble. At the inauguration of the monument to Victor Emmanuel II the Catholic members of the city council had been present. As Victor Emmanuel was the king under whom the Papal States were actually taken from the pope, the church in which his remains were buried was, on that account, still under an interdict and the whole situation between the Holy See and the kingdom of Italy remained, after twenty-five years, as delicate as might be. Some of the clergy of Milan had protested publicly against the action of the Catholic councillors, and now the council in reprisal threatened not to allow any of these priests to teach religion in the public schools. The archbishop once more turned to Don Ratti, and marvellously, considering the way passions ran and the height of feeling the incident had aroused, he managed to secure that the priests remained on the list and that the city council was satisfied. It was again a victory for the personality of a man who was tact itself, patient and, apparently, incapable of saying the wrong word.

From this time onwards, young as he was, Don Ratti was one of the cardinal's intimates. He was to be found on all the various diocesan commissions, he was named Synodal Examiner and Synodal Judge, and Canon of St. Ambrose. So it was that Don Ratti became, and remained for twenty years, a real power in his own diocese, though a power that rarely appeared in its public life.

It was an essential part of the great scheme of Cardinal Federigo Borromeo, that the doctors of the Ambrosian Library should be writers, making known to the general and the learned public the fruits of their life of study. Mgr. Achilles Ratti was, in his own field, an exceptionally prolific writer, and some account must be given of what he accomplished. For all his work is original work, " a real contribution to existing knowledge " to use the trite academic expression, and almost all of it is, for the general educated public, buried out of sight in learned reviews or in the reports of learned societies. This last circumstance is all the more to be regretted in that through all this vast and varied mass of scholarly writing there runs an insistent kindly humour, something that at times recalls a quality rarely associated, by us, with any but our own people, the whimsical touch of the author of *Obiter Dicta* or of Elia himself.

The total output is indeed vast, for all that it does not include a single book properly so-called, and it was written over a period of twenty-three years, 1890-1913. It consists, in the first place—if one may begin with a general survey—of contributions to the reports of the Royal Lombard Institute of Science and Letters, and eleven articles in the *Archivio Storico Lombardo*, besides different scientific reviews done for this same quarterly. There is also the magazine produced, edited, and largely written, by him to celebrate the third centenary of the canonisation of St. Charles Borromeo—" S. Carlo Borromeo e il III Centenario della sua Canonizzazione "—seven articles in the *Giornale Storico della Letteratura Italiana*, and another twenty-one separate publications of all kinds : something like seventy published articles and brochures in all.

For the most part these articles describe, annotate and give a critical judgment on the value and the importance of his own various discoveries in the Ambrosian and the other libraries of Europe. Apart from this—for Mgr. Ratti never scorned to write popularly for readers who were not scholars by profession—the more popular part of this rich output is concerned with the local history of Milan, the local history, that is to say, of one of those cities that for the best part of fifteen hundred years has played a leading part in all the crises of European life. Some of these papers are already known in this country from the translation of them made some years ago,[1] and the report on the famous climb of Monte Rosa has also been translated.[2]

A more or less complete list of all these various productions is printed by Dr. Novelli,[3] Don Silvio Vismara has published a brief description of them all,[4] and Senator Malvezzi has drawn, from these writings, a truly delightful portrait of his friend the one-time librarian in *Pio XI nei suoi Scritti*.[5] We should like, following the useful description of this last work, to give at least some elementary notion of the wide range of the pope's intellectual interests, show something of the justification of those who hailed him at his accession as the most cultured pope since Nicholas V,[6] and appreciate, if only indirectly, the fruits of that skill as palæographer and textual critic of which we have heard. But from the fragmentary nature of this vast work it really defies mere summary treatment.

Two works—not so far mentioned—however, must have a notice apart, the great edition of the *Acta Ecclesiæ Mediolanensis* and the *Missale Ambrosianum Duplex*, the last word —to the world of scholarship—in proof of Achilles Ratti's claim to pre-eminence there.

Everywhere, in all this varied work, one sees the fruit of an instructed curiosity, an active critical spirit, and in drawing the portrait of such another spirit, one of his predecessors at the Vatican Library—a predecessor whose career strongly resembled that of Mgr. Ratti, for he passed from the Vatican to be Nuncio to Poland—the writer, Achilles Ratti, has drawn his own. It is too characteristic a piece of writing not to quote in full. The subject of it is that same Giuseppe Garampi whose great index is known to all who have any acquaintance with the Secret Archives of the Holy See. Mgr. Ratti is reviewing a life

---

[1] *Essays in History, written between the years 1896–1912* by the Rt. Rev. Mgr. ACHILLE RATTI, now His Holiness Pope Pius XI. London, 1934.
[2] *Climbs on Alpine Peaks*, by ABATE ACHILLE RATTI. London, 1923.
[3] *Pio XI*, pp. 50–52.
[4] *L'attivita scientifica del cardinale Ratti*, in *Vita e Pensiero* for October, 921.
[5] Milan 1923 (Fratelli Treves, Editori).
[6] *Cf.* the brilliant opening chapter of MALVEZZI, *op. cit., Pio XI e Nicolo V.*

of Garampi by I. P. Dengen, *Mons. Jos. Garampi in Germania.*[1]

"His intelligence was quick and readily sympathetic, open indeed to every ray of truth, no matter what the source whence it came. He never, apparently, tired of his desire to better the great knowledge he already possessed nor, in the midst of all the negotiations and his complex diplomatic activities, did he cease to be interested in the hunt for books and manuscripts. By word of mouth and in all he wrote, in his confidential letters and in his official reports themselves, he proclaimed incessantly the urgent need to further and to better the intellectual formation of the Italian clergy of his time. This, he declared, was the means, the one and only means, by which they could be made fit to do a priest's work in the changed times in which they were living. With his splendid gifts of mind there went an endowment of heart and will equally precious and no less attractive. He was conscientious and zealous in his duty, no matter what the proof to which he was put. He had the highest possible sentiment of responsibility where authority, and the great interests committed to him, were concerned. As a priest he was a model for all his brethren. Consummate prudence, a most delicate tact, a spirit of patience, of long-suffering even, a love of peace and the means to bring it about, before such a character how can we not be carried away by wholehearted admiration?"

Of these numerous articles we may be allowed to translate the titles at all events. For the *Archivio Storico Lombardo* he wrote, first of all, *A Word or Two About Bombs* (1891). *The Work of Dom Ermete Bonomi of the Cistercian Order* (1895) recalls the immense services to learning of this monk who, during the dispersal of his order in the chaos that followed Napoleon's conquest of Lombardy, "in tempi torbidi e travagliosi, senza strepito e senza pompa, con diligenza per più lustri invariata, con lena instancabile e sempre fresca, accumula e prepara a facili studii dei posteri, tesori inestimabili de erudizione e di

---

[1] The review is in *Archivio Storico Lombardo* (1905), iv, p. 200.

dottrina, continuando in modo degnissimo le più gloriose tradizioni monastiche. Coscienzioso fino allo scrupolo nel riconoscere a ciascuno l'opera sua, quando se no vale ; modesto fino a dirsi non più che dilettante di diplomatica, quando tutti lo stimano professore dottissimo e ne ambiscono l'opera e gli scritti, e se ne valgono ; aperto ai nobili sentimenti dell'amicizia e della gratitudine ; devoto alla sua vocazione, così da sembrargli esiglio il forzato ritorno nel mondo." [1]

The passage is not interesting merely as a slight specimen of Don Ratti's mastery of his mother tongue, but also as yet another unconscious piece of self-portraiture. For a lifetime the monk who is the hero of this article copied and annotated manuscripts, with notes that reveal a wealth of critical ability and exact general learning, thus preserving, through an evil time, and under stupendous difficulties, not only a valuable tradition of scholarly work, but an immensity of facts and valuable documents. For seventy years the very name of this man on whose labours a whole vast edifice of learning was built, had been forgotten. Now Don Ratti, at the price of hard drudgery in a dozen archives, restored his memory and established, scientifically, his claim to the admiration and gratitude of posterity.

There are two papers (in 1895 and 1896) on the great abbey of Chiaravalle itself—where Dom Bonomi once functioned as archivist—in whose church all the kings of Sardinia and Dukes of Savoy lie buried. *A diploma of an archbishop of Milan and an unpublished legend of San Gemolo di Ganna* (1901) is a title that hides an interesting piece of

---

[1] " This monk, in a troubled and turbulent time, without any noise or fuss, with even care through many years, with a vigour that was ever fresh and seemed incapable of fatigue, collected and prepared for the greater facility of later students, treasures of learning that are priceless, continuing in the very best way the most glorious traditions of the monastic life. He was conscientious to the point of scrupulosity in the matter of attributing to its real author the earlier work that at times he had to use. He was so modest that he judged himself to be no more than a dilettante in this work of textual criticism, at a time when the learned world recognised in him one of the most learned professors of the science, envied him his achievement and readily made use of it. To the noble feelings of friendship and of gratitude he was ever open. To his vocation he was so devoted, that his enforced return to the world seemed to him very exile."

historical criticism and a little masterpiece of palæographical reconstruction. Another piece of fine critical analysis, exercised on a minute detail of mediæval history, is to be seen in the three articles on Ariberto, an eleventh-century Archbishop of Milan, *The probable route of Archbishop Ariberto's flight—from an unpublished autograph letter of the Archbishop* (1902) ; *Some more facts about the probable route of Archbishop Ariberto's flight* (1902), (this is Don Ratti's reply to his critics) ; *An original bull of Ariberto, Archbishop of Milan (1040) recently discovered* (1904).

The work published in the *Rendiconti*—" Transactions " we might render the term—of the Lombard Institute of Science and Letters is more varied, and if we regard the chronological order of its matter, it covers the whole field of ecclesiastical history.

For it begins with a description of *An antique Latin Inscription recently discovered at Milan*, a relic of the first century A.D., and the last contribution is Mgr. Ratti's éloge of his immediate predecessor in the Institute, the distinguished neurologist, psychiatrist and penal reformer, Serafino Biffi (1902).

Next are two papers which illustrate the kind of thing a learned archivist's recreation may be. When the ancient church of St. Vincenzo di Galliano, near Cantù, was destroyed, during the Napoleonic Wars, there were discovered in the high altar the little packets of relics placed there, centuries before, by the bishop who consecrated it. These relics were protected by a padding of old paper and the whole enclosed in little parchment envelopes. In later years the relics, which had somehow been sent to the Ambrosian Library, were made over to another church at Cantù. There they still were when Mgr. Ratti inspected them in 1908. With the utmost care he unfolded the thin, rotting paper that wrapped them round and proceeded to decipher, written on it, the names of the saints whose relics it had enclosed. How old that paper was ! The style of the handwriting revealed that it was thirteen hundred years since those names were traced, and also, an interesting detail, that one of the relics had come from the Holy Sepulchre. There remained the parchment envelopes. What had become of them in the course of a century no one knew. Angelo Fumagalli, a one-time librarian, had once seen them and from him there had come down the information that on these parchments there were some verses of Juvenal. The tradition was true. When Mgr. Ratti found the old envelopes—as ultimately he did—he found also that the manuscript of which they were fragments was as old as the turn of the fifth century—older then, these scraps, than any manuscript of Juvenal so far known—and, more remarkable still, the verses were the famous passage where the satirist sets out the ideals of a youth's education.[1]

An almost unknown bishop and council of Milan (1900) deals with the first years of the seventh century, and *The so-called Charlemagne's Book of Homilies and the Book of Homilies of Alano Abbot of Farfa* with the tenth. *Milan in 1266 : from an unpublished original document in the Vatican Archives* (1902) we have seen in preparation already.[2] To that same century belong three studies on the poet Bonvesin de la Riva : *Did Bonvesin de la Riva belong to the third order of the Humiliati or to that of St. Francis ?* (1901) ; *Bonvesin de la Riva and the Gerosolimite Brothers ;* and a review of Biadene's edition of the *Carmina de Mensibus*.[3]

The century of the Avignon papacy is commemorated by *The politico-religious condition of Upper Italy in 1317, as seen in the, unpublished, report of the Apostolic Legates Bertrand della Torre and Bernardo Guy* (1902) ; *The year of Matteo Visconti's excommunication, according to documents in the Secret Archives of the Vatican* (1903) ; and *A manuscript from Prague at Milan with the text of an unpublished life of St. Agnes of Prague* (1896).

One of the most distinguished figures of the next, fifteenth, century is the humanist pope, Pius II. The

---

[1] *The papers of the old basilica of San Vincenzo di Galliano near Cantù* (Series II, vol. XLI, 1908) ; *The remains of an ancient manuscript of Juvenal's Satires* (Series II, vol. XLII, 1909).
[2] *Cf. supra*, p. 16.
[3] In the *Giornale Storico della Letteratura Italiana* (vol. 40, p. 184), 1902.

librarian who would one day be Pius XI discovered no fewer
than forty-two letters of the earlier pope, all relating to the
war of the Neapolitan Succession in 1460–1463, and throwing a new light on most of the personalities concerned in it.
These he first published in the *Rendiconti* (1896) and then,
with a more elaborate commentary, in the *Miscellanea de
studi e documenti*, presented in 1903 at the International
Congress for Historical Studies.

Mgr. Ratti's interest in the century of the Reformation
is represented elsewhere than in the works published by
this learned society.[1] Here, however, we find a study of the
Poems of Carlo Maggi—a poet of the seventeenth century
—from a Roman manuscript (1900) and also—a matter of
more general history—" *The Life of the Lady of Monza*,"
*a sketch by Cardinal Federigo Borromeo with an autograph
letter from the " Lady " to the Cardinal* (1911). This was
really a " find " and Mgr. Ratti's treatment of it deserves
to be disinterred. Readers of the *Promessi Sposi* will recall
Lucy's companion in the prison and the story the nun tells
of her seduction and fall. It is this lady who is the subject
of Cardinal Federigo's " Life." As her bishop, when the
case came before him officially, he had had to act with
severity, and the unfortunate woman passed to a stricter
convent in his episcopal city. There she gave herself so
generously to amending penance that she reached the
heights of sanctity. It was the cardinal himself who was
her master and guide and after her death he planned to
write her life, as part of an anthology of sanctity he had
in contemplation. It is his summary of the proposed
chapters that Mgr. Ratti discovered and published in 1911.
Manzoni knew only a part of the story. He was too merciful
to tell the whole of what he knew, since, knowing only
that, he could not but condemn. Hence a certain reserve.
But suppose Manzoni had known the whole story ?
Suppose he had known of this sketch ? Would he then
have told the whole story ? Would he have altered his

---

[1] The periodical *S. Carlo Borromeo* mentioned already, and the *Acta Ecclesiæ
Mediolanensis*.

tale and added to the chapter where the burning tears of the *Innominato* fall upon the spotless scarlet of the cardinal, another of like kind? Mgr. Ratti raises this interesting literary question and gives his opinion for the affirmative.[1]

A manuscript of Volta at the Ambrosian Library (1901) proves the claims of the great scientist to the authorship of the notes that accompany his description of the pile he invented, against the publisher of the text Configliacchi. *The Resurrection of a Milanese Museum* tells the story of part of Mgr. Ratti's great work of reorganisation at the Ambrosian Library. It will be found in the volume of translations mentioned earlier.[2]

Mgr. Ratti also published, in separate form, in addition to the papers that make up that volume of 300 pages, *The oldest portrait of St. Ambrose* (1897), an argument for the authenticity of the mosaic portrait in the basilica, *The final fate of the Library and Archives of [the abbey of] San Colombano at Bobbio* (1901), *An old portrait of Petrarch at the Ambrosian*[3] (1907), *Petrarch's Copy of Vergil, now in the Ambrosian Library* (1904),[4] *The Life of Bonacossa da Beccaloe and a spiritual letter of Bianca Visconti di Savoia, An unpublished opusculum of Cardinal Baronius with twelve of his letters and other documents* (1910), *Some rediscovered fragments of an old Bobbio manuscript,*[5] *A contribution to the history of Milanese handwriting,* and *An autograph letter of La Morosina to Pietro Bembo.*[6] *A night excursion to Vesuvius* (Milan 1901) describes a climb made in order to see the dawn of the twentieth century from that spot.

---

[1] "La paterna verecondia e pieta sua verso la sciagurata creatura se ne sarebbero, chi sa in quale squisita e maravigliosa maniera, avvantaggiate; ed invece del breve, asciutto allinea del penultimo capo dei *Promessi Sposi*, soddisfacendo un'altra volta da pari suo alle piu squisite e difficili esigenze dell'arte, ci avrebbe dato tal pagina da stare degnamente allato a quella in cui vediamo le lagrime ardenti dell'*Innominato* cadere sulla porpora incontaminata di Federico."

[2] *Essays in History*, by Mgr. ACHILLE RATTI. *Cf.* p. 22.

[3] Two other studies that concern Petrarch must be noted : (1) *A supposed autograph of Petrarch in the Ambrosian* (*Archivio Storico Lombardo*, Series IV, vol. II) ; (2) *Another new portrait of Petrarch* (in the *Rassegna d'Arte*, Anno VII, n. 1).

[4] In *Miscellanea "Petrarcha e la Lombardia,"* Milan, 1904.

[5] In *Miscellanea Ceriani*, 1910.

In *Giornale Storico della Letteratura Italiana*, 1902 (Vol. 40 ,p. 335).

To his doctors of the Ambrosian Cardinal Borromeo gave a simple motto *Singula Singuli*—to each his own special work. Don Achilles Ratti's speciality was the publication in final, definite, critical form of all the decrees and legislation of all the archbishops of Milan from the first mention of the see sixteen hundred years ago to our own time. Such is the subject of the great work which bears his name, the *Acta* of the Church of Milan from its beginnings to our own time.[1]

There have been earlier attempts to order and print this great mass of legal and theological material, the editions of 1582 and 1843. What their value and what their shortcomings the preface of the new edition makes clear.

The greatest figure in all this history is the reforming Archbishop St. Charles Borromeo, archbishop from 1560 to 1584. Everyone knows that he was the nephew of that Pope Pius IV who finally steered to its close the adventurous business of the Council of Trent. The uncle made the young man of twenty-three his Secretary of State, Archbishop of Milan and Cardinal. As soon as he could obtain the pope's leave the youthful archbishop left the Curia for his see and there gave his whole life to translate into act the reforming decrees of the great council. The practical application of the Tridentine law in the scores of regulations enacted in the synods held by St. Charles was, for bishops throughout the world, a model eagerly copied for the next three centuries. It might almost be said that it was through St. Charles' use of them that the decrees of Trent were chiefly known.

It was with the work of St. Charles himself that Don Ratti determined to begin, and in 1890 his first volume (Volume II of the series) appeared—some nine hundred pages of double column, a carefully edited text and an abundance of notes. The next volume appeared in 1892—again nearly eight hundred pages—and a third in 1897,

[1] *Acta Ecclesiæ Mediolanensis ab eius initiis usque ad nostram ætatem.* Opera et studio Presb. Achillis Ratti (Mediolani, ex Typographia Sancti Josephi, MDCCCXC. Mediolani, apud Raphaelem Ferraris editorem MDCCCXCII. Mediolani, ex Typographia Pontificia Sancti Josephi MDCCCXCVII).

five hundred pages only. These last two volumes deal with the laws and decrees subsequent to St. Charles, and thus with the many signs in ecclesiastical legislation of all that long, mute conflict between the successive archbishops and those viceroys who, in the name of the cesaro-papist kings of Spain and emperors, ruled Milan in the seventeenth and eighteenth centuries. The second of Don Ratti's volumes won a special brief of commendation from Leo XIII.

There now remained for study the thousand years and more that stretched between St. Charles and St. Ambrose, *hoc opus, hic labor*. It was not until 1902 that Don Ratti was able to begin the great work of seeking out, collecting, deciphering, and critically establishing this immensity of texts. Here all his skill as palæographer and diplomatist— in the scholarly sense—would be called into play, for the material was all of it manuscript, and much of it unstudied and very primitive manuscript. He was still busy on this task that must take a lifetime to complete when he became, first of all, Prefect of the Library and then Prefect of the Vaticana. Some day some other doctor of the Ambrosian will complete what Pius XI began, and he will find in the Ambrosiana, carefully preserved, a mass of well-ordered documentation to assist him, the unpublished researches of Don Achilles Ratti.

" And now let the reader think a little, what a preparation for the high office of a bishop all this was—were his see the greatest in all the world—to have been the student who had transcribed, annotated, and corrected word by word in proof, such an enormous mass of the very documents that throw light on the episcopal office and must serve it as a guide. This is truly a case where we can say that the librarian, editing his texts, taught himself to be a bishop, and where critical scholarship was an apprenticeship to high command. Leibniz, whose kingly mind bent itself to collect documents of the Middle Ages, declared that history was of the highest value as a training for administration. Certainly we may be allowed to say that an ' archive-breaker ' can foresee and, what matters more, can provide for the future better than any facile and brilliant amateur." [1]

There is a second *œuvre de longue haleine* on which the name of Achilles Ratti appears. This is the *Missale Ambrosianum Duplex* (*Proprium de Tempore*),[2] and for this the prefect does, for a work of his great predecessor, the office of scholarly charity which another must one day do for his own work on the *Acta*. We have here a critical edition of the Ambrosian Missal with a wealth of notes bearing on every possible connected topic, the liturgy, theology, canon law, the language of the text, the history of the missal, its manuscripts and their writers, literary notes, philological notes—a very encyclopædia of learning. Mgr. Ratti's preface is a touching memorial of the great scholar who was to him, truly, a second father, and he pictures Ceriani looking smilingly on the completion of his work and blessing the sons whose piety has brought it about.

One of the many gaps in this study of Pius XI occurs here where there should be something like an adequate sketch, at least a sketch, of Ceriani, who was perhaps, humanly speaking, the major influence in the future pope's ultimate formation. Of the real love this great orientalist inspired in all who knew him, whether his scholarly colleagues, or the employees of the library, or the ragamuffins of Milan to whom, in his leisure, he taught the " dottrinetta " we have more than proof, in the annual pilgrimage to his grave in distant Uboldo. And of that great figure, whose dryly humorous, somewhat impatient, testy, intellectual countenance still interrogates from his bust the worker in the Ambrosiana, Don Ratti has left a sketch that regard for his own piety compels one to quote. It is to be found in his address at the unveiling of the memorial to Ceriani in the Ambrosian Library.

---

[1] MALVEZZI, *Pio XI nei suoi Scritti*, p. 87.
[2] *Editt. Puteobonelliane et Typice* (*1751–1902*) *Cum critico commentario continuo ex manuscriptis schedis Ant. M. Ceriani.* Ediderunt A. Ratti Ambr. Præfectus M. Magistretti Can. Ord. Eccl. Mediol. (Mediolani, Typis R. Ghirlandi A.D. MCMXIII).

"Mi pare de rivederlo, come tante volte in quasi vent'anni di vita convissuta, ritto in piedi dietro a quel tavolo ormai famoso come lui, la persona leggermente incurvata non tanto dagli anni quanto dall'abito di un lavoro assiduo, faticoso e paziente, un libro in mano, proprio quella sua mano assuta e robusta di vero lavoratore, la zimarra (sol per brevissima stagione da lui dimessa), scendente con bella negligenza dalle ampie e valide spalle, la canizie balzante in cespugli vivaci di sotto la modesta berretta a incorniciare d'argento quella vasta e bella fronte, quel viso in tutti i suoi tratti cosi fine e vigoroso, cosi buono ed arguto, dallo sguardo semplice e profondo, dal labbro casto ed energico. . . . Oh! 'la cara e buona imagine paterna . . .' " [1]

[1] "I seem still to see him as, in those twenty years we lived together, I saw him so often, standing, erect, behind that table henceforth as famous as himself, with that slight stoop due not so much to age as to the habit of careful, tiring, patient work. He has a book in his hands, those bony, robust hands of the real worker, his zimarra (never left off except for a very brief time) falling with a fine negligence from his wide, strong shoulders, the bushy white hair thrusting out from beneath his modest biretta, to make a silvery frame for that fine, broad forehead, and that face, every feature of which was finely drawn and vigorous. Oh! the goodness and the penetration. His look, so simple and yet so searching, those lips so pure, so forceful. . . . Oh! 'the dear, good picture of our father'." Quoted in NOVELLI, p. 68.

CHAPTER II

(i) *The Cenacle*

THE diocesan seminary and the Ambrosian Library were not the only fields to provide work for the talent of Don Achilles Ratti. At the same time that the Archbishop of Milan named him to a chair in the seminary he appointed him also to be chaplain to a community of nuns just established in Milan, the Society of Our Lady of the Cenacle. This post he continued to occupy as long as he remained in Milan, for thirty years all but a few months. This introduction to the work of the Cenacle was to have an importance all its own in the formation of the future pope.

The origins of " the Cenacle " go back to that heroic generation of French Catholicism which had to rebuild, in the early years of the nineteenth century, all that the years of the great Revolution had destroyed and wasted. The first founder was a contemporary of the Curé of Ars, a priest of the diocese of Viviers who bore the name of John Peter Stephen Terme. He was, in the 1820's, one of a small community of secular priests to whom had been made over the task of restoring religious observance in the wild, mountainous country of the Ardêche. These priests lived at La Louvesc, a tiny hamlet that crowned the highest summit of the region, 4,000 feet above sea level, difficult of access truly and, in winter, so forbidding in the isolation of its almost perpetual snow that few would live there from choice.

La Louvesc was, however, the religious centre of these mountains, for it contained the shrine of the great Jesuit, St. John Francis Regis, who in the early seventeenth century had, by an apostolate of fervent preaching and heroic personal sanctity, won back the people from Calvinism. This Abbé Terme who was to found the Cenacle was in many ways very like to the saint who was the patron of all his efforts. " I shall be satisfied with just this one thing," he once wrote, " I only ask to finish the work to which God has set me, without even trying to find out what that work may be."

He began by organising a tiny congregation of women to teach in the little schools he had founded in the different mountain villages. In 1825 he was preaching at Sablière and in the congregation there he discovered the ideal novice, in the person of Marie Victoire Thérèse Couderc. She was one of the twelve children of the most prosperous farmer of the neighbourhood, nineteen years old, *petite*, shrewd, with a lively wit and with a natural resolution and power of endurance remarkable even among the peasants of that hard countryside. Within twelve months her father's opposition had yielded and Mlle. Couderc was one of the Abbé Terme's teaching sisters.

A new inspiration now came to him. One effect of the revival of religion brought about by the activities of this band of missionaries was a new influx of pilgrims to the shrine at La Louvesc, a renewal of the great days before 1789. The accommodation of the few inns began to be overtaxed. As always, along with the pilgrims of purely spiritual intention there went others for whom the occasion was partly pilgrimage and partly picnic, and others still for whom it was wholly a jaunt. Soon there were unpleasant tales, and even scandal, reported from the overcrowded inns. M. Terme won his bishop's sanction to a plan of building some kind of hospice for the women pilgrims. He would put the nuns in charge of it.

With great difficulty the hospice was built, and immediately the pilgrims flocked to it. No doubt it was, what such convent hospitality remains, so inexpensive as to be irresistibly attractive. The food would be as good as one got in the inn, the lodging be very much cleaner. In no time the inevitable happened. All the women pilgrims were lodged in the convent, or rather they had turned the convent into an inn. When beds and rooms ran out they lay on straw in the hallways and corridors. They were peasants, the most of them rough and coarse. It was impossible to keep even the beginnings of order with them. From morning to night it was *kermesse*, with the nuns in attendance to provide food and lodging.

Then came to Mother Thérèse the inspiration, whence was to develop the special *rôle* of the Cenacle among the many new religious orders, " only to lodge those who are willing to make a novena or a triduum in honour of St. Regis." The women had come on pilgrimage, what more reasonable than this suggestion that the time be spent in prayer ?

Abbé Terme was, of course, immediately enthusiastic, and then, a short time afterwards, returning from a visit to the Jesuits at Vals near Le Puy, where he had gone to follow the Spiritual Exercises, he made the proposal which completed the new idea of Mother Thérèse, and really made the Cenacle. These novenas or triduums which the pilgrims would make in the hospice at La Louvesc should be made after the manner of the Spiritual Exercises of St. Ignatius, and to give these exercises should be the chief occupation of the nuns. " This work is our principal, our essential work " he was later to set down in the first draft of the little society's rule.

These Spiritual Exercises with which, at the age of thirty-eight, Abbé Terme was in 1829 making his first acquaintance, are more familiar to-day than they were a hundred years ago, for they are the peculiar possession of the Society of Jesus and in 1829 the Jesuits, restored a matter of fifteen years before, were only just coming to life again after the half century or so of their suppression. Nevertheless, since they are at the very heart of the Society of the Cenacle, since the main object of this Society is " for *each* of its members . . . to exert herself with all her strength for the salvation and perfection of her neighbour by the giving of Spiritual Retreats," and since we are now about to consider the close co-operation of Don Achilles Ratti in this work through a period of thirty years, to recall something of what the Exercises are will help our understanding of the pope to be.

The *Spiritual Exercises* is the name of a book written by St. Ignatius Loyola, the founder of the Society of Jesus. It is not by any means a bulky volume—it would make, perhaps, 120 pages of such a size as this—and its object is extremely practical, namely, to bring whoever uses it to a complete and total surrender of himself to whatever the will of God wills for him. The method by which the book seeks to assist a man to achieve this happy choice is to propose to his consideration, systematically, all the great truths of faith, the leading events in the history of man's relations with God, the principal happenings in the earthly life of Our Lord, and especially of His passion and death. Upon these all the powers of the mind are in turn brought to bear, the imagination, the memory, the reason, that the will may thereby be moved and the choice made.

The book called the *Spiritual Exercises* can be read easily in an afternoon, but even after much more careful reading than this it must still withhold its ultimate secret. The reason is very simple. The Exercises are meant not to be read, or studied, but to be *made*, that is to say, whoever wishes to profit by all they have to give must submit himself to the fullness of their discipline, to the long month of daily exercises, the carefully arranged order of meditations, and other spiritual practices carried out under the guidance of a director experienced in this particular craft which we may call the Ignatian Art.[1] It is for this director's use that the book is really written ; it is the programme he

---

[1] *Cf.* the title of a Spanish commentary on the *Spiritual Exercises* : *Ars Ignatiana animarum ad Deum per Christum adducendarum quæ latet in libro Exercitiorum Spiritualium ; i.e.,* The Ignatian Art of leading souls through Christ to God which lies hidden in the book of the *Spiritual Exercises* : quoted in Morris, S.J., *Meditation : An Instruction for Novices*, Manresa Press, 1889. It should be stated that the Exercises are meant to be adapted by the director to the special needs, and capacity, of the person who makes them. Not all can profit from the full four weeks, and it is left to the director to quarry from the whole, Exercises enough to last for retreats of shorter time.

is to follow. Also it is, to some extent, true to say that the book is but the letter of the Exercises. The spirit that gives life to them is the domestic tradition of the great religious order founded upon them and formed by them through, now, four centuries. For anyone not bred in that tradition to put forth his own description of the Exercises from any mere study of the text would be to risk blunders innumerable. Elementary prudence bids a writer here trust to the specialist, to any one of the many Jesuits who have written explanations of this celebrated method.

The spirituality of St. Ignatius may be resumed in one word, says the able author of the latest life of the saint.[1] It is a doctrine of combat. If man is ever to come to God he must first conquer himself. Now it is the great misfortune of most men that they do not wish to conquer themselves. The Exercises are designed to help a man first of all to a new frame of mind so that he desires that conquest. They help to bring it about, and finally to consolidate the spiritual gain. Man's self is the scene of the war, and the arms offered to him are daily meditation, daily examination of conscience, a habit of penance, frequent confession and frequent reception of Holy Communion. The mind is to be brought into harmony with the mind of the Church, a particular loyalty to the directions of the Roman See in all matters of belief and conduct being not only a safeguard but an essential condition of success.

Retreats are the ideal means to secure that the victory once gained endures—that is to say, the deliberate withdrawal for a time from the ordinary business of life, from friends, from family, to some monastic house, there to exercise oneself during that time according to the method prescribed. The effect of the Exercises, faithfully carried out, is to bring about a great generosity of soul. In this lies the secret of their proverbial effectiveness in converting sinners to a life of goodness and in turning good men into saints. The careful, not to say minute, self-examination in God's sight, the resultant self-knowledge, the self-control,

---

[1] *Cf.* Fr. PAUL DUDON, S.J., *Life*, pp. 274–309.

self-denial, self-conquest which is the essence of the system, have this surrender to God as their only end.

It can be readily grasped that the essentially Ignatian thing is a new technique, a new way of organising and using a discipline as old as the Church itself. And to use that technique perfectly calls not only for careful training, and a knowledge of God's ways with man, but for an initial innate capacity to understand human nature itself. Not all men have this by any means, and it is on record that St. Ignatius himself declared he knew only one man who could really " give the Exercises " with all their fullness of profit. For there is nothing automatic in the operation of this method. Like everything else of St. Ignatius' construction, the method called the Exercises is, in its application, flexibility itself, capable of a thousand adaptations to suit the needs and circumstances of the different individuals who are to be helped by means of it.

Whence—to return at last to Abbé Terme fresh from the dazzling revelation of the system's possibilities—great alarm at the notion of nuns " giving the Exercises," an alarm that still persists in quarters less well informed, and an alarm that the nuns were themselves the first to feel. It will be useful here, completing the description of the work of the nuns whom Pope Pius XI served for thirty years as chaplain and whose life was to influence so profoundly his own spiritual development, to quote the Abbé Terme and his co-foundress, Mother Thérèse, describing the first days of the new apostolate.

" Just say to the pilgrims," it is the abbé, stilling the nuns' alarm at his announcement of their new duties, " that if they like, when they have satisfied their devotion at the tomb of St. Regis, and to make use of the free time left over, you will come and do some spiritual reading with them, and you will explain what you read a little, if you see they would like it. For the subjects of your reading you will take by preference the End of Man, the Importance of Salvation, the Fall of the Angels, the Fall of our First Parents, etc. You might then advise them to make one quarter or one half-hour's reflection on these subjects, and without guessing it they will have made a little retreat. . . . "

" They [the pilgrims] accepted gratefully " writes the co-foundress, " and all said they would like to make use of [the offer] adding that they did not know how to meditate. We fastened on that to explain to them that with a little good-will it was no harder to reflect on a truth of religion than on their temporal concerns. Without mentioning the word ' retreat,' so frightened were we of that, we made them follow an order of the day, giving three daily meditations as well as we could to the retreatants, and we gave them a written synopsis, like the one Fr. Terme had brought us. At the same time we showed them passages suited to the subject for reading. The fervour with which they all made their retreat plunged us into amaze. The good country women were especially enchanted with the way in which they had done their ' novena '. . . . When they left the house they did so most regretfully. ' Ah ', they said, ' we shall certainly come back next year ! We are too happy '." [1]

From this moment the little society grew daily closer and closer to the image of the Jesuit order itself. When Abbé Terme—*anima naturaliter Jesuitica*—died, prematurely, in 1834, on the eve of his reception as a Jesuit novice, he left the care of his nuns to the Society. The then Father Provincial " took up the child from the straw." He provided priests to teach the nuns the meaning of the Exercises and the fullness of the Ignatian methods of prayer and other practices of devotion and asceticism. He put others at their disposal for their own spiritual direction and that of the retreatants who came to their houses, and finally it was a French Jesuit who first put into formal, detailed shape the Cenacle rule. " Certainly the Institute of the Retreat is not the only one which . . . has borrowed considerably from that of St. Ignatius . . . but we think no one of them has drawn more largely from it than the Institute of the Retreat," wrote a later father of the Society

[1] In C. C. MARTINDALE, S.J., *Marie Thérèse Couderc*, London, 1921, p. 31.

of Jesus.[1] This is not merely, nor principally, due to the innumerable textual coincidences of the two rules, the model and the derivative, but to the part played in the life of both by the *Spiritual Exercises*. For if to give the Exercises was the very *raison d'être* of the first Jesuits, the same is true of the nuns of the Cenacle.

It was in 1879 that the first Cenacle Convent was founded in Italy, in the Eternal City itself. Two years later a second was founded in Turin and in 1882, through the generosity of three noble ladies, a third in Milan. It was in this very year that Don Achilles Ratti returned to Milan to teach in the seminary, and the archbishop, already impressed with his somewhat precocious maturity, gave him to the newly-established convent as its first chaplain. " This is to be your parish," were his words. The time has perhaps not yet come to tell the detail of that gradual initiation for the young priest into the many-sided activity that centred round the convent of these Ignatian nuns in Milan. When that day comes the story of a remarkable mutual spiritual influence will be made known, something, if one dare say it, parallel in its way to that classic collaboration of St. Francis de Sales and the nuns of the Visitation, an association in which if the priest did much to extend the community's field of apostolate, the nuns' life in its turn did much, in the early years especially, to shape the priest's spiritual development and to fix its direction.

We must for the moment be content to recall something of the pope's day to day work as chaplain and co-worker at the Cenacle. Every morning he said mass for the community and exposed the Blessed Sacrament. Every afternoon at five he gave Benediction. Every Wednesday he took a class in Apologetics and every Thursday a kind of Christian Doctrine class for adults. On the first Sunday of every month there was a Day of Retreat—meditation, intimate sermons or conferences with opportunities for confession and for consultation—for schoolmistresses. Don Ratti was himself the initiator of this particular, good

[1] FELIX, S.J., pp. 72–73.

work at Milan, and during all his thirty years of chaplaincy this was the work nearest his heart. On the second Saturday of the month there was a similar day for Children of Mary, on every third Sunday one for " working " girls and women, and it was Don Ratti who charged himself with these too. He prepared for their first Communion the hundreds of children who, during these years, made their first Communion at the Cenacle ; he preached a general retreat annually at Easter, and he preached the annual novena in preparation for Pentecost. Every year he preached the " month of May," that is to say, a sermon on Our Lady each evening of the month, and every year too he preached in similar fashion all through June, the month of the Sacred Heart. To this must be added sermons unnumbered to the community of nuns, sermons at professions and for the many different events that marked the convent's own domestic history during all those years in which the youthful priest developed into the elderly scholar of European fame.

Many of these sermons remain in the archives of the Cenacle, verbatim reports taken down by some one of the auditory. They are all remarkable for the fund of matter they contain. All have a doctrinal base, nowhere is sentiment allowed to run wild, nor any imaginative development to obscure reality. They were delivered slowly, with leisure almost, one might say, the speaker never unwilling to hesitate while the word was found that expressed his exact shade of meaning, and never unwilling, to that same end, to risk repetition. They are the sermons of a thinker, sermons that provoked thought in all who heard them.

The directions given by Pius XI to the whole Church in this matter of retreats are then, as are so many of his directions, the fruit of long personal experience. " We know directly, from our own experience of such an apostolate," the pope writes to the Superior General of the Cenacle,[1] " that there are no fruits of Christian piety and of Christian

[1] Letter of 9 August, 1935, *La Devota Lettera.*

life that we may not look for from it. We know how many
inner and deep-rooted conversions frequently result from
it. We know how many fruitful inspirations productive of
good have had their origin in some retreat."

Even before his election to the supreme pontificate the
pope had given evidence of his high appreciation of the
Ars Ignatiana in an essay on St. Charles Borromeo and the
Spiritual Exercises [1] written for the magazine *S. Carlo
Borromeo nel III centenario della cannonizzazione*. The
Exercises, says Mgr. Ratti, " are a method which rests on
the finest shades of experience and a marvellous, not to say
miraculous insight into the deepest and most complicated
psychological processes," [2] and again he speaks of the book
as " the wisest and most universal guide in spiritual direction, an inexhaustible spring of deep and solid piety, an
irresistible stimulus and the safest guide to conversion and
to the highest spiritual perfection." [3]

This would be written in 1909–1910, and the priest who
wrote it had then had twenty-seven years and more of
practical experience in the value of the Exercises for all
classes of Catholics. Twelve years later, as Pope Pius XI,
he gave them the highest praise any Catholic work can look
for in the Apostolic Constitution *Summorum Pontificum*,[4]
which names St. Ignatius as the patron of all retreats and
indeed of the whole retreat movement. Here the pope hails
the saint as the first to systematise the practice of retreats
and to organise it. His method has the place of honour [5]
among all those many aids to piety which the centuries have
produced, and in this our own time, afflicted with ills of
every kind chiefly because " there is no one that thinketh
in his heart," [6] nothing could be more profitable than the
foundation everywhere of houses to which Catholics could
retire, whether for a week or for a few days, to make there

---

[1] Translated into English in *Essays in History* by MGR. ACHILLE RATTI,
pp. 163–174.
[2] *Op. cit.*, p. 169.
[3] *Op. cit.*, p. 174.
[4] 25 July, 1922.
[5] Insignem sibi locum vindicant.
[6] Jer. XII, 11.

these *Spiritual Exercises*.[1] The same preference for " these Spiritual Exercises " is set forth more openly still in the Letter of 3 December, 1922,[2] where the pope speaks of them as " this most perfect code of laws, which every good soldier of Christ ought to make use of." Other systems there are, and these deserve praise too, but in the Ignatian system " so wisely are all the parts arranged and ordered, so closely are they knit together, that if only a man will not offer any resistance to grace, the Exercises will renew him as from his very roots, and lead him to give complete and full obedience to God's authority." [2]

A distinguished diplomatist, for many years accredited to the Papal Court, who knew Pius XI well and admired him greatly, has left a delightful sketch of the pope's personality in the last pages of his memoirs. Writing several years after the termination of his mission to Rome, he speaks of an old colleague who calls on him at Brussels with the latest news from Rome. " Il résumait ainsi la situation au Vatican : il n'y a plus qu'un mot dans toutes les bouches, *obedire*, obéir." [3] Obedience is indeed the virtue in which the world instinctively recognises the principal occupation of the Society of Jesus. For thirty years nearly Achilles Ratti obeyed, with that completeness, that simplicity, and that apparent unawareness that any other course is possible, which reveal the ideal product of the Ignatian Art. Like all who have so obeyed, authority, when it came to him to command, has been exercised as thoroughly, with the same completeness and simplicity and the unconscious assumption that perfect obedience attends the command. In the Apostolic Letter to the General of the Jesuits on the tercentenary of the canonisation of St. Ignatius Loyola and St. Francis Xavier, just quoted, the pope stresses the greatness of soul, the high-mindedness, that distinguished the founder of the Society. But whoever

[1] Ut usus horum Exercitiorum Spiritualium latius in dies diffundatur.

[2] Apostolic Letter, *Meditantibus Nobis*, 3 December, 1922, to the Jesuit General on the Tercentenary of the canonisation of St. Ignatius Loyola and St. Francis Xavier.

[3] BARON BEYENS, *Quatre Ans à Rome*, p. 287.

examines more carefully the achievement of that great saint, he continues, will find that there was in Ignatius a most unusual spirit of obedience, so that it seems as though God had assigned to him this as his peculiar *rôle*, namely, that he should bring mankind to greater zeal in the cultivation of obedience.[1] Pregnant words to whoever recalls the state of religion when Ignatius was born at Loyola in 1491, and words that come spontaneously from the very depths of Pius XI's personality, and light up all the ideals and the methods of his reign.

The pope has told us in his own words something of what he owed to the years at the Cenacle : " Our revered Pastor and Archbishop, receiving Us on Our return from Rome, confided to Us the spiritual direction of the Cenacle at Milan. ' This will be your parish,' he said, and so it was to be for many long years. In this way the Lord gave Us, as a change from study and immersion in books, those souls ' in fossil ', this spiritual contact with living souls.

" We could not, at that time, know that this essential activity of the Cenacle and of its daughters for the formation of souls, for the restoration and the deepening of Christian life, its collaboration, not only subordinate to but co-ordinate with the work of the priesthood, We could not then know that all this really constituted, was in its essence and most perfectly, a beginning of that Catholic Action which, much later, was to have so large a place in Our cares and in Our will." [2]

(ii) The Italian Scene

In 1917 Mgr. Ratti celebrated his sixtieth birthday. In all likelihood his seventieth also, should he live so long, would find him in those same quiet studious employments which had occupied him all his life. " If the Papacy was the Dufour Peak he had not even reached Macugnaga." [3]

---

[1] *Meditantibus Nobis.*

[2] *Pius XI : Address at the reading of the Decree on the Heroicity of the Virtues of the Ven. Marie Thérèse Couderc*, 12 May, 1935.

[3] CIVIS ROMANUS, p. 50: for the Dufour and Macugnaga cf. § (iii) of this Chapter.

But it was so ordered that what would happen would be the unlikely thing, the most unlikely thing of all. The librarian was, within twelve months, to be transformed into a diplomatist, and the diplomatist within another four years into the pope himself. His sixty-fifth birthday he would celebrate as Pius XI. It is rare indeed that a great man comes so late in life to the cross-roads of destiny, that such greatness as this is thrust upon him so speedily. Before the story is told of the vital three and a half years that link the prefect of the Vatican Library with the ruler of the universal Church, something ought to be said, and this seems the place to say it, of the Italy in which the sixty years of Mgr. Ratti's life *in minoribus* was spent.

Of his own action in the national life, his share in the controversies of his time, political, religious, intellectual, there is not much that can be said. There is not much accessible evidence. But this we do know, that he was not of that race of scholars who are unaware of the world outside their books. His interests were always universal, nothing that touched man ever failed to interest him. He was, during all his long years in Milan particularly, in constant contact with the leaders, the actors as well as the thinkers, of his time, and of the national life as it presented itself there was no keener observer and none better qualified to understand what he observed. For thirty-four years he watched in the town which is the heart of modern Italian life ; and for another six he watched, scarcely noticed, in the capital, and here, from his suite in the Vatican, he could note too the hundred currents of life in the heart of Catholicism, and could mark the action upon Catholic development of the great ecclesiastical personages of the day.

The first important fact to recall about Achilles Ratti is that, born not ten miles from Milan, he was born a subject of the Emperor of Austria, no other in fact than Francis Joseph.[1] His childhood saw all those events which we call compendiously the Unification of Italy. Nine years before his birth, in the great year of revolution 1848, the Milanese

[1] Emperor from 1848 to 1916.

had risen against their foreign ruler and after an amazing
five days of fighting had driven out his troops, to hail the
King of Sardinia, Charles Albert—the one wholehearted
anti-Austrian of the dozen or so rulers of Italy—as the
protector of their new freedom. That freedom lasted only
a matter of months. In August 1848 the Austrians returned.
Charles Albert, defeated badly at Custozza and Novara,
abdicated to save his kingdom, and by 1857 the Five Days
of March might have seemed for the Milanese no more than
a great memory. Reality and appearance, as often happens,
differed greatly. In 1859 the Sardinian attack on Austria
was renewed, with the support this time of the armies of
France. The allies were victorious at Magenta (6 June);
and two days later Victor Emmanuel II of Sardinia rode
triumphantly into a Milan delirious with joy.

This time there was no relapse. In the peace that
followed, Lombardy was made over to the Sardinian king.
The rule of the foreigner was ended for ever, after three
hundred and fifty years.

So far the situation, for any Milanese, was simple enough.
But the Sardinian king and his premier Cavour did not aim
solely at the liberation of Lombardy. Their agreement
with Napoleon III had had for its end the expulsion of
Austria from Venetia too, and the grouping of all the
Italian states in some kind of federal union, the pope to be
its nominal president. This scheme broke when Napoleon,
prematurely, brought the war to an end by offering Austria
easier terms on the morrow of his victory at Solferino
(24 June); and when the pope declined to consider the
suggestion of the presidency.

Cavour's diplomacy, meanwhile, made use of the revolutionary element in the central Italian states—including
those of the pope—and these in the later part of 1859 rose,
and by plebiscites of surprising, not to say suspicious,
unanimity, declared for union with Sardinia. In the spring
of 1860 it was Sicily's turn to rise. Garibaldi's legion
sailed to assist the rebels and by the end of the year all
Italy, except Venetia and the province of the Papal States

called the Patrimony of St. Peter, was united under the rule
of Victor Emmanuel, called now King of Italy.

For the loyal Catholic Milanese who was also a good
Italian the position was now somewhat complicated. The
royal liberator was also the spoliator of the Holy See.

Ten years of chronic strain followed, Italy awaiting her
chance to seize on the last remaining territories. Venetia
came to her, a gift from Bismarck, as reward for her fidelity
to Prussia in the Austro-Prussian war of 1866. In 1870
came the Franco-Prussian war. The French garrison in
Rome that had been the pope's main defence since 1849,
sailed away to the war, and on 20 September, 1870, the
forces of the King of Sardinia battered their way into Rome
at the Porta Pia. Italy was united and the Roman Question
born.

For the Catholic who was grateful for Italian unity
complication could go no further.

These were the events that filled the childhood of
Achilles Ratti. By the time he came to Rome, to be
ordained, in 1879, and begin his post-graduate studies, the
Italian occupation was a settled thing, and the kingdom's
policy towards the papacy fixed as it was to remain for the
next thirty years.

The political unity of Italy was now a fact, the goal of
forty years' effort had been attained. But not all those who
had dreamed of and worked for national unity and the
expulsion of the foreign rulers had had the same ideal Italy
in view. Some had been partisans of a federal union of
partly autonomous states. There had been Milanese who
dreamed of the republic of Milan, Genoese too and
Venetians whom the memory of like ancient glory inspired.
There had again been republicans whose object had been
an Italian republic. There had been the ambitious Pied-
montese who longed to see their own royal house ruling
the whole peninsula. Such were the politically divided
partisans whom a common hatred of the existing state of
things bound into mutual loyalty during the actual crisis of
1848–1870.

A further difficulty, which divided the victors once the unity was accomplished, was the new state's policy towards religion, that is to say towards the Catholic Church throughout the kingdom. This question was older than the Roman Question properly so-called—*i.e.*, than the question of a mutual accommodation of the political rights and claims of the dispossessed sovereign of the Papal States and the ruler of the new Italian kingdom. It is as old as the Catholic state itself, in this sense at least that there has hardly ever existed a Catholic state where, sooner or later, the state's jealousy of the Church's influence or its envy of the wealth the Church controls or its desire to use religion as an instrument of government, has not brought about a conflict with the Church.

Such a conflict had been raging for twenty years already in the kingdom of Sardinia at the moment when the new Roman Question came to disturb the national life. From 1870 onwards the two problems, to quote the useful phrase of a French writer, "se sont mutuellement empoisonnés." [1]

In the year of revolution, 1848, Sardinia had expelled the Jesuits and the nuns of the Society of the Sacred Heart. Two years later the funds of all religious charities had been taken over by the state, laws had been passed restricting gifts or legacies made to churches or for religious objects, and the privileges of the clergy in the matter of trials and of taxes had been suppressed. Criticism of these decrees, and any movement to procure their modification, was prevented by an act that punished heavily any priest who excited others to contempt of laws, an ingeniously vague device that was to appear again in later years. Next, in 1855, all the monasteries and convents of the contemplative orders were suppressed, the chapters of canons who served the collegiate churches and other " useless " institutions. This meant the closing of 2075 monasteries and convents, 31,649 monks and nuns turned out of their homes, 11,889 benefices suppressed and property of the capital value of something like £20,000,000 confiscated to the state.

<hr>

[1] PERTINAX, *Le Partage de Rome*, Paris, 1929, 10th ed., p. 99.

As the other provinces of Italy fell to Sardinia in 1859–1860 these laws were extended to them also. Thus in 1862 500,000 acres of Church lands in Sicily were confiscated, and in 1866–1867 all the monasteries throughout Italy were suppressed with the exception of five or six of the most famous, such, for example, as Monte Cassino.

As to the confiscation it is true that, in theory, the state merely took possession and continued to administer the revenues for religious purposes. What actually happened, is there need to say it? was very different. It was, for example, calculated in 1877 from returns officially made by the Italian government that only 31 per cent. of the revenues were going to the objects which were their lawful destination. The rest went in " costs of administration." [1]

Now in the first phases of the national revival in Italy there had been none of this hatred of Catholicism. " The programme of the early great exponents of Italian Unity had been to drive out the foreigner and to form an organic whole, in which religion would be looked upon as a beloved and wanted mother; nothing should be allowed to impede its spiritual action. Even Mazzini," this author points out, " at one time shared this ideal, if only for a moment." [2]

The tragedy came when, in the hour of their need, Victor Emmanuel and Cavour called to their aid, not Napoleon III alone, but Masonry. This " involved them in consequences they had neither foreseen nor desired, so that almost inevitably they were dragged at the heels of those who sought the destruction of the Papacy." This, says Count Soderini, was assuredly " not part of the programme of either the king or his able Minister " ; and he quotes Cavour as saying, only a few days before his death in 1861, "If on Rome's becoming the capital of the new Kingdom of Italy, the independence of the Holy See suffered, if such fears were founded, if really the fall of the

---

[1] PERNOT, Le Saint-Siege, p. 91, quoting Weber in the Kirchenlexicon of Wetzer and Welter.   Weber was not a Catholic.
[2] SODERINI, Leo XIII, Italy and France, p. 117.

Temporal Power would necessarily entail this consequence, I should not hesitate to say that the union of Rome with the State of Italy would be fatal, not only to Catholicism, but to Italy." [1]

When the Italian government occupied Rome and thus deprived the pope of all but the palace in which he lived, its way of regularising the situation was to pass an Act of Parliament decreeing the place of the pope in the new state of things and leaving it to him to accept or reject the compensations this law offered. This was the famous Law of Guarantees of 13 May, 1871. It declared that the pope's person was sacred and inviolable. At the worst Italy would not take his life nor imprison him. Any attempts against his person, or incitement to such attempt, would be punished as were punished the like attempts against the person of the king. Public offences and insults by speeches, acts and other means would be punished likewise. The pope is only considered as a sovereign to the extent that the new state will not deprive him of his customary guards. It will pay the pope an annual sum of three and a quarter million lire, specifying in detail what expenses of the Holy See this is intended to meet, and this sum shall always be free from taxation.[2] The Vatican, the Lateran Palace and the Villa at Castel Gandolfo the pope " shall continue to enjoy," free from taxes. The state pledges itself " not to violate the freedom of conclaves, or of General Councils," and such gatherings, as also the residence of the pope, enjoy immunity as against the official entrance of officers of the Italian government. The state papers of the various ecclesiastical offices are protected against seizure—so long as these offices " are endowed with attributions manifestly spiritual." The pope is free to exercise all his spiritual power, and also to publish the acts of such power. The diplomatic immunity of the envoys of foreign states to the Holy See is recognised,

[1] *Op. cit.*, p. 117.
[2] This clause, Article IV, seems to hint that the Government considers itself free to confiscate the various museums and art collections of the Vatican and provides that in such contingency there shall be no reduction in the annual grant.

though they are declared subject to the Italian state in the same way that the envoys to that state are subject to it.

It would be waste of time to repeat in detail, now, the many criticisms made of this notorious law. Its clumsiness and unsuitability are evident even to the lay reader of its texts. Apart from the major defect that it is tantamount to an attempt by one sovereign power to win from another a tacit abdication of its own sovereignty—for obviously, whatever the pope accepts under the law, he accepts the ruling of the Italian state, a ruling in which he has had no say as that state's equal; he does not consent to a treaty but is the conditional beneficiary of an Act of Parliament— the law is too full of ambiguities for anyone to risk his future on its promises.

It was an act of the Italian government and it bound the state that made it. It is nowhere bilateral. The state decrees certain things, it offers others. The status and protection it decrees are nowhere tied up with or made conditional on any acceptance of the offers. They are enactments then that bind the lawmaker absolutely. And the next thirty years were to see the lawmaker break his own fundamental law in the spirit and in the letter repeatedly. " Never did diplomacy employ with more skill the *double entendre*," it has been said of Cavour's manœuvres in 1859–1861, " the half truth, and even the direct lie." [1] Cavour had been dead ten years when the Law of Guarantees was passed, but that same genius of lying still walked with those who made the law and, for another generation yet, with those with whom lay its administration.

The attitude of the popes, faced with the Italian occupation of their states and capital, and safe from further violence and spoliation only so long as the victorious government chose, was from the beginning simple and logical. At all costs they would avoid any word or gesture that might lend itself to any interpretation of acquiescence in what had been done. They were the victims of violence and the

[1] A. J. Grant and H. Temperley, *Europe in the Nineteenth and Twentieth Centuries*, 1789–1932, London, 1935, p. 299.

E 2

world should never, from them, have reason to forget or to misunderstand that it was from a position where they lay at the mercy of further violence that the popes were exercising their spiritual authority. Hence they never ceased to protest against the loss of that civil sovereignty which was the outward proof of their freedom and its most obvious guarantee. From the beginning they refused to fall into the trap laid in the Law of Guarantees : " Guarantees which rest on no other foundation than the arbitrary and hostile will of a Government in whose power it is to apply them, to interpret them, and to carry them into effect as it may choose, and solely for its own purposes and interests." [1] They would not give even the faintest chance to those who would, after 1870, so willingly embarrass their *rôle* in the world by the ruinous gibe that the popes were now but chaplains and pensioners to the Italian king.

The first protestation of this kind was made by Pius IX on 15 May, 1871—just two days after the law was passed. It was to be renewed, for the next fifty years and more, on every occasion when circumstances were such that not to renew it might seem a revocation of papal policy.

The government of the new state did not fail to present the Holy See with ample opportunity for protest. The suspension of the religious orders and the confiscation of their property in Rome itself; the transfer of monasteries and colleges to the uses of the state ; the extension of the conscription laws to ecclesiastics, and the tacit permission to all and sundry publicly to insult and threaten the pope ; all this made the prospects of reconciliation indefinitely remote.

Nor did the death in 1878 of the two protagonists, Pius IX and Victor Emmanuel II, bring any change. The new pope, Leo XIII, set himself from the beginning to end the isolation of the Holy See. The Church's mission was to save the civilisation in which it was placed. The new conditions under which that saving work must be done were

---

[1] Pius IX, Allocution of 12 March, 1877 ; translation in MOORE, *Peter's City*, p. 251.

not of the pope's choosing, nor could he change them. Hence Catholic activity must be accommodated to them, and the Church and the world be once more brought together. "The Church," the pope declared, "is the best friend and the most generous benefactor princes and peoples can hope for. It is the Church which inspires the harmony that unites them one to the other." [1]

For the better execution of its high mission to humanity throughout the world, for the mere possibility of its success, it was essential that the Church be seen to be free from all external constraint. The papacy, first of all, must be free and therefore a solution must be found to the so-called Roman Question. As things were, declared the pope, "we are it is truer to say in the power of another rather than in the enjoyment of our own." [2]

Gradually the new pope's patience and tact won back the sympathy of the different Catholic powers alienated, for one reason or another from the Holy See in the critical years 1859–1878. Spain, Portugal, Bavaria, Belgium, Switzerland, and even Bismarckian Germany, renewed their diplomatic relations with the pope during the first ten years of Leo's reign.

It has sometimes been thought matter of reproach against this most distinguished personage that he made such use of those arts of diplomacy in which he was so eminent a practitioner. Catholics have not been lacking among his critics, and among these Italian Catholics, of an older generation, were perhaps somewhat conspicuous. No better answer to the critics who abhor any use of political arts by the popes can be found than that of the French writer who is the most recent historian of their policy. "We only need to look with unprejudiced eyes on the history of the past and to consider the world to-day attentively and dispassionately, and we shall see immediately that the papacy could not abandon the political position it

---

[1] Letter to Cardinal Rampolla, 15 June, 1887. PERNOT, p. 13.
[2] "*Verius in aliena potestate sumus quam nostra.*" Letter to Rampolla, 15 June, 1887, *op. cit.*, p. 11.

has for so long enjoyed without compromising its future and even without treason to some of its essential aims." [1] So far as concerns Leo XIII personally he has suffered unduly from all too zealous, but not too well instructed, partisans of the pope who followed him, a great pope too, but of wholly different temperament, younger than Leo by a generation and formed in a world that Leo hardly knew. Popes, like saints, may differ indefinitely from one to another without prejudice to their equal claim on the loyal admiration of those for whom they live and work. Now that we are half a century away from the great pontificate of 1878–1903 we can begin to see how Leo XIII used the whole machinery that is the Catholic Church to forward the Church's mission of saving civilisation.

The pope who was the diplomatist *par excellence* was also, it should be remembered, the author of those remarkable encyclicals, to this day too neglected by those for whom they were written, on the Blessed Sacrament, the Sacred Heart, the Holy Ghost, and as great a spiritual leader as any of his predecessors. And who is there who does not know him as the pope of the Rosary? When, in 1879, he sent to France as nuncio one of the greatest diplomatists in the papal service, Mgr. Wladimir Czacki, popularly regarded as the subtlest of all the beasts of the field, the pope, in the nuncio's secret instructions, bade him " to remember always that the good of souls must be the first consideration ; that this must be his first concern, without troubling about political parties, to none of which could the Church allow herself to be bound." [2] The pope did indeed play politics and use his diplomatic gifts to the full, but he found his ultimate resource, as truly as did his successor, in the prayers of the faithful throughout the world.

The Italian politicians saw this revival of the pope's international prestige with fear and with jealousy. They had planned to impose on the pope, through the Law of Guarantees, a sovereignty that would be merely nominal.

---

[1] PERNOT, *op. cit.*, p. 8.
[2] SODERINI, *op. cit.*, p. 144, note.

" By the terms of the Law of Guarantees the head of the
Church retained, despite the loss of all his states, the title
and the prerogatives of a sovereign. . . . Nevertheless it
was very evident that, in the minds of Italian statesmen,
most of these concessions were to be purely honorary.
Stripped of all real sovereignty the pope was to
abandon, at one and the same time, the exercise of
temporal government and all claim to pursue any political
activity abroad. . . . The Italians flattered themselves
with the thought that they would see the pope, for
the sake of their goodwill, brusquely abandon all political
activity. . . . " [1]

Somehow the statesmen had failed. As the years of
Leo's reign went by, their exasperation grew. If he was no
longer, in their eyes, an enemy he was a competitor. The
situation increased in bitterness.

In 1881 arrangements were made, with the knowledge
and approval of the Italian government, for the transport
of Pius IX's body from its temporary tomb in St. Peter's
to its final resting place in the basilica of St. Lorenzo. The
arrangements were those for a private funeral, a hearse and
four carriages for the officials ; the time chosen for the
departure, midnight. When the cortège reached the bridge
of St. Angelo, a mob of anti-clericals surrounded it, singing
obscene and blasphemous songs. Stones were thrown,
knives drawn, those who accompanied the funeral were
assaulted. At one moment it seemed that the coffin
would be thrown into the Tiber. Nor did the police
interfere.

The funds of the Church's department for Foreign
Missions—the Congregation De Propaganda Fide—were
seized. The different Catholic social societies throughout
Italy were dissolved. A reformed penal code introduced
new penalties for the clergy who in any way spoke against
this new legislation or criticised it, the Minister declaring
in the Italian Parliament, that " to speak of the Roman
Question as an open question is equal to claiming the right

[1] PERNOT, pp. 5–6.

of rebellion and insurrection." [1] The premier, Crispi, in
1887, in a famous speech at Turin,[2] openly avowed his
intention of bringing the pope to his knees and other
ministers were no less outspoken in their insults to the
protégé of the Law of Guarantees. " The Vatican," one
of them declared, " was the enemy of Italy " ; and
another greeted a papal allocution that spoke of the
advantages Italy must derive from the settlement of
the Roman Question, with the words " To-day we
are threatened with new embraces from the patriarch of
lies."

Leo XIII understood quite well who were his enemies.
It is " not so much the hostility of the Italian nation as the
masonic conspiracy which has violated the just rights and
dignity of the Holy See," he declared in 1887.[3] How truly
he divined the source of his trouble a letter of the Grand
Master of Italian Freemasonry, written about this time
(1887), survives to show. " The loyalty of Brother 33
[Crispi] who is at the head of public authority, is a sure
guarantee that the Vatican will fall under our vivifying
hammer. . . . The G. O. calls on the Genius of Humanity
in order that all the brothers may do their utmost to scatter
the stones of the Vatican to build with them the temple of
the emancipated nation." [4]

Little wonder that at times the pope grew desperate
and studied the possibilities of governing the Church
from some other place than his palace of the Vatican.
No fewer than five times, in fact, between 1881 and
1891, did he sound the governments of Austria and
Spain as to the chances of flight from Rome and its
effects.[5]

One thing he could not do, consent to being in Rome as
the fourteenth-century popes had been in Avignon. For

---

[1] PERTINAX, *op. cit.*, p. 107.
[2] MOLLAT, *La Question Romaine*, p. 385.
[3] Allocution of 23 May, MOLLAT, p. 381.
[4] Quoted in SODERINI, *op. cit.*, p. 76.
[5] In 1881, MOLLAT, p. 375 ; PERTINAX, p. 94 ; 1882, MOLLAT, p. 376 ; PER-
TINAX, p. 95 ; 1888, MOLLAT, pp. 388–391 ; 1889, MOLLAT, p. 391 ; 1891, MOLLAT
p. 397.

Leo XIII the Avignon residency represented the very nadir
of papal influence.

From this summary view of the papacy as it planned and
strove and suffered during the earlier years of Achilles
Ratti's priestly life, when, at Milan he was gradually gaining
for himself a very definite place in the life of that most
important of all Italian cities, we may turn to the question
of the effect of these revolutionary changes and of the
victory of the Liberals upon the generation in whose childhood the great events had come to pass, the generation
precisely of Don Achilles Ratti.

The biographer of one who was considerably his senior,
though yet not of the older generation, Antonio Fogazzaro,
has described very eloquently the general spirit of these
years, and its effect upon the more generous minded
idealists among the Liberals.[1]

He describes the dominant political party, that party of
the Left which we have seen so busily endeavouring to
imprison the papacy in the accomplishment of 1870, as in
no way enamoured of real democratic change. For all the
splendid phraseology its real aim was the maintenance of
the present state of things, social and political. It lacked
ideals to stimulate it to reforms. Some of its adherents were
doubtful of the wisdom of what had been accomplished,
others were only interested in the opportunity they now
enjoyed of satisfying local needs at the national expense.
To the welfare of the masses they were supremely indifferent.
Such problems as that of the wretched peasantry in the
south, or of the general high average of illiteracy, they left
alone, and the constant inflammatory denunciation of the
Vatican as the source of all evil served to distract the nation
from their own shortcomings.[2]

It was a generation languid and weary to the point of

---

[1] TOMMASO GALLARATI-SCOTTI, *Vita di Antonio Fogazzaro*, Milan, 1920.
[2] GALLARATI-SCOTTI, *op. cit.*, pp. 148–149.

death, showing all the signs of that unhealthy lassitude that
follows a great, and premature, effort. For fifty years after
1860 the soul of the nation slept, a troubled sleep stirred by
uneasy dreams. There were no great ideals, no confidence
in oneself or in others, a general lack of faith and an indifference to the right and wrong of things. " Grey hours in
the national history," says the writer, " spiritual twilight."
The universal tendency was to let things have their way
since there was no hope in effort. Scepticism and inertia
were the dominant characteristics of life. The only way to
save one's soul was to ignore the world without and to look
within oneself for guidance.[1]

Achilles Ratti was by nature of sterner stuff than the
man here taken as typical of these wretched years. His
Catholicism had deeper roots, his disciplined, orderly soul
had drawn new strength from the objectively real doctrine
of his religion and from regular obedience to its law of life.
Nowhere, ever, in the accounts of his early life is there so
much as a hint of contentment with superficiality, nor of
pose, nor of satisfaction with anything short of work
finished and well finished. He was indeed by nature, by
intellectual formation, and by choice " of that learned
Milanese world in which Manzoni still lived as a kind of
invisible tutelary deity," [2] that world whose romanticism
was anything but subjective, and from the first he would
gladly proclaim himself partisan and child of that " arte
cattolica Manzoniana," [2] which for the vague-minded,
uneasy, self-exploring, self-occupied jeunesse of his day
must give place to a new and more " interesting " sub-
jectivism.

Something of this same futility that characterised so much
of that generation's endeavour, dogged the attempts of the
" enlightened " Catholics of the time in their efforts to end

---

[1] GALLARATI-SCOTTI, op. cit., pp. 40, 41, 156.
[2] Ib., p. 45.

the real discord between the Church and the Italian state
and also the alleged antagonisms between the traditional
faith and the discoveries of the new critical sciences. The
biographer of Fogazzaro speaks of " a certain superficiality
which characterised the moment. . . . It was the day of
Americanism, of a state of mind vague in the extreme and,
philosophically speaking, poverty-stricken. . . . Whatever
came in from across the seas suddenly seemed a revelation."
So it was, for example, that the Darwinian [1] theories of
Evolution found a welcome from such Catholics, and to
meet the new attacks on revealed truth and the traditional
beliefs, like-minded Catholics produced the theories and
the system condemned as Modernism.

If we ask what part Don Achilles Ratti took in the
burning controversies which filled Italian life during the
years of his maturity, political controversies, politico-
religious controversies and controversies about philosophy
and Catholic doctrine, or if we seek to know in detail how
these affected him we are, at the moment, bound to be
disappointed. His career, during these long years that
preceded his sudden appearance as a personage in the public
life of the Church, was, by reason of its very nature, hidden
and withdrawn. Never was there a man who found in his
own business more than enough to occupy his whole life
than this busy, reserved scholar. It was never his office
to make pronouncements on the questions that troubled his
contemporaries and, perhaps, himself. Nor did either his
duties or his tastes plunge him into the various controversial
activities.

We are not surprised to know, from the chance references
that occur in his various writings and political conferences,
that he was ever a patriotic Italian. While loyally leaving
to the Holy See the choice of the moment and the manner
of Catholic intervention in the political life of his country,
he was never a disinterested spectator of that life. Still less
had he any sympathy with those extremist Catholics who,
like the sons of Thunder, would have called down fire

---

[1] I use the word in its popular sense, of course.

from heaven upon the system that, to all appearance, refused so persistently to hearken to the divine message. The prudence of his uncle, Don Damiano Ratti, had found a way, even in the difficult days of the sixties and the seventies to serve his country and the Church together. The nephew whom this patriot churchman did so much to form developed a like prudence and a like trusting patience.

Don Achilles Ratti was of too practical a mind to group himself with the *intransigenti* who, until the day the last of them disappeared, seemed to welcome every new act of anti-papal hostility for the support it gave their thesis that the Italian kingdom must be destroyed. Nor can he ever have had much sympathy for those whom Manning described as the *miracolisti*.[1] On the other hand the solutions which the Catholics of professedly liberal inclinations so readily produced could never deceive his judgment. All of them had the defect that has so often ruined the hopes of Liberalism, that they took no account of the actual circumstance, of the concrete facts of human nature. Reconciliation would come when those conditions were realised in which alone reconciliation is possible, conditions that depend not on juridical acts but on a change of heart.

Meanwhile he was a patriot and a Catholic too. In the sad days that followed the catastrophe of Adowa he spoke publicly " of the unspeakable sorrow that to-day fills every Italian heart " and hailed the famous intervention of Leo XIII on behalf of the Italian prisoners of Menelik as the act of human sympathy it was—and this at a time when only too many Catholic writers in Italy seized on the incident as an opportunity to glorify the papacy by heaping insult on the Italian state. Again he could write that nothing that touched the history of the royal family could find any Italian unsympathetic. The war found him the Italian, decidedly anxious for the success of the allied cause. " If the Germans took Milan," he once said to a friendly

---

[1] *Cf.* Manning's Diary for 5 December 1883, in Purcell, *Life of Cardinal Manning*, London, 1895, Vol. II, p. 580.

colleague in the Vaticana, "I believe it would kill me."[1]
Another writer declares that as early as the first month of
the war Mgr. Ratti looked to the participation of Italy,
and this on the side of the allies.[2] Certainly his personal
relations with the royal officials were always good, and
during his mission to Poland, at the time of the plebiscites
in Silesia and elsewhere, he made no secret of his friendship
for the various Italian officers who were, in a sense, his
colleagues.

(iii) The Alps

The real cradle of the Ratti was, as has been stated, the
mountainous peninsula that divides the Lake of Como,
which is as much as to say that mountains and mountain
climbing were in the family's very blood. The future
pope's own love of this sport was shared by his brother
Edward and a near relation, Carlo Ratti, was not only an
active climber but, for seventeen years, editor of the publications of the Italian Alpine Club. No biography of
Pope Pius XI would be complete that was silent about this
side of his life. In recalling these incidents of his life the
biographer does something more than insinuate a description of the alpinist's character and habit of life. He recalls
one of the great feats of modern mountaineering, which,
for climbers, put those who achieved it in the first rank of
mountaineers. This was the famous ascent of Monte Rosa
from the Italian side in July 1889.

The story is fully told in Don Achilles Ratti's report
published in the *Bollettino* of the Italian Alpine Club for
that year[3] and translated into English by J. E. C. Eaton.[4]

The mountainous mass known as Monte Rosa is on the
frontier of Italy and Switzerland and its several peaks touch
very nearly the 15,000 feet line, the summit (the Dufour
Peak) reaching actually to 15,400. In the Alps, Mont

---

[1] BEYENS, *Quatre Ans à Rome* (1921–1926), p. 102.
[2] PERTINAX, *Le Partage de Rome*, p. 178.
[3] Vol. XX, iii, No. 56, pp. 1–29.
[4] *Climbs on Alpine Peaks*, by ABATE ACHILLE RATTI (now Pope Pius XI),
London, 1923, pp. 42–108.

Blanc alone is higher. The ascent from the eastern, or Italian, side, is particularly difficult, and from the frequency of the avalanches in this region it was generally considered to be extremely dangerous. There were not lacking alpinists who considered this particular climb " ought to be banned," and one authority (Bonney) gave it as a considered opinion that " under no circumstances however favourable" should it be undertaken. Two English climbers had, however, achieved the feat in 1872, and left it on record that " the width of the crevasses on the upper glacier and the continued threat of avalanches . . . filled them at times with absolute terror."[1] In 1880 an Austrian did the climb successfully, and in the next nine years there were four other alpinists who won through. None of them was, however, an Italian, and among the various motives that produced the expedition of 29–31 July, 1889, must be reckoned, undoubtedly, the patriotic desire that an Italian should at last conquer this most difficult Italian summit.

Don Ratti took the matter up in his characteristic, judicious way. It was a problem to be resolved, as problems of palæography or diplomacy, by careful study first of all. The records of previous climbers were examined, and the difficulties peculiar to the ascent ; the causes, for example, of the avalanches which are Monte Rosa's speciality on its eastern face were tracked down and the ideal conditions for an attempt determined. Then when these appeared to be realised, and the very weather the climb called for occurred, there was quick decision and the expedition was on.

Love of adventure, high courage, great power of endurance, are as evident all through Don Ratti's narrative as his great physical strength. But never does prudence desert him. All the acts of that queen of the virtues, as Aristotle describes them, are to be found in his careful preparation, as the scientist is written across every page of the later, meticulously exact report. For " we apply the name [of

[1] *Climbs*, p. 47.

prudent] to those who deliberate well in some particular field, when they calculate well the means to some particular good end, in matters that do not fall within the sphere of art. So we may say, generally, that a man who can deliberate is prudent." [1] The acts of prudence are counsel which discovers the means, judgment which chooses the best of these and command which lays its duty upon the will; all are evident in operation in the alpinist as, indeed, they are everywhere throughout this astonishingly ordered life.

⌐ "The idea of attempting a gambler's throw, as it is called, never entered our heads," the climber writes. [2] This particular climb, he recognises, "is not to be undertaken lightly." [3] All the same "Mountaineering is not a breakneck pursuit, but . . . merely a question of prudence and of a little courage, of love of nature and her most secret beauties," and when these qualities are to be found in the climber, with favourable conditions of terrain and weather, "there are few recreations which are more wholesome for body and mind, and more to be recommended than a little mountain climbing," [4] though the writer goes on to admit that getting up Monte Rosa by the eastern face is much more than "a little mountain climbing."

This famous climb of July 1889 was made together with a priest friend, Dr. Luigi Grasselli. The guides were Giuseppe Gadin and Alessio Pranert. The party set out from Macugnaga at one in the afternoon of 29 July, and by 7 p.m. had reached the Marinelli hut, 10,000 feet up. Here they rested until one in the morning, sleeping for the last two hours. Then began the real work. Don Ratti describes the scene: "Solemn silence reigned around, the stars shone brightly in the infinite, azure, almost velvety sky. The huge masses of the mountains and their sublime summits towered in majesty about us and their gigantic shadows stretched

---

[1] *Nichomachean Ethics*, Bk. VI, ch. v, trans. F. H. PETERS, London, 1916, p. 187. *Cf.* also "Statesmanship and prudence are the same faculty," *ib.*, ch. viii, p. 192.

[2] *Climbs*, p. 58.

[3] *Ib.*, p. 45.

[4] *Ib.*, p. 96.

forth and intermingled on the white expanses of snow and ice."

Steadily they climbed for twelve hours, with scarcely a halt, over the couloir where the famous guide Marinelli had met his death a few years earlier and across the glacier. Then, after a rest sitting in the snow with before them " a huge massive wall of pure ice, whose brow projected, and extended above our heads a regular canopy of crystal," the expedition resumed, to reach its first objective, the peak called the Ostspitze, at 7.30 p.m. It was too late now to make for the actual summit, the Dufour peak which with the Ostspitze forms a kind of enormous double tooth of rock. Hence, " driven by the wind, which was now insupportable and by approaching night " they began to descend, their goal a ledge of rock, almost free from snow, 100 feet or so lower down. Here at 8.30 they took up their station for the night, 15,180 feet up.

It was not the most comfortable of resting places, the writer admits,[1] but it was perfectly safe for anyone who was reasonably sure of himself. " It was impossible to take a step in any direction. Anyone sitting down found his feet dangling in space ; we had, however, every facility for stamping them, provided we were careful not to lose our balance. And these elementary gymnastics were most necessary. . . .

" The cold was intense ; without being able to reckon the exact degree, I may mention that our coffee was frozen hard, and our wine and our eggs resembled it, in that they were respectively neither drinkable nor eatable.

" We again had recourse to our chocolate, and to a generous quantity of excellent *kirsch*, which we still had with us.

" In such a place and such a temperature, it would have been the height of imprudence to allow sleep to overcome us.

" But who would have slept in that pure air, which pierced our marrow, and in face of such a scene as we had before us ?

[1] *Climbs*, pp. 79–80.

" At that height, in the centre of the grandest of all the grand Alpine theatres, in that pure transparent atmosphere, under that sky of darkest blue, lit by a crescent moon and sparkling with stars as far as the eye could reach, in that silence. . . . How could we even think of the fatigue we had endured, much less complain of it ?

" We stood there absorbed in our thoughts ; when the perfect silence was broken by a sound like a mighty thunderclap.

" It was an avalanche which was breaking loose and falling below us, but too far away to cause us any trouble.

" Awestruck and amazed, we listened attentively to the terrible sound of destruction, the sight of which was denied us, as the mass, ever increasing in volume, hurled itself downwards, with ' un fracasso d'un suon pien di spavento,' as Dante says, till it came to rest on the lower glacier. . . .

" And we were to have the opportunity of enjoying from that height the spectacle, everywhere beautiful, of the dawn of a splendid day ; we were to witness the first diffusion of light, to see the loveliest tints growing in the east, the sun appearing in splendour between the summits, and its rays spreading like a fiery mantle over a thousand slopes of ice and snow, lighting them up with a wondrous medley of splendid tints !

" It was enough to drive a painter mad . . . and for us it was time to be moving, and to climb the peak once more." [1]

At five in the morning of the 31st, they left their rocky resting place and returned first to the Ostspitze and thence by the intervening ridge, " at times literally straddling the ridge," to the Dufour itself which they reached at 8.20 a.m. They had the satisfaction that they were the first Italians to have stood there, and also, a more important point for Don Ratti, that they had made their way by a new route. They were pioneers too in what followed, the negotiation of the pass between the Dufour and the Zumstein peaks, for this was the first traverse of the second highest of the

[1] *Climbs*, pp. 79–82.

Alpine passes. It had been reached three times before only, and then from Zermatt. From the Italian side it had never even been reached, let alone crossed. The patriot in Don Ratti could rejoice, and the practical man feel justified when, a few years later, a party of fully armed soldiers, using his route, showed that it had a certain military practicability.

At this point the party met with misfortune. Their guide—one of the great guides—was half-blinded with the glare, and the moraine, " a regular desert of snow " on which no trace of the path could be found. So yet another night had to be spent in the open " on the hard stones of the moraine. . . . We slept peacefully."

Such, in brief *résumé*, is the story of what Mr. Freshfield calls " Two prodigious days . . . arduous to the last degree." [1]

Achilles Ratti's last words on the whole subject of Alpinism were to come many years later. In 1923 the Bishop of Annecy was organising his diocese to celebrate worthily the tenth centenary of the birth of St. Bernard of Menthon, the Archdeacon of Aosta who for forty years evangelised the mountainous regions of the Valais and Tarentaise, and who founded the celebrated hospice to assist Alpine travellers in the pass that ever since bears his name. From Rome the pope himself joined in the celebration, sending to the bishop a special Apostolic Letter for the occasion.[2] In this letter he who was Don Achilles Ratti, now as Pius XI sings the praises of mountaineering after praising God for the life of the great St. Bernard, to whom, he confesses, he has had all his life a great devotion. " At an earlier period of our own life," the pope writes, " whenever circumstances made it possible, it was our custom to attempt the ascent of these sublime peaks, to refresh the mind wearied by study and to gain new bodily strength. We know therefore by frequent personal experience those places which formed the immense stage on which the saint's exceedingly practical charity displayed

[1] *Climbs*, p. 23.
[2] *Quod Sancti Bernardi*, 20 August, 1923,

itself. The very sight of the mountains where he laboured, and where the traces remain, still deeply impressed, of his holy life, so that one may be said still to breathe there his very spirit, used readily to fill us with admiration and indeed affection for such heroic virtue."

There follows a beautifully written eulogy of the saint's life and character, and then, to fix the memory of his achievement more securely than ever, the pope names him patron saint not only of those who travel through the Alps, but also of those whose pastime it is to attempt their very summits. " For one may truly say that of all the sports in which men seek recreation there is none healthier than this, whether for the mind or the body, provided always that foolhardiness is kept in check. The hard work involved and the ascent into an air that is purer and finer, renew and increase the body's forces. The soul, on the other hand, gains a new constancy to face the duties of life from the necessity mountaineering entails of conquering difficulties of every kind. Finally, from the sight of that beauty and immensity which the peaks of the Alps present to those who seek them, the mind readily moves upwards to think of God Himself, Nature's creator and lord." [1]

[1] The Sacred Congregation of Rites has also published—14 October, 1931— a form for blessing the alpinist's equipment, alpenstocks, ropes, ice-axes, etc. *A. A. S.*, xxiii, p. 446.

CHAPTER III

THE detail of Mgr. Ratti's next promotion after his appointment as prefect of the Vatican Library—promotion, if one may so style it, of a most unusual kind—has not, so far as I know, ever been made public. That in the course of three and a half years he had become personally well known to the new pope, Benedict XV, is true, true also that Mgr. Ratti found Pope Benedict always very willing to second his schemes for the improvement of the library. No one, least of all such a cultivated man of affairs as the war-time pope, could fail to be impressed by Mgr. Ratti's personality, his gifts, his encyclopædic knowledge, his immense energy and his unfailing courage before tasks involving hours of drudging hard work. Also he was a linguist.

In the spring of 1918 the Polish bishops asked Benedict XV to send out some high official to consult with them about the religious restoration of their country, free now, for the first time in a century, from the yoke of the anti-Catholic tsardom. For this task of observation and consultation the pope chose the librarian—to the librarian's vast surprise. However, all that the pope would say to his protestations was " What day can you leave ? " There was nothing for it but acceptance. Mgr. Ratti was appointed Visitor Apostolic for Poland on 25 April, 1918. His first care was to betake himself to the archives of the Secretary of State to prepare himself by studying there the history of Poland's relations with the Vatican since the Congress of Vienna.

Mgr. Ratti left Rome on Whit-Sunday (19 May), 1918. He broke his journey at Milan, and again at Munich, Vienna and Berlin, where he was commissioned to sound the Chancellor about the reality of recent proposals for a peace. On the last day of May he arrived at Warsaw, the centre of a world where all was in a state of flux, and seemingly separated by the thinnest of partitions from a state of complete anarchy, political first and then economic and social. Nor was the life of the country to which his new mission had brought him, really to pass from this stage of crisis until the last few months of his stay in it.

The political circumstances of the Polish nation when the war, now nearing its close, had broken out had been such as, at first, to threaten this unhappy race with suffering more tragic than anything that had so far been its lot. For just one year short of a century the territory of the ancient kingdom had been partitioned between the three empires of Russia, Austria and Germany. The settlement of the Congress of Vienna in 1815 had given to Russia not only the Lithuanian and White Russian provinces of the one-time Polish kingdom, but the greater part of Poland proper. Austria, with the Ruthenian provinces, had also received provinces that were purely Polish, and the German Empire of 1871–1918, including as it did the kingdom of Prussia, took in the Polish provinces of Pomerania and Poznan made over to Prussia in 1815.

For a century Poland proper had been partitioned among these three powers, and now for four years Poles, conscripted into their several armies, had been fighting Poles on the different battle-fronts of the war. No more tragic situation can be imagined.

During the century of partition, furthermore, the three divisions of Poland had been governed in very different fashion, and there were beginning to be three different kinds of Poles. The Russian rule was the most oppressive of all, but the oppression was not uniformly effective. In Prussian Poland, on the other hand, the movement to de-polonise the Poles was continuous and systematic, applied with proverbial German patience and thoroughness. The most fortunate division was that which fell within the Habsburg empire. Not only was there here the tie of a common religion, the Poles and the Austrians being alike Catholics, but to patronise the Pole and to keep him Polish suited the policy of Vienna, always aiming at internal peace by balancing the rival non-German nationalities of the empire.

One result of this difference of treatment was the growth of a serious division of opinion among the patriotic Poles who dreamed of and planned a restoration of Polish independence. For, although none looked for assistance of any kind from Hohenzollern Germany, there was one party that the liberal *régime* of the Habsburgs made very pro-Austrian, while another looked to Russia, moved by the kinship of blood that united the two Slav peoples and by the facts of recent Russian policy gradually working towards a bloc of Slav states closely united in amity against German and Austrian alike.

It was, then, but a natural consequence of developments already in process for some years before the outbreak of the war that the hostile powers, almost from the beginning, began to make bids to draw to their side, by lavish promises of a future freedom, the whole Polish people.

The first to do this were the Russians, and in 1914 military proclamations of the commander-in-chief of the armies invading German and Austrian Poland announced that a reunion of all the old Polish territory in some kind of independent state would follow upon the Russian victory. The promise was generous, but vague, so vague, indeed, that it produced no effect at all. The fortunes of war soon disposed of this first, Russian, suggestion of a resurrection of Polish independence. The German victory of Tannenberg in the autumn of 1914 and the German successful counter-offensive in the spring of the following year entirely reversed the situation. Warsaw, the capital of Russian Poland, fell to the Austro-German allies in August 1915, and by September the whole of Russian Poland was in their hands. Poland was, *de facto*, reunited, but under a military occupation.

In the next twelve months, as the situation of the German allied empires became ever more serious, it was not unnatural that, in their anxiety for new supplies of troops, their thoughts should turn to the population of Russian Poland, now under the rule of their own generals. Conscription was out of the question, but were Poland independent it could hardly refuse to be the ally of the powers who had made it so. It was political reasons of this nature that motived the first real declaration of Polish independence, made on 5 November, 1916, by the Austrian and German governments. The details of the settlement were somewhat vague. But the new state was to include Russian Poland only. Neither Austria nor Germany consented to restore the Polish provinces they had occupied since the settlement of 1815. Nor was the military occupation to cease. While the new state was given a Council of State, and, until its status as kingdom or republic was determined, a Council of Regency to preside as its ruler, Warsaw continued to be the seat of a military administration for the German zone, and Lublin of a second military administration for the Austrian zone. And the division between the Polish patriots deepened over the question of co-operation with the new *régime*.

Only four months after this first Declaration of Independence the Russian revolution began, in March 1917. Tsardom fell and, for the moment, liberal conceptions of foreign policy were given a hearing. One of the first acts of the provisional government in Russia was to declare Poland independent, which, in practice, meant a surrender of all claim to the old Russian Poland now in German occupation.

The next twelve months (March, 1917–March, 1918), saw successive confirmations of the new fact, when, one by one, all the different forces at war, for their own several ends and in their own way, each declared for the principle of Polish independence. The Allied Powers—France, England, Italy and the rest—and the President of the

United States in his famous Fourteen Points, all pledged themselves in this sense while at Cracow, the ancient capital, since 1846 an Austrian city, a movement began which demanded specifically a restoration and reunion of the whole Polish kingdom.

In November 1917 occurred the second Russian revolution, and under the new Bolshevik *régime* Russia, deserting the allies, made peace with Germany in the Treaty of Brest-Litovsk (1 March, 1918). The parties to this treaty were the governments of Germany and Austria, on the one hand, and the new revolutionary government of Russia on the other. Poland had no part in it. Russia surrendered all the old Baltic provinces, Esthonia, Livonia, Courland, Lithuania, with the Ukraine and Poland. The Germans thereupon advanced their forces and occupied Riga and the province of Podolia.

It was at this moment that, finally and definitively rid of even their *de jure* subjection to Russia, the bishops of what had been Russian Poland approached the Holy See and asked for a Visitor Apostolic. Just three months after the Treaty of Brest-Litovsk he entered Warsaw in the person of Mgr. Achilles Ratti.

For the first time for more than a hundred years the bishops of Poland were able to communicate as they wished with the Holy See. The Apostolic Visitor was to survey the whole field of ecclesiastical activity, to take counsel with the bishops and to send on his information and recommendations to Rome. In the territory for which he was commissioned—Poland, Lithuania and the other regions which, previous to the Treaty of Brest-Litovsk, had formed part of the Russian Empire—there were perhaps 20,000,000 Catholics in all. Poland proper accounted for nearly two-thirds of this total, something like 12,000,000 Catholics organised in the seven dioceses of Warsaw, Wloclawek, Plock, Kielce, Lublin, Sandomierz and Sejny. In Lithuania there were the sees of Vilna and Kovno, in White Russia Mohilev and Minsk, in the Ukraine Luck-Zhitomir and Tiraspol.

This ecclesiastical arrangement dated back to an agreement made between the Holy See and the Russian government in the days of Alexander I (1801–1825). The intervening century had seen the agreement broken almost
continually in the spirit and very often in the letter too.
Time and again, for example, the government of St. Peters-
burg had kept the different sees vacant, Warsaw, from
1831 to 1837, and again from 1838 to 1857, and from 1863
to 1883. The Uniate see of Minsk had never been filled
at all and the Latin see was left vacant after 1869, while
Kamenetz was arbitrarily suppressed in 1866. Not a see
but at one time or another had thus suffered, and when sees
were not actually vacant the bishops were often in exile.

Another way in which the anti-Catholic tyranny of the
Russians worked, was to forbid the development of the
religious orders of men and the establishment of contemplative orders of nuns. In all Poland in 1914 there were
only thirty-nine regular clergy (to 2,731 seculars) and only
666 nuns, the vast majority of them Sisters of Mercy or
Sisters of Charity.

Even though the active persecution of Catholics for their
faith, the fines, the imprisonments, exile and the floggings,
had come to an end, administrative oppression and the
prohibition of any continuous direct relation between the
bishops and the Holy See was an extremely serious check
on the religious life of the country.

The Visitor lost no time. Within three weeks of his
arrival he summoned the Polish bishops for a first conference (19–21 June, 1918), and a month later they came
together again when, in the cathedral of Warsaw, a bishop
was consecrated for the see of Minsk, vacant just fifty years.
In December there was a third episcopal reunion.

Between that second and third bishops' meeting Mgr.
Ratti had been continually in movement. On 17 July he
was at the great national shrine of Our Lady of Czenstochowa and thence, a few days later, he passed to the
episcopal city of Kielce. In September it was the turn of
the sees in the south, Sandomierz, Lublin and—a personal

visit outside the area of his mission—Cracow which, in September 1918 was still an Austrian city, where the Visitor was hospitably received by the Prince-Bishop. The month closed with visits to the western sees of Wloclawek and Plock.

The Visitor continued to show himself a tireless traveller, always *en route* to inquire personally and to see for himself on the spot the personalities, the populations, and the districts which the projected rearrangement in ecclesiastical affairs would affect. Before the year 1918 was ended, Mgr. Ratti, in close collaboration with the Polish bishops, had been instrumental in restoring the sees of Riga, that had disappeared in the sixteenth century, of Janow and Kamieniec. Moreover, the long vacant dioceses of Minsk, Vilna and Lublin were given bishops and, a matter to which the old Tsarist government had offered continuous and effective opposition, the bishops of several sees in Poland were provided with auxiliary bishops, namely, Warsaw, Sejny, Plock, Wloclawek, Lublin and Sandomierz. In all, twelve new additional bishops were consecrated in a matter of six months.

By this time (December, 1918) anxieties of another order had been added to those which already occupied the Visitor Apostolic. Poland was now free and independent in fact. The allies had won the war and while the armistice of 11 November had deprived the Austro-German forces— still at that date in occupation of Russian Poland—of any right to their position, the revolutions in Berlin and Vienna and Budapest deprived them for the moment of any real interest in actually maintaining it.

For the moment there were no fewer than five governments contending for Poland's allegiance. There were the two military administrations of the occupying armies, there was the Council of Regency at Warsaw, and a socialistic counterpart of it at Lublin, and there was the Polish National Committee at Paris which had negotiated, earlier in the year, the allied recognition of Poland as a belligerent power. The German and Austrian armies retired from

Russian Poland to take their share in the revolutions at home, the Regency Council declared for the independence of the whole of Poland; and then began the disarming of what Austrian troops were left in Austrian Poland and—a matter that involved weeks of fighting—the expulsion of the German troops from Prussian Poland, *i.e.*, from Pomerania and Poznan. The arrival of Pilsudski, the experienced politician and soldier, set free from the confinement at Magdeburg to which the Hohenzollern *régime* had sentenced him, put an end to the period of uncertainty. The socialists of Lublin submitted and soon, except for eastern Galicia, the whole of Poland—Russian, Austrian and Prussian—was momentarily tranquil and obeying the provisional government at Warsaw.

Eastern Galicia was to remain a trouble for some time more. Here the population was almost wholly Ruthenian, but the great towns such as Lwow (Lemberg) and Przemysl, were just as Polish. The Austrians, before they abandoned the province to its own fate, had handed over its armaments to the Ruthenians, and these, making common cause with their compatriots of the old Russian Empire—now organised as the West Ukrainian Republic—laid siege to Lwow (Lemberg). This new war dragged on all through November and December, but by the end of 1918 the Polish army was master, and all Austrian-Poland subordinated to Warsaw. The assembly to form a constitution for the now united Poland was elected in January 1919, but before it met (February, 1919) the army had crossed the eastern frontier of the old Russian Poland to occupy those lands which, before 1772, had formed part of the ancient Polish kingdom and which Russia, in March 1918, had given up at Brest-Litovsk. The Poles met with little difficulty, and soon had pressed forward several hundred miles, occupying territory as far as the line Vilna—Kamieniec-Podolski.

Meanwhile, at Versailles, the detail was being fought out as to what territories, hitherto under German, Austrian and Russian rule, should be recognised by the victorious allies as forming the new Polish state. The question was settled, so far as concerned German Poland, by the Treaty of Versailles (28 June, 1919) while the Treaty of St. Germain (10 September, 1919) settled what provinces of the old Austro-Hungarian empire were to be given up. The question of the Polish-Russian frontier the Conference did not touch, but left to the mutual arrangement of the parties concerned—ultimately to the arbitrament of war.

On 30 March, 1919, while the details of the various frontiers were yet wholly undecided, the Holy See recognised Poland as an independent state, and negotiations began for the establishment of a nunciature at Warsaw. At the request of the Polish government the post was conferred on the Visitor Apostolic (19 June, 1919), and there opened for Mgr. Ratti one of the most difficult chapters of his whole career.[1]

He had not any longer to deal only with the more or less homogeneous problem of Russian Poland, but to assist now at the first reactions when there came together, after a separation of a hundred and fifty years, populations which, for all their common Catholicity had, in all that long time, developed and been shaped by widely different circumstances.

It was in December, 1918, that the first meeting of the bishops of the reunited provinces took place, and a second meeting followed in the following March. At both of these reunions Mgr. Ratti presided, and his habitual calm, his patience, and that impartiality which derived from his simple loyalty to the Faith which was what all had in common, to the Roman directions and to the Code of Canon Law upon which the restoration was to be built, wrought wonders in the matter of interpreting to each

---

[1] Nuncios, in the normal course of things, are invested with the dignity of titular archbishops. Mgr. Ratti received the title of Archbishop of Lepanto. He was consecrated on the feast of SS. Simon and Jude, 28 October, 1919, by the Archbishop of Warsaw, Mgr. (later Cardinal) Kakowski. The co-consecrators were the (Latin) Bishop of Przemysl, Mgr. Pelczar and the Bishop of Wloclawek, Mgr. Ruszkiewicz. The President of the Republic, the Cabinet, the diplomatic corps, the twenty-two bishops of the regions of his jurisdiction as Visitor Apostolic, were all present and the ceremony was treated as an event of national importance.

other the different members of this great Polish family so cruelly separated for generations and now so marvellously brought together again.

Three very grave matters called for the Nuncio's careful attention, the question of a Concordat, the problem of the Church's position relative to the land reforms which the new government was now pushing forward, and the new state's attitude with regard to the extensive Church domains which the several previous governments had confiscated and which had now come under the dominion of Poland. Feeling ran high on these, as on all other questions. National anxiety as to the outcome of the negotiations still in progress at Versailles, anxiety as to the fortunes of the army in the field against the Bolsheviks, the remains of old hatreds and a very natural suspicion of non-Polish influences, with, later on, a really desperate revival of national feeling aroused by the plebiscites which were to determine whether certain important areas were to go to Poland or to Germany, all these turned the Poland of 1919–1920 into a very hell of primitive human passion, where at times the furies seemed to reign supreme.

It was the Nuncio's business, in this perilous time, to keep himself aloof from the several factions, to win and to retain the confidence of all, to keep the Polish bishops true to the one thing that mattered, the welfare of religion, and with their co-operation to secure that, in the very foundations of this new Catholic state, Catholicism should be given public recognition, every possible opportunity of free and healthy development, and just compensation where rights were surrendered. The day will come when the history of these critical years will be set out in all its detail and in its proper perspective, and in that history Mgr. Ratti, Nuncio Apostolic, will be recognised as one of the founders of the new state.

The new state was Catholic, undoubtedly, but it contained a very large non-Catholic minority, and even Catholic opinion was by no means unanimous as to the precise form the relation between Church and State should take for the future. Religion was now freed from the shackles laid on it by the protestant government of Prussia and the orthodox *régime* of the Tsars, but as to the future status of the Church there was the greatest uncertainty and in that uncertainty a hundred dangers lurked. There were Catholics who desired a concordat with the Holy See that should recognise the new state as heir to all those rights of intervention in ecclesiastical affairs which the old monarchy of the Habsburgs had been able, in an evil time, to secure from the weak and helpless papacy of the eighteenth century and the Restoration. There were others whose opinion, at the other extreme, was that, while the Church should be absolutely and in every respect free of government interference in all its own concerns, there should be no governmental recognition of religion and no such recognition of Catholicism as a public thing as would be implied in any concordat.

In the lively controversies this great question provoked, the Nuncio, once again, managed to steer clear of both extremes. His wonted thoroughness studied every aspect of the case, all the complications introduced into it by the three-fold system that had obtained previous to 1918. The problem was too vast to be solved all at once, and thanks to the general goodwill of the Polish people towards Rome and the reality of their traditional devotion to the Holy See, there was not that danger in delay which otherwise there might have been room to fear. One of Mgr. Ratti's last acts was the nomination of a commission of bishops and heads of religious orders appointed to treat with a similar governmental commission and to draw out the preliminary conditions of an agreement. The concordat ultimately arrived at was completed and signed four years later.[1]

But if the matter of the state's recognition of the Church's status could wait yet awhile, the case was far different with the other problem of the effect on Church property of the projected reforms in the tenure of land.

Poland has always been a land of villages, and even to-day

[1] It is described in a later chapter. *Cf.* pp. 175–190.

two-thirds of its people are villagers. The land has been owned in the past by a relatively small number of great proprietors, lords of vast estates of tens of thousands of acres, and, in the old kingdom before the partition of 1772, the Church had been one of the greatest landowners of all. Many of these Church lands had been confiscated by the partitioning powers and they were now in the possession of the new republic. Nineteenth-century Poland inherited a *régime* of large landed proprietors upon whose vast domains there lived hordes of peasant serfs. The towns were impoverished, there were no industries worth mentioning, trade was utterly decayed. But, by the end of the century, even in Russian Poland, the worst administered and the most oppressed of the three divisions, things had greatly changed. Industries there had so developed that Poland was become the workshop of the Russian Empire. Trade flourished. There was a prosperous middle class, an active intelligentsia, and the beginnings of a strong movement to organise the town workers. But the system of great estates and peasants remained, despite the growth of a powerful class of small farmers.

One inevitable effect of the new political divisions effected at Versailles in 1918 was to cut off from Poland its two natural markets, Germany (from the provinces of Poznan and Pomerania which no longer formed part of the Reich) and Russia (from the industrial centres of Warsaw and Lodz). Between the industrial districts of Poland and their best markets there now intervened a political frontier, and there would one day intervene a tariff barrier too.

Almost the first task to which the new state had to set its hand was then a reorganisation of the whole system of national economy. The industries whose markets had so suddenly shrunk must, somehow, be preserved. Trade must be fostered and encouraged. Above all the question of the land must be faced.

And this for other reasons besides those of national economy.

Whether Bolshevism be a boon or a curse such distant

western states as France and England could, twenty years
ago, afford, perhaps, to look on at the Russian experiment
with academic curiosity. Not so Poland. For the new
state, in such painful gestation during the three years of
Mgr. Ratti's mission, the huge Russian Empire where every
socialistic theory was now steadily going into practice, was
a menace (or example) whose effect was immediate.
Poland, until within a few months since, had actually been
a part of that empire. Its agrarian *régime* was similar. The
grievances of the peasant in the one had much in common
with those of the peasant in the other. There was no
frontier of any kind whatever between the two peoples.
The new *régime* in Russia was actively militant, proposing
to aid the oppressed in all countries to rise and destroy
their oppressors. By the time Poland saw its first freely
elected Parliament in session at Warsaw (February, 1919)
an agrarian revolution in Russia had made the peasants
masters of the land they tilled. It was inevitable that this
immense change should have its echo in Poland too. The
new government had to consider how most speedily to
emancipate the peasant and make him owner of his farm
and yet avoid such a sudden dislocation of agricultural life
as would lead to its ruin. The latifundia must go and yet
no injury be done to the standard of agricultural production.

The difficulty of the problem was, of course, greatly
increased by the fact that it was not in a time of ease and
general peacefulness that it came before the government,
but in a time of grave political anxiety, where any false
move might bring down the whole fabric of the nascent
state, and in a time of serious economic crisis that bordered
on famine. A million and a half of the farms of Poland
had been destroyed as the hostile armies marched and
counter-marched across its territory in the years following
1914. A third of the livestock had gone, there were almost
no horses to be had anywhere. Three years after the
armistice it was only an importation of seven million tons
of foodstuffs in 1921 that kept the country alive.

MGR. ACHILLES RATTI
Prefect of the Ambrosian Library, " En Route "

It was in July, 1919—the month of Mgr. Ratti's appointment as nuncio—that the question of the redistribution of the land first came before the Parliament, and the Constituent Assembly passed a resolution adopting the principle of this policy. The next year saw a drastic bill pass into law, making sales compulsory and fixing a maximum acreage beyond which no one individual might own. This was later modified, and by the Act of 1925 the maximum was fixed at 450 acres. Along with this revolution in the ownership of land there has gone on simultaneously—but more slowly—a second revolution to ensure that a man's holding of land shall, as far as possible, be in one piece. Under the old system the strips that made up a farm were usually separated and were often at no small distance one from another. How great this evil was may be judged from the very moderate ideal which this movement, called " commassation," has before it—namely, that each owner should have at least one connected acre of land. There were, in 1918, 28,000,000 acres in need of this rearrangement, and even now, after nineteen years, the problem is far from its final solution.

The revolution in land tenure just described brought Mgr. Ratti into the very heart of the great political controversy of the day. No nuncio was ever so little the ornamental diplomat as the man who had now to guide the action of the bishops and clergy during changes that affected intimately the daily life of some nine-tenths of their flock.

The Church was concerned in the matter in two ways. Often the endowment of a parish was in the shape of land, and to sell this in any great amount would be to destroy Church property for ever in a country where the mass of the faithful were extremely poor—peasants for the most part whose staple food was a diet of rye bread, potatoes and cabbage—and, in an age when new endowments in any quantity were hardly to be hoped for, to throw on these poor people a new and heavy burden. To this very serious aspect of the question of land reform, other complications were added that made the inevitably difficult negotiations still more delicate, such a complication, for example, as that arising from the fact that much of the land was Church property, confiscated by the three foreign powers who had once partitioned Poland, but in right, and in Canon Law, still the property of the Church, and not to be subjected to further expropriation without some kind of understanding with the Holy See.

It is not necessary to point out what an unusual combination of firmness, tact, patience and wide knowledge of a many-sided problem were called for in the man who, hailed from his first coming into the country as the providentially sent harbinger of a new age, had now, in the very first enthusiasm of restored life, delicately but firmly, to recall duties and obligations of justice.

Here again it was not given to Mgr. Ratti to complete the work. But the solution ultimately arrived at, which he sanctioned not as nuncio but as pope, owed very much indeed to his great gift of hard work which in these years 1920 and 1921 brought him through whole seas of projects, plans and petitions with their hundreds of documents and their thousands of detailed arguments. The lifelong habit of system, the clear head, the scientific impartiality, secured that the examination was complete and that in the final decision not a single one of the myriad factors involved was overlooked.

The final settlement of these, and of other questions, is to be seen in the Concordat of 2 June, 1925, made as its opening words declare " In the name of the Most Holy and Undivided Trinity." Article XXIV of the Concordat deals with the matter of the Church's landed property. The question of Church properties once confiscated by the three partitioning powers and now in possession of the Polish Republic is left over for final settlement, but until such settlement the state agrees to annual payments, not inferior in value to the similar payments made of old by the governments of Austria, Prussia and Russia. An annex to the Concordat sets out the details. The sums, need it be said, are not such as to attract fortune-hunters.   Should these ancient Church lands meanwhile be broken up, then sees, seminaries and parishes which are actually without any landed endowment, or whose landed endowment is insufficient, shall receive up to 445 acres (in the case of sees and seminaries) or 37 to 74 acres (according to the quality of the soil) in the case of parishes : in case of such distribution the annual money grant from the state is to be proportionately diminished.

As regards the question of compulsory sales of estates in lots to the peasantry, the Holy See has consented, " in order to better the economic and social conditions of the peasantry and to promote to the best of its power religious peace in Poland," to allow the different ecclesiastical owners to sell what arable land they hold over and above 37 to 74 acres in the case of parishes (according to the quality of the soil) and 445 acres in the case of chapters, seminaries and sees.   The choice of what parts of their estates they shall retain is left to the ecclesiastical authorities concerned.

The Concordat has also finally regulated the rearrangement of the different sees.   No part of Polish territory now falls within the jurisdiction of a foreign see, and no Polish see has any territory outside the Polish frontier.   There are five ecclesiastical provinces and fifteen suffragan sees of the Latin rite.   The see of Sejny has been suppressed, there are new sees at Lomza, Lodz, Pinsk, Czenstochowa and Katowice ;   Vilna and Cracow are raised to archiepiscopal rank.

Mgr. Ratti's new offices, the new dignity and the new experience of being one of the day's public figures made scarcely any difference to his habitual way of life.   For thirty years at Milan and at Rome, he had filled a post that placed all his working hours at the service of others.   As Visitor Apostolic and Nuncio he continued to be universally accessible.   To see everyone who called on him had once been very largely the secret of Abraham Lincoln's success, and for all that in the nunciature at Warsaw there was an appointed limited hour for audiences, it soon became known that almost any hour of the day that found the Nuncio at home found him ready to receive whoever called. This meant, very often indeed, the sacrifice of the last of his scanty leisure. But he would never restrict the steady flow. " I am the first envoy of the pope to live here for more than a hundred years," he would say, speaking of that feature of Russian persecution which had most wounded the Poles, namely, their enforced isolation from Rome, " it is only right that I should give to them all every possible chance of seeing me and of meeting me." Did he, one may ask, recall Cardinal Federigo " These souls are mine. Perhaps they may never see my face again. Would you not have me embrace them ? " [1]

Like Lincoln, too, Mgr. Ratti understood that a visitor with a grievance, or a complaint, or one who came laden with anxiety, needed leisure if he was really to tell his story, and be effectively helped. A full and patient hearing, the nuncio would say, is always a consolation and, rather dryly, perhaps some compensation when authority has to make an inevitable refusal.

During these years he usually said mass at 7.30, and then, his coffee taken, went to his desk working or receiving visitors until one. He lunched with his secretaries, and by two was once more in his study, occupied through a long afternoon until six. Then followed a stiff walk. He dined at eight, and about ten he said good night to his household and retired for a last time to his desk, to compose his despatches and reports for Rome, working steadily up to midnight, and, when matters pressed, often until two and three in the morning. These long official despatches he wrote in full himself, and the future historian of Poland to whom, in fifty years or so from now, these more recent sections of the Papal Archives will be opened, will find an

---

[1] *I Promessi Sposi*, ch. xxii : " Sono mie anime, e forse non vedranno mai più la mia faccia, e non volete che gli abbracci ? "

immense amount of his material written in the hand of a future pope.

The papal nuncio is a diplomatist, and universally [1] the doyen of the diplomatic corps in the capital to which he is accredited. To him it often falls to represent his colleagues and to speak in their name, and about his person much of the diplomatic life turns. The advantages can hardly be exaggerated of having, in these pioneer days of the new state, as doyen of the diplomatic body a man of such unusually wide interests, of such a knowledge of Europe and European culture in all its variety, who spoke with ease its principal tongues. Whence a certain affection and even veneration for their colleague that peeps out more than once in the chance references to him of those diplomatists who have, since those days, written of their own career in Poland.

But the nuncio is not a diplomatist merely. He is a priest and a bishop, and from the very beginnings of his stay in Poland Mgr. Ratti showed himself, as ever, most of all at home in the country's religious life. Visits to orphanages, hospitals, colleges and seminaries, sermons and conferences to clergy and to religious, the administration of Confirmation and Holy Orders, scarcely ever was an invitation of this kind refused. The busiest man has always the most leisure.

He continued to live in his little suite at the clergy house attached to the great church of St. Alexander in Warsaw, thriftily, even in a certain poverty as hardly needs telling, considering the state of the papal treasury in these years when so many millions had to be found for relief work in eastern Europe. " You'll have to make do on next to nothing," Benedict XV had warned him, and then, with a characteristic touch, " but when you must spend, spend well. Poor indeed we are, but still with a certain dignity." It is not without interest to know that these three years in Poland passed without the Nuncio ever having a holiday. The first summer he was continually *en route*, the next year the immense detail of the establishment of the nunciature

[1] By the Final Act of the Congress of Vienna, 1815.

filled the whole summer, and in 1920 those same months saw the crisis of the Bolshevik invasion. His only holiday was the time spent in the train between one appointment and another.

Before we come to speak of the most delicate situation the Nuncio had to face, the matter of the plebiscite in Upper Silesia, something must be said about his work as Visitor in the other parts of his jurisdiction, Lithuania, Latvia, Esthonia and Finland.

At the time of his arrival in Poland, June, 1918, the territories that to-day form the states of Lithuania and Latvia were in German occupation and when the Visitor Apostolic sought the necessary permission to enter this provisionally German province it was politely refused, the reason given being the antipathy of the Lithuanians to anything or anybody associated with Poland. How much of truth there was in this piece of bureaucratic diplomacy may be doubted. Whatever the feeling of Lithuanians against Poles, and their fears in 1918 that the new Poland would stand in the way of Lithuanian independence, the Visitor Apostolic was no Pole and stood to Poles in precisely the same relation as he stood to Lithuanians. Before long catastrophe came and in their hour of difficulty it was to Mgr. Ratti that the German authorities in Lithuania turned, inviting him to Kovno and Riga as insistently as, a short time before, they had kept him out. But to leave Poland in the critical November of 1918 was impossible. The next year saw the re-establishment of the nunciature, and it was not until January, 1920, that the Nuncio found his opportunity to cross the northern frontiers.

By this time Lithuania was an independent state and bitterly hostile to Poland, whose armies since the anti-Bolshevist advance of 1919 had occupied Vilna, a city whose inhabitants were no doubt almost entirely Poles but which, none the less, was the historic capital of Lithuania. It was one of those situations where the peacemaker can hope for very little. Lucky indeed he is if he himself escape the combined suspicions of both parties as plot and counterplot succeed each other. The see of Vilna had just been filled after a vacancy of fifty years. The new bishop, for all that his life had been spent in Poland—he was the Superior-General of the religious order to which he belonged—was by birth a Lithuanian. This nomination, made while the German occupation was still a reality, was anything but welcome to the newly-roused nationalism of the Poles, and once they had occupied Vilna a tense situation speedily developed. The new bishop was the choice of the bishops of Poland and the Visitor Apostolic had assented to it.

To Vilna then Mgr. Ratti went in January, 1920, staying there for five days and paying his visit to the famous shrine of Our Lady—the Black Virgin of Vilna—where he knelt in the snow with the crowd of pious peasants, remaining in prayer for a matter of two hours, prayer who can doubt it, for the reconciliation of these two Catholic nations called by their geographical situation to be the first defence of Christendom against the militant atheism of the new Russia.

At Vilna the Nuncio used every chance that came to him to study the thorny question of the hour, delegations from one party and the other filing continuously into the bishop's residence where he was lodged. All were patiently heard, encouraged to be patient and to understand that this kind of difficulty can only be solved by the exercise on both sides of the charity that comes from the love of God.

On 29 January, a bitterly cold day—the thermometer registering forty degrees of frost, and the very railway engine covered with icicles—the Nuncio set out for Kovno, the actual capital of the Lithuanian state. As the mission proceeded the pace grew even slower until finally the frost was too much for the locomotive, for a succession of them even, and it was only after a matter of several hours that the short fifty miles between the two cities were covered. At Kovno there were the usual succession of conferences, the bishops, the diplomatic corps, the President of the Republic, and a great ceremonial banquet in which the

Nuncio's tact was taxed to the full in replying to the speeches of responsible ministers which invited assent to a denunciation of the Polish enemy.

Six weeks later the Nuncio returned, to make another passing visit on his way to Riga, the capital of Latvia, where he had been instrumental in restoring the bishopric. At Riga, as at Kovno, this visit saw laid the foundations of understandings between the Holy See and the new states which, a few years later, Mgr. Ratti was to sign as Pope Pius XI.

In these visits to the north the Nuncio had every chance to understand by personal experience the ruin and misery that war leaves in its track, whether it shows in the hunger of whole populations, in the ruins of villages and towns, or the inconvenience of the breakdown of communications. Once again it took the special train eighteen hours to go a matter of a hundred miles, and the journey ended on an army service lorry.

Finland the Visitor Apostolic never reached, nor was he any luckier in regard to Russia. To all his endeavours the Soviet government turned a persistently deaf ear. His one success, if that is the right word, was to secure the liberation from his prison of the much persecuted Archbishop of Mohilev, the Metropolitan of the Latin Catholics in Russia, Mgr. Edward de Ropp.

Internal conflicts in yet another part of the new state called for the Nuncio's peace-loving intervention. This was in those provinces, once governed by Austria, known as Eastern Galicia. Here there is a mixed population of Poles and Ruthenians, these last the same people racially and linguistically as the Ukrainians who occupied the adjacent territory just beyond the frontier in Russia. Ruthenians and Poles, who were about equal in numbers, the superiority being with the Ruthenians, were further divided by the fact that although both were Catholics, they were Catholics of different rites, the Poles being Latins, like the vast majority of the Catholics in western Europe, and the Ruthenians using a Greek liturgy akin to that used by the

Orthodox Church throughout eastern Europe. This complication is the reason why in more than one town of Galicia there are two Catholic bishops, one for each rite. Thus Lwow (Lemberg), the chief town of the province, has a Latin archbishop who rules over 1,014,321 Catholics of his own rite with 802 priests : and also a Ruthenian archbishop with another 1,344,355 Catholics and 1,321 priests.[1]

The six months that followed the armistice of 1918 saw Galicia the theatre of a bloody struggle between Poles and Ruthenians until finally the Poles got the upper hand. Mgr. Ratti's intervention was a letter to the Latin and Ruthenian Archbishops of Lwow exhorting them to use all their influence to bring about a general peace and meanwhile to lessen the horrors of this struggle, to whose unusual savagery a host of stories, from both sides, seemed to bear witness. The two prelates thanked the Visitor Apostolic, as he then was, for his letter, but whatever their differences, agreed in the reply that, given the circumstances, nothing remained but for the two parties to fight it out to the end. Mgr. Ratti could but await the moment when it would all be over, and then use all his influence with the victorious Polish government to move it to a policy of clemency towards the Ruthenians.

No disputes, however, of all these critical years exceeded in bitterness those which centred round the decision of the Peace Conference that the future of Upper Silesia should be decided by plebiscite. "In consequence of this announcement," a distinguished Polish historian has written,[2] "the province became a veritable witches' cauldron of political passion and propaganda on both sides." This area—some 4,000 square miles, with a population of some two millions —had not formed part of the Polish state since the Middle Ages. It had been under Habsburg rule until Frederick the Great's successful theft of it from Maria Teresa in the

---

[1] Lwow has also a third, Catholic, archbishop for the Catholics of the Armenian rite, some 5,000 in number.

[2] ROMAN DYBOSKI, *Poland* (1933), p. 95.

eighteenth century, and thenceforward from 1742 to 1918 it was a part of the kingdom of Prussia. Now, in 1918, the Poles laid claim to at least a part of it, alleging that the population was two-thirds Polish. The province has an immense strategic importance, but what was more the reason for the Polish claim was the fact that the nineteenth century had shown Upper Silesia to be one of the world's great industrial regions. In the years just before the war its annual production of coal was something like 44 million tons, three times as great as that of Germany's other great coalfield in the Saar. The region is likewise immensely rich in iron and lead and zinc. The preliminaries to the plebiscite could hardly fail to be seriously disturbing.

The first sign of trouble was a Polish rising against the German authorities in the autumn of 1919. This produced the Inter-allied Commission for Upper Silesia and a small international force with which lay the responsibility for maintaining order until the plebiscite had taken place.

The population of the disputed territory was, in the mass, Catholic, and under the jurisdiction of the Bishop of Breslau, Cardinal Bertram. Naturally the Poles regarded him as anti-Polish, and the government at Warsaw, fearful that his authority as bishop of the diocese might influence the situation, asked the Holy See to appoint a special commissioner for Silesia, whose duty it should be to promote the cause of peace and to see that ecclesiastical influence was not allowed any undue share in the campaign of propaganda now in full swing. The government proposed the nuncio at Warsaw for the post, and, since the German government, too, found him acceptable, he was appointed to the unenviable position, March, 1920. Had Mgr. Ratti's own ideas prevailed, the commissioner would have been chosen from some country that had played no part in the war, or, if it had to be himself, he would have had associated with him the then nuncio to Germany, Mgr. Pacelli, the present Cardinal Secretary of State.

The new task began with a brief unofficial visit of a week or so to the scene of the dispute. Mgr. Ratti arrived at

Oppeln, the chief town of the region, on 4 April, 1920, went on the next day to visit Cardinal Bertram at Breslau, and spent the remainder of the time in his usual fashion, gathering information from all sides and weighing up the general situation.   Even in this short time he came to the conclusion that if the plebiscite was to pass off with even a chance of peace it must not be long delayed.   Four or five months, he thought, was the longest delay possible.   In the event it did not take place for a whole year.

As papal commissioner in Upper Silesia Mgr. Ratti had but one duty, to do all he could to prevent anything like a civil war between the German and Polish sections of this Catholic population.   With the plebiscite itself he had, as a commissioner, no connection whatever.   Nor had he any special ecclesiastical jurisdiction.   The rights of the Bishop of Breslau to rule his diocese and provide for its welfare as he judged best remained in every respect intact.

But Mgr. Ratti had instructions to confer with the Cardinal and in his public action to do nothing without such consultation.   The Cardinal was similarly instructed.   The whole aim of the mission was to prevent, in this burning matter of politics, any intervention of ecclesiastics which might prejudice the interests of religion.   The association of the papal commissioner with the German bishop would protect from any suspicion of partiality whatever intervention was thought necessary.

In June 1920 Mgr. Ratti returned to Silesia, this time in his official capacity.   He issued a letter, in German and in Polish, which was read at mass in all the churches of the territory on Sunday, 13 June.   In this he explained carefully the precise nature of his mission and exhorted the faithful to co-operate in the good work by an endeavour to understand the position of the other side and to remember that, Poles or Germans, they were to the Holy Father first of all Catholics and equally his children.

For a whole fortnight the Nuncio busied himself in his arduous, and more or less thankless, task.   Feeling ran too high for any but new partisans to be really welcome to the extremists whose passions, not unnaturally, coloured the whole life of the district. On both sides there was some dissatisfaction already that Mgr. Ratti had failed to see that right lay entirely with their own party.

· Then, on 21 June, he had to leave for a week to make a visit to an area further north, in East Prussia, where also plebiscites were in operation and where his presence was required. Here, in Marienwerden and at Allenstein, feeling was happily not so bitter, and the Nuncio had the opportunity of visiting in his ancient cathedral city the primate of Poland, Cardinal Dalbor, Archbishop of Gniezno-Poznan. From East Prussia he went on to Warsaw, and after a week in the capital, returned yet once again to Silesia on 6 July.

This time his visit was short, for at the news of the defeats of the Polish army[1] and the rapid advance of the Russians towards the capital, he hastened to regain Warsaw. Apparently the end of the new state was now in sight. The western powers, who a short twelve months before had called it into being, were now deaf to all appeals for assistance. It was not unnatural that the German faction in Silesia used its opportunity and the rumours began to spread of a complete collapse of Poland. The Poles in Silesia replied by another armed rising (August, 1920) that was only quieted by the substitution of a mixed force of Germans and Poles for the German police.

The political situation kept the Nuncio close to Warsaw all through the next six months. Actually he was never again in Upper Silesia.

The plebiscite took place in March 1921, when 479,359 votes were cast for inclusion in Poland, and 707,605 for inclusion in Germany. Protestations poured into the League Council from the Poles, allegations of undue influence, especially on the part of the German owners of the mines towards their Polish workmen, and then, on the rumour that to Poland were to be adjudged only some of the agricultural districts (whereas the industrial block was

[1] *Cf. infra*, pp. 95 seq.

almost wholly Polish) revolt flared up again. There was a
general strike in the coal mines and an armed rising that
developed into a miniature war and continued for another
three months (May–July, 1921). In October the decision
was announced. It gave to Poland, besides certain agricultural regions in the south, the industrial area that
centres round Katowice. Oppeln and the half million or so
Poles in its neighbourhood remained German. On the
other hand Poland in gaining Katowice gained a town with
a large population of Germans.

What the final decision meant to Poland may be gathered
from these few facts. Of 67 coal mines in the area Poland
received 53; of 37 blast furnaces 21; of 14 steel mills 9;
and 70 per cent. of the zinc-producing mines and plant.
The League, however, insisted that Polish Silesia should
enjoy a kind of Home Rule through an elected provincial
Legislative Assembly, while a special international arbitra-
tion commission was set up to deal with German-Polish
disputes arising in the new province. Finally, in June
1922, Polish troops marched into the new possession.
After almost eight years Poland's wars were finally over.

The final settlement of the Silesian question did not,
however, take place without causing to the Nuncio what
was probably the gravest embarrassment of his whole life,
and certainly an occasion of weeks and even months of
anxiety and pain. In November 1920 the Cardinal Bishop
of Breslau issued an instruction to his clergy in which,
under pain of suspension to be incurred *ipso facto*, he
forbade any priest to take part in any political action without
the previous consent of the parish priest of the place concerned. Furthermore, priests from outside the diocese
were strictly forbidden to take any part in the controversy
about the plebiscite. The numerous Polish subjects of this
German bishop interpreted the decree as an anti-Polish
manœuvre.[1] Their indignation knew no bounds, and, the

---

[1] It has been said that 75 per cent. of the parish priests in the plebiscite area
were Germans. *Cf.* PERNOT, p. 150, who, however, gives no authority for the
statement.

decree having been published as " with the approbation
of the Holy See," [1] their indignation included the papal
commissioner as well as the cardinal.

As a matter of fact Mgr. Ratti had had nothing whatever
to do with the preparation or publication of the decree.
The cardinal had judged such action to be necessary. He
had foreseen the storm it would provoke. And to keep
the neutrality of the commissioner free from any suspicion
he had carefully refrained from notifying him of what he
was about to do. When the storm broke, fierce invective
and denunciation of the Nuncio in the Press and in the
Parliament, it was not for Mgr. Ratti to explain the situation
and, clearing himself, perhaps compromise the cardinal.
There was but one course possible, complete silence, and,
for the rest, to hope that one day the truth would be known
and his name cleared. And before his mission to Poland
came to an end the Nuncio was happy in the knowledge that
he was already vindicated in the minds of all but the
extremists, and that the Holy See's office to be the reconciler
of nations rather than a partisan in their conflicts was more
and more gratefully recognised.

Mgr. Ratti's mission to Poland gave him three years of
life packed with adventurous realism. They were years
spent among an imaginative and passionate people in the
first dawn of their emancipation. A host of problems
clamoured for solution. Rival interests intrigued and fought
for predominance. Idealism on all sides was often in closest
alliance with opportunism. And beyond the eastern
frontiers of Poland the age-long enemy of her culture, her
faith and her freedom awaited its hour. Once this foe
moved, the fate of the Poles might be only a matter of
weeks.

The Polish military occupation of the lands surrendered
by Russia in 1918 proceeded, during 1919, without any
notable opposition. The Soviet government was too
occupied with its own internal troubles to be able to pay
much attention to what was happening on its western

---

[1] PERNOT, p. 150, but again without any authority for the assertion.

boundary. Towards the end of that year, in fact, the Bolsheviks made proposals for a peace, but Pilsudski, who was now the all-powerful force in Polish affairs, refused, believing in his heart that no lasting peace with the Soviets was possible until they had been crushed in the field.

The new year, therefore, saw a new Polish offensive, this time in co-operation with the new anti-Bolshevik government set up in the Ukraine under Ataman Petlura. Once more there was little opposition and in May 1920 the allies took Kiev.

But the Bolsheviks were by this time delivered from the menace of the counter-revolution within, and the fall of this great city of the south was the signal for a vigorous counter-offensive, whose aim was something far greater than the mere recovery of Kiev or even than the conquest of Poland. "Had the Soviet forces overcome Polish resistance and captured Warsaw," writes Lord D'Abernon,[1] "Bolshevism would have spread throughout Central Europe, and might well have penetrated the whole continent." That this is not the wild exaggeration of an anti-Communist partisan, anxious only to make the bourgeois flesh creep, is evident from the language in which the Commander-in-Chief of the Russian army himself described his ultimate objective. Lecturing on the campaign of 1920 to the students of the Military Academy at Moscow in 1923, Marshal Tukachevsky [2] declared "There is not the slightest doubt that, if we had succeeded in breaking the Polish army of bourgeois and seigneurs, the revolution of the working class in Poland would have been an accomplished fact. And the tempest would not have stopped at the Polish frontier. Like a furious torrent it would have swept over the whole of Eastern Europe. The Red army will not forget this attempt to carry the revolution outside our

[1] *The Eighteenth Decisive Battle of the World*, London, 1931, p. 11. Lord D'Abernon was in 1920 British Ambassador at Berlin, and in these months of July and August resident in Warsaw as the British Diplomatic representative on the Allied Commission to advise and support the government of Poland.

[2] The lecture is quoted extensively in D'ABERNON, *op. cit.*, pp. 152–168. The title of the lecture is itself significant, viz., "The Advance beyond the Vistula."

frontiers, and if ever the European bourgeoisie braves us to new fights, the Red army will crush it and spread revolution throughout Europe."

In something less than forty days the Poles retreated four hundred miles before the new advance. In June it was Zhitomir that the Bolsheviks captured, with immense stores, thousands of prisoners and almost all the Polish heavy artillery. At the same time the enemy broke through the resistance on the northern front along the Dwina. Whole regiments of the new Polish armies broke in panic, and the demoralisation began to spread universally. Then in July Minsk fell to the enemy, Vilna and Grodno. Lemberg was threatened and, crossing the Bug, the Bolsheviks made straight for Warsaw.

The situation of Poland was now desperate, and it was almost universally regarded as hopeless. As to the condition of its army both Tukachevsky and Pilsudski tell the same tale. " Our brilliant successes," says the Russian commander,[1] " and the continued retreat of the Polish army had finally destroyed the latter's fighting capacity. We were no longer opposed by organised troops ; the complete demoralisation, the absolute want of any confidence and the impossibility of success, had undermined the morale both of leaders and men. The Poles sometimes retired without reason ; there were hundreds of deserters ; no Provost-Marshal could restore order or discipline ; and above all there was the antagonism between class and class. Workmen's centres had been strangled by the mobilisation, but the murmur of revolt continued among them."

Pilsudski's testimony to the demoralisation is equally to the point. " The nightmare of defeat and the excuses of poltroons were sweeping over the whole town. . . . I hesitated to place my trust in the morale of the troops and the inhabitants, and I could not be sure of the military and civil authorities. . . . I noted, moreover, a very poor state of the equipment and uniforms of the troops. I had never in all my experience of warfare seen such ragamuffins as I

[1] D'ABERNON, op. cit., p. 152.

called them. In the 21st Division, half of the men appeared before me, at Firlej, practically naked." [1]

To such an experienced observer as Lord D'Abernon, then actually on the spot, "Nothing could appear more certain than that the Soviet forces would capture Warsaw." [2] It is safe to say that all Europe shared that expectation. As the Anglo-French mission passed through Czecho-Slovakia President Masaryk actually did his best to persuade them to abandon the enterprise. "By openly siding with the Poles in their hopeless position we would do them no good and we should do ourselves much harm." The population here was more friendly to the Bolsheviks than to the Poles, and the whole atmosphere secretly hostile to Poland.[3] Socialists and Communists everywhere watched the Russian advance with the most eager sympathy. In Germany the workers could not be relied on to handle supplies destined for the Poles. At Paris the D'Abernon Commission was regarded as no more than a last despairing gesture of futile sympathy. English politicians had one preoccupation only ; to keep clear of any entanglement, whether Warsaw fell or not. Lord Curzon could speak of the executioner's axe as already within an ace of Poland's neck.

As the weeks of constant tragic loss went by, and the realisation grew that Poland was to be left to defend herself —though in defending herself she defended all that Europe knows as civilisation—preparations were hastily made to evacuate the capital. Archives and government offices were transferred to Poznan and the diplomatic corps prepared to follow suit. The Nuncio, who presided daily at their reunions, knew well what the prospects were. Diplomacy, for the moment, was at the end of its resources. The hour had come when man has no hope but in God. Mgr. Ratti telegraphed Rome for leave to remain in Warsaw whatever happened. The Catholic bishop could be of service even

---

[1] D'ABERNON, *op. cit.*, pp. 126, 127, 142.
[2] D'ABERNON, *op. cit.*, p. 18.
[3] D'ABERNON, *op. cit.*, pp. 21–22, 48, 113.

though the Nuncio had no longer any function. "I am not, like yourselves, a diplomatist only. As a priest I have the duty of helping to keep up this people's courage," he told his colleagues.[1] And indeed, at such a crisis as this, a Christian capital beset by an infidel horde, where else could an Archbishop of Lepanto be if not with the defenders in the very breach? He got off his archives, and his staff; with the English ambassador, Sir Horace Rumbold, he saw to the departure of his colleagues, and then, with the skeleton cabinet, he awaited, in the patience and hope that comes of prayer, what Providence would send.

For days now the menaced city had given itself to prayer, and on 6 August, the Feast of the Transfiguration, a great nine days of prayer began, to end on the Feast of Our Lady's Assumption, and as in some city of the Middle Ages, processions singing litanies of intercession filed continuously through the streets. This spirit seems to have been universal. When the Nuncio asked the French military adviser of the Allied Commission, General Weygand, what his expectations were, the soldier replied that all that was possible had been arranged. "The rest remains with your good prayers."

The Bolsheviks had already nominated the officers who were to govern the recaptured Poland. In the west, high political opinion was so unanimous in its expectation of the worst, that the Bolsheviks would win, that the crisis cost Poland a certain amount of territory, valuable industrial territory that were it granted to Poland would, evidently, within a matter of weeks, be a Bolshevik possession. So the western part of Teschen went to Czecho-Slovakia as a matter of obvious practical political sense.[2]

On 14 August, 1920, the Bolshevik attack on Warsaw began. There was heavy fighting all that day in the suburbs, parts of which were lost, retaken and lost again. The Poles

[1] BEYENS, p. 101.
[2] The Spa Conference of 1920.

were holding their own, but hardly realised that they were not defeated. Discouragement reigned supreme and urgent messages were sent calling for the return of Pilsudski who, two days earlier, had left the capital to take over the command of the desperate manœuvre on which he had staked all. He refused to return, hoping against hope that Warsaw would hold out yet another day while he made his great move, an attack on the enemy's flank from a position well to the south of the capital. His one concession to the situation was to begin his advance a day earlier than he had intended. At dawn on 16 August he moved forward and, after two days of incredibly rapid marching, his ragged and bootless army came up with the rear of the besieging army. He had succeeded beyond all human right of expectation.

To save themselves, their communications now seriously threatened, the Bolsheviks rapidly withdrew, in great confusion, and after a momentary hesitation, due to their genuine inability to grasp the fact of victory, the Poles fell on them in pursuit. The whole position was transformed. Had there now been reserves who were fresh, had there been normally decent equipment, there was a chance, seemingly, that an end might have been made for ever of the military power of the Red government. Even as it was, the Poles drove the enemy before them for hundreds of miles. Of the twenty-one divisions engaged they captured seven, six were utterly broken, and the rest retired in the greatest disorder. Sixty thousand prisoners were taken, 200 guns, and 1,000 machine guns. In September a second battle was fought on the Niemen, in which the Poles were again victorious, and on 21 October the armistice was signed from which came, in March, 1921, the definitive Treaty of Riga.

Not for centuries had a papal envoy thus stood with the army of Christendom in its desperate hour defending the frontier. Who shall speak of the fruits of such an experience and such a victory upon the mind of the scholar-diplomatist, the culminating adventure of these three wonderfully filled years that link the librarian with the pope ?

Although Mgr. Ratti knew it not, his term of office in Poland was, in March, 1921, drawing to a close. In that month, when by the Treaty of Riga and the plebiscite in Upper Silesia two of the major questions of Poland's future were settled, he had only been nuncio a matter of twenty months. To be given high promotion after so short a service is not usual. But a few weeks earlier, on 2 February, there had died Mgr. Ratti's one-time superior, Cardinal Andrew Ferrari, for twenty-seven years Archbishop of Milan. He had been one of the greatest Italian prelates of his generation, and now, almost immediately it would seem, it was to the nuncio in Poland—the one-time canon of Milan and prefect of the Ambrosian—that Benedict XV turned to fill his place.

CHAPTER IV

13 June, 1921—6 February, 1922

THERE is not much room, in so slight a study as this, for any detailed account of the brief episcopate of Mgr. Achilles Ratti in the city of St. Ambrose and St. Charles.

He left Warsaw on 4 June, 1921 ; on the thirteenth he was created Archbishop of Milan and cardinal with the title of St. Martin *ai Monti*. He stayed on in Rome for a month, busy with the formalities that closed his life as nuncio and with the deluge of congratulatory letters that had poured in. On 25 July he left for Monte Cassino, to spend a whole month in the quiet of the great Benedictine monastery, organising his thoughts and preparing for the new life and responsibilities that lay ahead. Here he wrote his first pastoral letters, one for his new subjects in general and the other, a Latin letter, for his clergy. He was once more in Rome, on 25 August, for his farewell audience of Benedict XV, before taking possession of his see, and he left Rome for the last time as the leader of the Italian national pilgrimage to Lourdes.

The night of 7 September he spent in his native place, Desio, and on the morrow, the feast of Our Lady's nativity, he made his solemn entry into Milan and was enthroned as archbishop. It was a great day of public rejoicing. The whole city gave itself up to celebrate this return to Milan, as archbishop and cardinal, of one of the most loyal of Milanese, who had drawn from its great library the wealth of learning and culture and from its ecclesiastical tradition the force of character that had, since he left Milan seven years before, made him a figure in the international world. There was the pontifical mass sung in the Duomo by the new archbishop, his sermon, banquets, speeches, illuminations, and in the afternoon the inauguration of a new work of charity. The city and the whole archdiocese turned to happy thoughts of the great episcopate now opening so auspiciously. The new archbishop had all the gifts, as the Press, with ample detail in proof, pointed out. What might not be expected of his reign? Alas for Milan! Cardinal Ratti took for his motto the punning device *Raptim Transit*.[1] It was to prove prophetic. Five months barely from the day of Milan's festivity he was elected pope.

There has since been published a letter, written from Warsaw by Mgr. Ratti some days before he left for Rome, a letter of thanks for a friend's congratulations. "As to my own affairs, what can I say except what St. Martin said, '*Non recuso laborem*,' new work unaccustomed and immense as it will be. I do not, however, let myself be overcome either by the pastoral dignity or the cardinalate. With the first the Holy Father has wished to give satisfaction to the many, oh, too many friends, who wish me well, and the second is a gesture of sovereign courtesy from him to that noble Polish nation, lately risen from the dead and still palpitating, and to my own dear city and diocese of Milan.

"The pope's decision, serious as it is for me, leaves me in peace and even gives me a great trustfulness in the help of men and of God Himself, the more so since my own will was altogether absent from the decision, as was indeed any possibility of choice on my part."

The pope's own words were a great help: "In this appointment God and myself alone had a say." [2]

If there were, in the great archdiocese, any who expected a hermit-archbishop, his days given over to his books, they were rudely and rapidly disillusioned. From the first week Cardinal Ratti began to show himself everywhere, and pastoral visits of one kind or another filled every day of the next five months. His official diary for that time does not show a single day free from some official engagement. As

[1] He passes hurriedly.
[2] "In questa nomina non ci sono entrati che Dio ed io," NOVELLI, p. 176.

in Poland, his first thought was to make himself personally acquainted with every aspect of the new task. Week by week in a series of receptions he made the first contacts with his clergy. Sundays invariably found him in some country parish. Wherever he went he preached and spoke, and he gave liberally of his leisure to callers of every kind. The lasting literary memorials of this short, well-filled, episcopate are the address delivered at the inauguration of the new Catholic University of Milan and the first part of the joint pastoral letter of the bishops of Lombardy published in January, 1922.

Benedict XV's death was sudden and unexpected. The news that he was seriously ill broke on Rome like a thunderbolt on the evening of 18 January, 1922. Less than four days later he died, early in the morning of Sunday the 22nd. No one who was in Rome during those days will forget the anxiety that held the whole city, nor the spontaneous grief that sent hundreds of thousands to St. Peter's to pay their last respects and offer a prayer at the bier of the dead pope. He had endured so much, the tragedy of the war had broken all the beginning of his reign, and now, just when his gifted spirit might look to accomplish something of its brilliant promise, death, wholly unlooked for, had taken him.

Little by little Rome began to receive the non-Roman members of the Sacred College and their suites. The columns of the newspapers were almost equally divided between lengthy accounts of the solemn requiems in the Sistine Chapel, the actual funeral of the dead pope, and the prospects of the different cardinals in the coming conclave. It is no exaggeration to say that, sooner or later, every one of the Italian cardinals found some paper to mention him as *papabile*. From the beginning the Archbishop of Milan had—may the term be allowed—a good Press. In any combination of half a dozen names his was sure to be found. As I read and re-read, the words of Cardinal Gasquet, describing his one-time subordinate, in a conversation only a month before the pope's death, came to mind : " The Archbishop of Milan . . . immense ability . . . a marvellously hard worker . . . the greatest ecclesiastical personality in Italy."

Cardinal Ratti left Milan on 24 January after preaching at the solemn requiem for Pope Benedict, on the text " He was a burning and a shining light " (John v. 35). At Rome he was lodged in his old Alma Mater the College of the Lombards. He paid a visit to the Roman house of the Cenacle nuns, where he made a very dry reply to some unfortunate well-wisher anent the coming election, and amongst other visits, a long one to Cardinal Gasquet, whose kindly insistence on seeing him to the door " at the last visit you will ever pay me " seemed rather to startle him.[1] Stories are told that seem to show he had some kind of presentiment of the dignity in store. But when two noble ladies of Milan brought a bouquet of white flowers—an augury of the white papal robes—to go with him into the conclave, he merely said " They'll look better before the Tabernacle in the little chapel," and there, of course, they went. The Rector of the college took his fourteen students into the cardinal's room for his blessing as he was about to leave for the conclave. " We shall be with Your Eminence in prayer," he said. " That is the best way to be with me," was the reply, and after a pause, " Thy will be done, Thy kingdom come." The students went out, and then to the Rector he said " And now let us go to prison." [2]

The evening of 2 February, the feast of Our Lady's Purification, fifty-three cardinals entered the conclave. The voting sessions began next day, Friday. It is matter of common knowledge that the cardinals are bound by a rigorously drawn oath not to reveal anything that passes in the conclave, even after the new pope's election. This must always be borne in mind, and the fact that at the voting sessions in the Sistine Chapel the cardinals alone are present. With these reserves and the remark that the account now given is said to derive " from the papers of a cardinal who died recently and who played a prominent part in the

---

[1] Cardinal Gasquet to the author.

[2] " Ed. ora andiamo in gabbia," NOVELLI, p. 214, which may be only a jesting way of saying " Now for the conclave " !

conclave of 1922," the following passage from Mgr. Fontenelle's *Pie XI* [1] will no doubt be of interest.

" If we can believe certain indiscreet ' revelations '—now public property—that derive from the papers of one of the last cardinals to die, who himself played a prominent part in the conclave of 1922, the struggle was lively enough from the moment it opened. There were two groups confronting each other. The one, centring round the two cardinals Merry del Val and La Fontaine, could count on 23 votes, the other—whose inspiration was the cardinals Gasparri and Maffi—counted 24. Neither of these groups had any chance of gaining the two-thirds majority which the law requires for the election of the pope, that is, in this case, 36 votes. A name which to begin with had never obtained more than 5 or 6 votes soon began to impose itself on the general opinion of the conclave. Cardinal Ratti, on the third day of the conclave, received 11, 14, 24 and 27 votes. [2] On the fourth day he received first 30 votes, and then (in the fourteenth ballot of the conclave), 42, which made him pope with 6 votes over the necessary two-thirds."

In carefully chosen words, slowly, haltingly almost, he accepted the election, and chose his new name of Pius, in memory of Pius IX, in whose reign he was born, baptised and made the first steps of his ecclesiastical career, and of Pius X who had called him to Rome, nearly ten years before. He then said, after a pause, " There is something else. I protest before the members of the Sacred College that I have at heart the safeguarding and the defence of the rights of the Church, and all the prerogatives of the Holy See ; that being said I wish that my first blessing should go out, as a pledge of that peace for which humanity is longing, not only to Rome and to Italy, but to the whole Church and the entire world. I shall give it from the outside balcony of St. Peter's."

The Monday of the election—6 February—was cold, wet and stormy. The square in front of St. Peter's was, for

---

[1] P. 70.
[2] There were two sessions daily, and at each session two ballots.

most of the time, deserted by comparison with the scene of
the sunny day before, and the crowd was massed under the
great colonnade. When the white smoke was at last seen
pouring thinly from the famous chimney, there was a
moment of doubt and then a general shout of " E fatto "
and a rush towards the church. Not for another half hour
or so did anything further happen, except the gradual
appearance, on the terrace that crowns the colonnade, of
various dignitaries of the Vatican, and then the lackeys of
the papal court came out to prepare the balcony in the
centre of the basilica's façade for the proclamation. Gradually the news crept round who it was had been elected.
But names shouted from house-tops, or telegraphed man-
ually by prearranged codes, are sometimes confused. There
were whispers of " Ratti " and also of " Tacci," and by the
time the senior Cardinal Deacon came out with his escort
to proclaim the new pope, a newspaper was selling a special
edition with an account of the life of Cardinal Tacci and a
photo of him in the pontifical robes ! [1] An old Italian
priest, I remember well, looking over his neighbour's
shoulder and at the picture—and his astounded exclamation
" Giovanni Tacci ! Madonna ! "

The proclamation was made in the usual style, and then
there was a rush for the church to get a good place inside for
the new pope's first blessing, always given inside since
1870. And then, slowly at first but soon with the speed of
fire, the marvellous news came through the crowd. It was
from the outside *loggia* that Pius XI would bless his people.
The next twenty minutes passed for most of that crowd—
it had swelled into tens and tens of thousands by now,
blocking the whole piazza, the Piazza Rusticucci and the
Borgo—in a very delirium of joy. Then the great moment
came, and, amid shouts that must have reached the Sabines,
the new pope appeared and solemnly gave his blessing,
and then, as he went, turned back to fling his arms wide
towards the crowd in a vast gesture of affection.

[1] Cardinal Tacci, one-time nuncio at Brussels, received the red hat at the
same consistory as Cardinal Ratti. He died 30 June, 1928.

Pius XI was crowned on the following Sunday, 12 February, a simple enough ceremony at the conclusion of a mass sung by the pope with all the traditional stately ceremonial.

To what burden and responsibility he had come ! And how dark and uncertain was the future, how very real the menace that hung everywhere over the Catholic Church ! The new countries of eastern Europe still struggling in the first efforts of new life, Austria facing an economic breakdown that threatened to destroy her utterly, Germany, embittered if unarmed, fighting her old enemies now in the matter of reparations, Italy torn with civil strife—wherever the new pope turned there was little to console or to encourage him.

He drew his own picture of the frightful legacy of the war in his first encyclical,[1] published eleven months after his election.

" The fact is patent to all. Even yet nowhere, since the catastrophe of the recent war, has man found the peace he seeks for, whether we consider individuals, or groups or nations. That active, fruitful peace which all desire still evades our grasp." In these words Pius XI supplies the future historian with the key to all his policies and the events of his reign. He begins his reign haunted by man's failure to secure that peace without which civilisation cannot endure. As pope it must be his first duty and his chief aim to work for the restoration of peace.

" If in Europe," the sombre analysis continues, " the weapons of war are laid aside, in the Near East threats of new wars are piling up. In those lands, and over immense areas, every horror and misery imagination could invent are to be found. Multitudes of unhappy people, of old people especially, of women and of children, daily fall victims to famine and to plague.

" Wherever the recent war raged, in all the nations that took part in it, the old jealousy has not yet died down. It

---

[1] *Ubi Arcano Dei*, 23 December, 1922 : translation in *The Pope and the People* Catholic Truth Society, London.

shows itself disguised in political manœuvres and in the fluctuations of the exchange, and, more openly, it shows in the articles that fill the newspapers and the reviews. These old hatreds have even invaded a part of life which of its nature has nothing in common with such bitter strife, the domain of art and of letters.

" This mutual enmity, these attacks of one state on another, are choking the people of the world. Not only are the victors still at war with the vanquished, but among the victors themselves there is an equally active mutual hostility. . . . The consequences of the war grow daily more terrible, as the innumerable conferences and congresses of statesmen fail to provide any remedy and, indeed, aggravate the trouble. The fear of a return of war is growing, of a war that will be worse than the last, and the nations are, all of them, haunted by the necessity of living under arms. Thence comes an exhausted treasury, a waste in physical strength, and a wholesale decline in the intellectual life as in morals and religious zeal.

" To this must be added the still more deadly hate of civil discord within. . . .

" The evils from which human society, as such, is suffering react upon the lives of all its members. No one will deny that, in every rank of society, at every age, the minds of men are restless, embittered, sullen. Insubordination and laziness are almost the fashion. The levity of women and girls has passed all the limits of moral decency, in dress and in dances especially, and their increased thirst for luxurious living stirs up the hatred of all those in want. Nor finally can we forget how the number of these last miserable creatures steadily increases, and that from their ranks there is daily recruited the vast army of future disturbance.

" Where once was trustfulness and security, there is now but anxiety and fear, activity and hard work have given place to apathy, to idleness ; the orderly calm in which peace dwelt has gone and on all hands it is strife and confusion that reign. Whence that slowing down of industrial enterprise that is evident to all, the decline in international commerce, the feebleness, manifest too, in all that belongs to literature and to art. Whence also, what is more serious still, the traditional Christian way of life has been so weakened in many places that not only does human society not move forward there to further heights of achievement, but it seems really to be turning back to the savagery of barbarism."

CHAPTER V

PIUS XI : THE PROGRAMME, THE INSTRUMENT

It is a kind of convention that a newly-elected pope makes known something of his general aims in the first of his encyclical letters. The key to all the complex pontifical action of the last fifteen years is to be found in the letter *Ubi Arcano Dei*[1] of 23 December, 1922. Not to know this lengthy document is to be ignorant of the goal towards which Pius XI has steadfastly set his face, it is to know nothing of the spirit which animates his every word and gesture and gives unity to an infinitely varied public action.

The date of the encyclical must be borne in mind, just four years and one month after the Armistice of 1918, barely three years and a half after the signing of the peace treaties. Peace, the new pope notes, " the active and fruitful peace that men everywhere crave," has somehow not yet been achieved. To bring that peace, to bring this universal desire of mankind to fulfilment is, he goes on to say, the one object to which he proposes to dedicate his whole pontificate. The letter will explain the nature of the obstacles to such true peace and the means by which alone they can be overcome.

The opening pages of the document are taken up with that survey of the Europe of 1919–1922 from which we have quoted, and then the pope passes to his analysis of causes, prefaced with a few phrases, Tacitean in their economy, that set out the essentials of the problem. " *Reconciliatio specie facta non re . . . invidendi consuetudo vim naturæ iam obtinuit . . . homo homini non frater sed extraneus et hostis . . . nihil pervulgatius quam bona sempiterna.*"

[1] Translation in *The Pope and the People* ; Catholic Truth Society, London.

This last sentence sums up the whole matter. The problem before the world is one of goodness in living and therefore of a right estimation of values. The fact is that the spiritual is everywhere despised and the whole energy of man is set on temporal gains. The pope, making no attempt to invest these ancient truths with any new subtlety, reminds all who will listen that the modern enemy of man is his ancient triple danger " the lust of the flesh, the lust of the eyes, the pride of life." [1] These, nowadays, go too often masked as patriotism, are carefully fostered and cultivated as virtues. Mussolini has not yet appeared on the European scene nor the Nazi when the pope makes for the first time the declaration that is to sound so frequently through his vexed and troubled reign, that even love of country, if it passes the limits of justice and equity, is the seed of innumerable evils. For, of nations no less than of individuals is it true that it is neither lawful nor politic to sever what is profitable from what is right. Whatever the gains may be, to the state as to any other community, no matter how brilliant they be in men's sight, if they are bought with the ruin of others, they cannot endure. Nor can they fail to bring to the victor the menace of future disaster. " Joys, they are indeed like glass," the pope quotes from St. Augustine, " fragile in their splendour, fearsome still more from the dread that they may suddenly shiver into splinters." [2] Fifteen years ago the victorious allies had yet to learn the full price of their success, and this bold reminder did not fail to irritate more than one of those for whose greater happiness it was penned.

We must, however, probe deeper still if we are to discover the source whence this great evil comes. Very simply the root of it all is man's apostacy from God. " They that have forsaken the Lord shall be consumed," said the prophet,[3] and man has not so much forsaken God as, to the best of his ability, he has banished Him from the life of this

[1] Jas. ii. 16.
[2] *De Civitate Dei*, iv, 3.
[3] Isaias i, 28.

world.   God's will is no longer a factor in the public life of the nations.   Laws are made and administered, treaties arranged without even the form of a discussion as to their accordance with the will of God.   The divine thus banished, there disappears the chief reason why man should obey, the chief justification for a government's claim to command.

Secondly, God is banished, in the modern world, from that pact which is the very foundation of all society, namely, marriage.   Thereupon there disappears from family life all that preserves it from the fires of selfishness and passion. Marriage is exposed, defenceless, to every assault of self-interest, and life is poisoned at its very source.

Finally, God has no longer His due place in the education of youth.   Inevitably the growing child looks upon religion as a thing of minor importance, that avails little or nothing in the matter of a successful career.   Can children really be trained, in such a system, to avoid evil and to live virtuously ?   Can we hope for the continuance of a supply of good-living citizens, faithful husbands and wives, good fathers and mothers ?

The first step towards a way out of the critical and dangerous state of things that now obtains is to realise that the peace needed by the world is a real appeasement of spirits and not a mere general restoration of mutual international politeness and tact.   The only peace that will serve, that will bring forth the awaited fruit is, in fact, the peace of Christ, and this there cannot be except through justice, that is to say, the rendering to every man that which is his due.   It is not an inflexible, iron justice that the pope speaks of here, but justice tempered by an equal measure of brotherly love.   The supreme reconciliation, of God and man wrought through the death of Christ Our Lord, should be our pattern and this, if a work of justice, was even more a work of love.

This true and lasting peace does not flow from any abundance of temporal goods.   On the contrary the natural lust for these must be sternly controlled, and its due primacy given to what is spiritual.   It is in this way that there will be produced the desired revival of obedience in the life of the home.

The pope has no new doctrine to suggest. In an age when novelty is so widely regarded as the first justification of social and political remedies, as of artistic and literary production, he has the courage to take his stand by ancient truth, to recall the old and well-known fundamentals. All that is new in his message is the unusual hardiness of its simple statement.

He goes on, in the same direct and simple way, to remind the world that has for centuries done its best to ignore Catholicism except in so far as it is the conscientious belief of certain individuals, that those precepts of Our Lord on obedience to which the possibility of lasting peace depends, and which He came down from heaven to make known, were by Him committed to the Church, whose whole function it is to preserve them and to explain them. To the Church God has given a certain infallibility in its work of teaching, and upon the Church He has imposed the duty of teaching them at all times and to all men. The Church is necessarily the most powerful agent for the attainment of peace that this world knows. This is, in fact, a work which the Church alone can do.

As for the efforts of the various governments, the age of peace will not begin until these, too, once more begin to acknowledge that they also are subject to God's law. Merely human efforts must fail in the future as they have failed in the past and the pope pertinently cites, as an instance, the impossibility of finding any merely human authority that shall impose a common code of law on the universality of mankind. Against this inevitable weakness in the purely human organisation of the world he proceeds to set in contrast the Catholic Church. Here is a divinely appointed guardian of the sanctity of international laws, which has relations with all the nations and is yet identified with none, and which possesses immense authority and prestige.

There can then be no real peace, the much desired peace

of Christ can never be realised—and here is the key
sentence to the encyclical and to the whole of Pius XI's
pontificate—unless mankind faithfully holds to the teaching,
the commandments and the example of Christ in matters of
public life no less than in the private life of the individual.
And thus in the comity of men, now related to its real
foundation, the Church, playing its divinely appointed part,
will be in a position to defend the rights of God over
individual men and over human society as such.

This ideal condition of things the pope describes, in a
phrase now celebrated, as the reign of Christ.[1] Jesus Christ
reigns over the minds of individual men by His teaching,
over their wills by love, over their whole activity when
they obey His law and imitate His example. He reigns over
the family when this is founded on Christian marriage. He
reigns over the state when the state gives to God the
highest homage in its power by acknowledging God as the
source of all its authority and its rights, and when the state
recognises the place assigned by God to the Church He
has instituted, its character as a perfect society, the mistress
and the guide of all other societies.[2]

From all this it follows clearly that the peace of Christ
can only flourish where Christ reigns.[3] Nor can we do a
better work for peace than by striving to restore this reign
of Christ. Pius X had proposed *the restoration of all things
in Christ* as his goal, Benedict XV *the reconciliation of peace.*
Pius XI, combining these two, will set himself *to seek the
peace of Christ through the reign of Christ.*[4]

The encyclical closes with a warning destined to be
repeated more than once in the addresses of Pius XI. The
new pope showed from the very beginning of his reign that
he was under no illusion as to the quality of Catholicism as
practised by some of his subjects. He proceeded to describe
a type of Catholic who, while never rejecting the traditional

---

[1] His enim continetur, quod brevi dicimus, *Regnum Christi.*
[2] The Church's status does not in any way lessen the power of the state, the
pope notes. It rather perfects the human organisation as grace perfects nature.
[3] Ex his liquet nullam esse Christi pacem nisi in regno Christi.
[4] Id maxima contentione studebimus, *pacem Christi in regno Christi*, quærere.

teaching of the Church, acts, and especially in public life, as though the teaching of recent popes, Leo XIII, Pius X and Benedict XV had lost its force. Such a Catholic is a modernist in morals, a social and juridical modernist.

Questions of pure politics are, it is true, no concern of the Church, but statesmen must not, under the pretence that their action is purely political, do anything which will hinder the Church's mission, nor can they legitimately object when, in such circumstances, the Church defends itself against their action.

Finally, the pope pledges himself that never will he as the price of a concordat, surrender any of the Church's freedom of action, and he concludes with a renewal of the protest, traditional since 1870, against the grave inconveniences that are the result of the loss of the temporal sovereignty of the Holy See.

This great letter has been followed by a twofold action designed to keep before the mind of every Catholic the need to bring back the world to the reign of Christ and the need that he himself shall play his appointed part in that movement. The pope, in 1925, by the letter *Quas Primas* [1] instituted the feast of Christ the King, to be celebrated henceforth every year on the last Sunday of October. In the letter that set up the new feast Pius XI returned to the subject of his first encyclical and, linking up the programme of *Ubi Arcano Dei* with the doctrine of the kingship of Christ, and the Church's liturgical life, gave evidence, yet once again, that the aims of the modern papacy are wholly spiritual, that its ultimate care is the sanctification of souls. A study of this second encyclical will also make clear all that the pope means by Catholic Action—a phrase one reads to-day on every page of every Catholic newspaper and magazine—and all that he expects from it.

Christ is King and reigns in the minds of men because

[1] 11 December, 1925.

He is Truth itself, to whom, necessarily, men must obediently turn for the truth which is the life of their intelligence. Christ reigns in the wills of men, and He reigns in their hearts. The ancient Jewish scriptures foretold Him as a king in whose days justice and peace should flourish, and whose kingdom should know no frontiers. In the New Testament too we find support for the truth of this idea. Our Lord Himself claims to be a king. It is but a natural consequence of this doctrine that the Catholic Church, which is the kingdom of Christ on earth, should solemnly and publicly acknowledge and hail Him as king. Scattered through offices and ceremonial of the liturgical year many such acts of homage are to be found. The new feast is but the crown of a long development.

This kingdom of Christ, or reign of Christ, is chiefly concerned with spiritual matters. " My kingdom is not of this world," are His own words about it. Into this kingdom, so the Gospels bear witness, man can only enter by a preparation of penance, and then by faith and being baptised, the sacrament itself effecting a true rebirth. The kingdom's one rival and enemy is the kingdom of Satan, and the faithful subject must not only wean his heart from desire of wealth and earthly goods, practise kindness, strive for justice, but give up his own will and carry his own cross.

Has Christ then no power in temporal matters ? It would be a singularly inept conclusion to draw. His rights over all creatures are absolute, since He is God. But as during His life on earth He left such concerns to those whose special function it was to care for them, so does He continue to do. The hymn in the office for the Epiphany expresses this truth with point and charm : *Non eripit mortalia, qui regna dat cœlestia.*[1]

It would be erroneous, also, to think that none are subject to the kingship of Christ but those who are baptised into His visible earthly kingdom the Church. As Leo XIII declared in the encyclical which accompanied his famous

[1] " He does not grasp at mortal realms, Who gives celestial realms away."

dedication of mankind to the Sacred Heart,[1] " the empire of Jesus Christ embraces the whole human race," and men not only as individuals but also as beings whose nature is social and as organised into the societies we call states. " There is not one source of happiness for the citizen and another for states," says St. Augustine [2]; and it is thus the duty of the rulers of the world, personally, and again officially in the name of their peoples, to pay public homage to the sovereignty of Christ.

The pope then describes the fruits that such an acceptance of the kingship of Christ must bring to princes and people alike, just liberty, order, tranquility, concord, peace. The primal submission to Christ ennobles and dignifies and makes more easy all the necessary submissions of man to his fellow man, the subject to his ruler, the wife to her husband, the child to the parent. Again, if rulers exercise their power not so much as though this was some manifestation of their own personality and right, but rather an office through which they themselves obediently made manifest the will and sovereignty of God, a new spirit would be evident in the public life of the world, a new wisdom, a new care for the common good and for the dignity of human nature. On the side of the subject there would be a readier obedience, once he understood that it was not to just another man, like in everything to himself, that he was asked to give his will, but to the sovereignty of Christ of Whom the earthly ruler is but the image. If the reign of Christ were *de facto* the universal thing it is *de jure*, no man could despair of the realisation of that peace which He came to bring.

Here Pius XI turns once again for words to express his thought to the incomparable latinity of his predecessor of thirty years ago, Leo XIII.[3] " Tum denique licebit sanare

---

[1] *Annum Sacrum*, 25 May, 1899.
[2] Epistle to Macedonius, ch. iii.
[3] Encyclical Letter, *Annum Sacrum*, 25 May, 1899. I venture to translate: " Then, at length, it shall be possible to heal all these wounds, and right shall everywhere flower again with all its one-time power; peace shall appear in its wonted array, the swords shall fall and the arms from men's hands, when men, in willing obedience, put on the yoke of Christ, and when every tongue shall confess that the Lord Jesus Christ is in the glory of God the Father."

tot vulnera, tum ius omne in pristinæ auctoritatis spem revirescet, et restituentur ornamenta pacis, atque excident gladii fluentque arma de manibus, cum Christi imperium omnes accipient libentes eique parebunt, atque omnis lingua confitebitur quia Dominus Iesus Christus in gloria est Dei Patris."

Such are the doctrines and the ideas that the new feast is designed to keep before the minds of Catholics. This annual commemoration will speak to millions whom no papal letter, however important, will ever reach. The new liturgical solemnity will enlighten their minds, strengthen their allegiance and inflame their hearts with deeper and deeper loyalty to the King and lead them to ever more devoted service in His cause.

In the office and the mass written for the feast of Christ the King, one comes very close to the mind and heart of Pius XI. The lessons [1] bid us recall in gratitude that Jesus Christ is the one Mediator through whom we are redeemed, that He is " the image of the visible God, the first born of every creature . . . the head of the body, the Church, the beginning, the first-born from the dead " ; in whom it has pleased God " that all fulness should dwell . . . through him to reconcile all things unto himself," and narrate Our Lord's dialogue with Pilate. " Art thou the King of the Jews ? . . . Art thou then a king ? " The collect prays that " all the communities and the nations, scattered by the wound of sin may be made subject unto His gentle yoke," and the prayer after the Communion that " we who glory to fight under the banner of Christ the King may come to reign for ever with him where he dwells in heaven." The preface is new, written for the feast. " It is truly the proper thing to do, Thy right indeed, O Lord our God, always and everywhere to praise Thee and give thanks, Who with the oil of gladness didst anoint Thine only begotten son our Lord, Jesus Christ, as priest eternal and universal king ; so that, offering Himself, a spotless, peace-making victim on the altar of the cross, He might achieve the mystery of

Coloss. i, 12–20 and John xvii, 33–37.

man's redemption; so that all creatures being made subject to His command, He might present to Thine infinite Majesty a kingdom all embracing and eternal, a kingdom of truth and of life, a kingdom of holiness and grace, a kingdom of justice, of love and of peace."

The liturgy has always been a great means of teaching the truths of faith, but never before has the personal initiative of a pope so explicitly instituted a feast in order to bring home to the whole Church the importance of a doctrine vital to the well-being and indeed to the very existence of civilisation as we and our fathers have known it. The solemn celebration of the feasts that commemorate the mysteries of faith is evidently, with Pius XI, a well understood means of propaganda. In this very encyclical, explaining to the bishops of the world the reasons that led him to institute the feast of Christ the King, he recalls the revival of religion that has followed on the public celebration of the feasts of Our Lady at different periods of the Church's history, and again the fruits of the feast of Corpus Christi, of the solemnities of the different Eucharistic Congresses, and of the institution of public devotions to the Sacred Heart of Jesus.

To-day it is not in the morose and melancholy theories of Jansenism that the danger to the faith of Catholics lies. The plague of our time is the rejection of the supernatural, the de-supernaturalising of man's life,[1] a poison that has long been maturing in the secret places of the body politic. Its first stage is to deny that Christ is sovereign ruler of all peoples, then to deny, what follows from the rights of Christ, the right of the Church to teach the whole human race, to make laws for it, to rule the peoples and so to lead them to eternal happiness.

[1] Pestem dicimus ætatis nostræ Laicismum, quem vocant, eiusdemque errores et nefarios conatus : (the plague of our age is this thing they call " Laicism," its erroneous ideas and its mischievous activities). *Quas Primas.*

Little by little the religion of Christ is placed on the same level as the false religions. It is made subject to the civil power, or, even, there are some who go further still and would see substituted for it a purely natural religion and, even, a mere natural sentimentality of a religious tint. There are, also, some states that profess to manage without God, and whose religion, so to speak, consists in a deliberate, irreligious ignoring of God.

The duty of all Catholics faced with this menace of " laicism " is evident enough. Each must make it his life's work to fight the evil in his own particular walk of life. Many Catholics, it is true, seem not to possess that influence in their own milieu which defenders of truth and effective propagandists all need. This, says the papal realist, is perhaps due to apathy, perhaps to fear. They never resist the enemy's advance, or they do so half-heartedly. The new feast should enliven such Catholics and give them the courage they need.

Finally, this annual solemn observance will serve as an act of reparation for the long-standing universal apostacy of our Christian society. The name of our Redeemer is never mentioned in parliaments and international congresses. All acknowledgment of Him has ceased in public life. The greater reason for the feast and its call reof Christ's sovereignty.

The programme is clearly set out in the pope's first message to the Church, and the ideal to whose attainment he would direct all the Church's energy is enshrined in the new feast. It is now necessary to say something of the scheme through which Pius XI has endeavoured to organise the whole Catholic world for the attainment of that goal. This is the famous Azione Cattolica, a title which the literally equivalent English phrase—Catholic Action—hardly translates, for the Italian substantive suggests a spirit as well as the thing it inspires, and the thing is not particular but a universal.

One of the leading personalities of this new movement, Mgr. Pizzardo, the Chaplain-General of the Azione Cattolica of Italy, has described it in a single vivid phrase as "the mission within the fold." [1] The object of the mission is the realisation of the reign of Christ and the missionaries of Catholic Action are the Catholic laity. The clergy no longer suffice for this task. Vocations are scarce and, furthermore, the intercourse of the clergy with the ordinary life of the day is too restricted for clerical activity to produce the needed effect. This work of apostolate, the task of making Catholics out of non-Catholics, of making good Catholics out of careless Catholics is, properly speaking, the mission, and indeed the very *raison d'être*, of the episcopate. The clergy are their chief collaborators, and now the layman is reminded that his *rôle* in the Church is not merely a passive one. The layman is not an ideal Catholic if his Catholicism goes no further than attendance at mass, reception of the sacraments and observance of the ten commandments. He must take an active part in the Church's work for souls, "sharing the apostolic mission of the hierarchy," [2] the co-worker of the priest.

To play his part in this apostolate is for the layman not a matter of choice but a duty. This duty derives from his reception of the sacraments of baptism and confirmation, especially the latter. Every Christian enjoys the supernatural life which flows in the veins of the Mystical Body of Christ—so, too, every Christian should transfuse some of this life that is in himself into those others who either have none or only a modicum. [3] The obligation is a consequence

---

[1] *Cf.* his address of 8 December, 1930, translated in *The Pope and Catholic Action*, published by the Catholic Truth Society of London. This pamphlet also contains the four pontifical Letters to which constant reference is made in this section, viz., Letters to (1) Cardinal Bertram, Archbishop of Breslau, 18 November, 1928; (2) Cardinal Segura, Archbishop of Toledo, 6 November, 1929; (3) the bishops of the Argentine, 4 February, 1931; and (4) the Patriarch of Lisbon, 10 November, 1933. These are referred to in the notes as B, S, A, and L respectively.

[2] PIZZARDO, *op. cit.*

[3] L.

of the divine precept: "Thou shalt love the Lord thy
God with thy whole heart and thy neighbour as thyself."
Society is, in fact, becoming increasingly paganised and
vast numbers live without any knowledge of the Christian
heritage, so that without its inspiration the worth of faith
and morals is ignored.[1] It is therefore essential that, to-day,
every Catholic should be an active apostle.

The aim of the new movement is not the personal
sanctification of its members. Their own efforts in this
direction must, of course, continue unceasingly if they are
to be effective units of Catholic Action, but Catholic
Action presupposes them as already rooted in virtue and
men of good desires ; " without this formation in Christian
virtue Catholic Action is not only fruitless but lifeless." [2]
Hence associations whose direct objective is the spiritual
advancement of their own members, religious guilds for
example, and confraternities, cannot be described as parts
of Catholic Action. Nor can those Catholic societies whose
object is the professional advancement or social recreation
of their members. The criterion by which to judge whether
any society can be considered Catholic Action is its relation
to the pastoral ministry of the bishops. Is the object of
such a society a " participation of the laity in the apostolate
of the hierarchy " or not ?

This high mission, it will be said, differs little from the
mission of the clergy, and in so many words the pope
himself admits the truth of this.[3] The difference between
the two is a difference of function in the general work and
of the means of work open to each. But both clergy and
laity are co-operators " with the bishops in the extension of
the reign of Christ " [4] ; and the pope sees the beginnings
of such collaboration in St. Paul's references to the women
" my fellow labourers . . . who have laboured with me
in the gospel." [5] Catholic Action, he says, " was born with
the Church, but it has recently undergone fresh direction." [6]

There is nothing so dear to Pius XI as Catholic Action,

---

[1] S.   [2] A.   [3] Letter to Cardinal Van Roey quoted in S.
          [4] A.   [5] Phil. iv, 3 .   [6] A.

" the apple of our eye," as he wrote to Cardinal Bertram. How does the pope envisage the practical realisation of this stupendous ideal ? He calls for definite organisation. " All those who know and live the life of to-day will grant that there is no sort of initiative or activity, from the more spiritual and scientific bodies to the more material and mechanical ones, which does not find the necessity of organisation and of organised action." [1] The high enthusiasm, the generous resolve must find concrete embodiment in societies with a definite aim and a plan to realise their aim. This organisation will, of course, be varied according to the needs and the circumstances of different countries. In time new forms of apostolate will be created. Meanwhile, in most countries, there are already societies whose end is an apostolate of one kind or another. Catholic Action will here be a central unifying thing, establishing mutual understanding between these societies, and, while leaving them the autonomy that is proper to them, dictating, in the manner of the staff of an army's higher command, the manner of their collaboration and the place they are to fill in the general scheme. There will, then, be in every nation one single organisation of Catholic Action which will co-ordinate all Catholic activities towards " the peace of Christ in the reign of Christ," [2] and the establishment of this central direct organisation is recommended as the first step in the movement.

The work calls for workers who are trained, and the pope has insisted that quality here is better than quantity, and also that the success of the movement is bound up with the thoroughness of the training given to its members. Everything will depend on the ecclesiastical assistants, the chaplains appointed by the bishops to guide the movement. The word " assistants," the pope's own word, should be noted. [3] Catholic Action is the layman's business, [4] essentially the task of the laity, [5] and the laity retain their respon-

---

[1] Encyclical *Non Abbiamo Bisogno* of 29 June, 1931.
[2] The pope as quoted by PIZZARDO, *op. cit.*, p. 29.
[3] Letter to Patriarch of Lisbon.
[4] PIZZARDO, *op. cit.*   [5] *Ib.*

sibility and " should be encouraged to retain their *sui iuris*
autonomy, particularly in civic and social matters—and to
act upon their own initiative in all that is approved by the
Church." [1]

There is a bewildering variety of particular objectives
before the movement and the pope has chosen to direct its
attention to some he considers of more immediate importance. He speaks of the formation of " centres of sound
teaching and social activity," of the training of leaders, the
formation of the young, the work of evangelisation by
means of Christian doctrine, " this generous apostolate of
the Catechism," and, a matter on which he lays great
emphasis, the production of good literature, *i.e.*, literature
which openly champions the Catholic faith and morality.
The greatest of all such services is the establishment of a
good Catholic daily newspaper, and to promote the success
of such a venture the pope recommends, where it is necessary, the suppression of smaller newspapers. Always, it
would seem, the pope comes back to the truth that ignorance
is the enemy chiefly to be fought. Instruction of the
members of Catholic Action and then the defence, diffusion,
application of Catholic principles in public as in private
life.

Catholic Action is then a body with the social obligation
to make its members into a sacred militia, and its aim is the
perfection of social life. It offers itself as the most effective
means by which the evils arising from the secular conception of civil society can be undone, and, if successful,
will do away for ever with " the reprehensible, but by no
means rare, practice of behaving differently in public and
in private life." [2]

There is one field where the need of Catholic Action is,
says the pope, most of all urgent. This is in helping the
working classes,[3] helping them in material ways as well as
in spiritual matters. Catholic Action will establish societies
devoted to bring about a realisation of the principles of
social justice and of the gospel and will guide existing

[1] *Ib.*   [2] Letter to Patriarch of Lisbon.   [3] *Ib.*

organisations in matters of principle. " Its special concern will be the infusion of definite Catholic principles and in particular the teaching of the Holy See as set out in the encyclical *Quadragesimo Anno*." [1]

The mention of social teaching brings us face to face with the relation of Catholic Action and political life. If the true principles of social justice make no further headway than frequent exposition in Catholic lecture rooms and churches, or applauded acceptance by debating societies, the world will remain as far from the sovereignty of Christ as ever. Ultimately these principles must inspire social legislation, and to make laws is the affair of politicians. How does Catholic Action propose to influence legislation ? One thing very clearly it will not do and cannot do, namely, enter the field of politics as an independent self-constituted party. Whoever engages in politics pledges himself, necessarily, to a particular concrete solution in which to embody his principles, and thereby to the acceptance of a particular technique, a thing in itself morally neutral. But Catholic Action is, by definition, spiritual not material, divine not earthly, religious not political. It has no place in political life and for it to attempt to make there a place for itself would be to change its whole nature. Abstention from politics, indifference to them is a root condition of its success.[2] All political discussion, even of matters involving its members, must be rigorously excluded. But its members are not forbidden to take part *as individual citizens* in the political life of the day. " It is the duty of everyone to further the welfare of the state to the full extent of his power," [3] and individual Catholics are bound to take part in politics in order to ensure government by Christian principles,[4] so that these foundations of all stability and happiness will guide political action.[5] The stricter private life of the apostle of Catholic Action, the respect for

---

[1] *Ib.*
[2] Letter to Cardinal Bertram.
[3] Letter to Patriarch of Lisbon.
[4] Letter to Argentine bishops.
[5] Letter to Patriarch of Lisbon.

authority as a thing divinely founded and for the civil law as its expression, the whole moral and intellectual formation which Catholic Action gives its members will make them all the more useful members of whatever political party they adhere to. Catholic Action has its Catholic moral principles but it has no politics. When religious or moral interests are at stake its members will, in their various parties, strictly observe the instructions *of the bishops* " regardless of any apparent conflict with party interests," [1] and Catholic Action itself, " can and must intervene directly, and by a full exercise of its strength lead an organised campaign in favour of the paramount interests of the Church and of the souls entrusted to its care." [2]

It is not, then, the business of Catholic Action to organise a Catholic political party, nor to elaborate official solutions of technical, political and economic problems, but to give individual Catholics—on questions involving Catholic principles—guidance as to their action within whatever party they have joined. A passage from the encyclical *Quadragesimo Anno* will illustrate the practical working out of Catholic Action in the work of social restoration. " We believe that a better social order will be the more certainly attained, the greater the number of those who are ready to contribute their technical, professional and social competence to this, and, more still, the greater the contribution made by Catholic principles and their practical application. We look for this contribution, not to Catholic Action (which excludes from its programme strictly syndical or political activities), but to those sons of Ours whom Catholic Action imbues with these principles and trains for the apostolate under the guidance and direction of the Church—of the Church, We say, which in the above-mentioned sphere, as in all others where moral questions arise, cannot forget or neglect its God-given mandate as custodian and teacher." [3]

The systematic division and co-ordination which Pius

---

[1] Letter to Cardinal Bertram (italics mine).
[2] Letter to Cardinal Segura.   [3] Section 96.

XI has in view in this great work can nowhere be seen to better advantage than in the new societies of Catholic Belgium, the Jeunesse Agricole Catholique (J.A.C.), Jeunesse Etudiante Catholique (J.E.C.), Jeunesse Maritime Catholique (J.I.C.), Jeunesse Ouvrière Catholique (J.O.C.), and the Jeunesse Universitaire Catholique (J.U.C.). Of the J.O.C. especially, the pope has said " This is the finished article." [1]

The basic principle of all the activity of this new apostolate is that expressed in the old saying *similia similibus curantur*, a man is helped best by those of his own class. " In order to bring back to Christ," says the pope,[2] " these whole classes of men who have denied Him, we must gather and train from amongst their very ranks auxiliary soldiers of the Church, men who well know their mentality and their aspirations, and who by kindly fraternal charity will be able to win their hearts. Undoubtedly the first and immediate apostles of the working-men must themselves be working-men, while the apostles of the industrial and commercial world should themselves be employers and merchants."

And again, speaking to the pilgrims of the Association Catholique de la Jeunesse Française, he speaks of Catholic Action as " an individual, specialised activity, whose *modus operandi* is closely related to that which we have put before the foreign missionaries, the method, namely, of converting the native races through a native clergy. Every rank and class and circumstance of life will therefore have its appropriate apostles, for the workers workmen apostles, for the peasantry apostles who are peasants themselves, for sailors sailors, and students for students." [3]

To seek out such lay apostles, to choose them with prudence and give them suitable training, both from among the working-men and among the employers, is the chief duty of the bishops and their clergy.[4] No easy task, as the pope himself remarks.

---

[1] FONTENELLE, p. 95.   [2] Encyclical *Quadragesimo Anno*, section 142.
[3] 6 April, 1934, *cf*. FONTENELLE, p. 94.   [4] *Quadragesimo Anno*, section 142.

CHAPTER VI

" A NEW PEOPLE "

" WE pray often for the conversion of England : not,
of course, that all Englishmen may become just such
Catholics as you and I, but real Catholics." So once I
heard a preacher say to his interested congregation. He
told a story from the life of the saintly Richard Challoner.[1]
The bishop was tried, once upon a time, by some unpleasant experience of anti-clerical feeling on the part
of Catholics whose pride, rather than submission to
authority, was keeping them true to Catholicism. When
the news was brought to him he slipped to his knees
in prayer. " There will be a new people," he said as he
rose.

The memory of this sermon and the story come back
vividly with the study of Pius XI's ideal of Catholic Action.
For it is indeed " a new people " that the pope is striving
to create out of the old, " fit ministers of the New Testament." He is under no illusion that all is well within the
Church and, to make Catholic Action the normal thing
for Catholics of the next generation, he is prepared to
consider the reconstruction of, and to improve, every
organ of Catholic life, every Catholic practice, every
institution.

The dignity, the efficiency, the very life of the Church,
are bound up with the well-being of its clergy. The
importance, in the matter of the salvation of souls, of everything that promotes their well-being or that works against
it cannot be exaggerated. Pius XI has devoted anxious
hours to the many questions bound up with this matter
and his ideals, his recommendations and his commands

[1] Bishop of Debra, Vicar-Apostolic in the London District, 1758–1781.

are set forth in some of the most eloquent of his many letters.[1]

The pope's concern is twofold, that the clergy shall be men of godly life and that they shall be professionally competent, trained to express the traditional faith in the idiom of their own time. It is this last aspect that concerns us here.

With regard to the fact that we live in our own age, Pius XI, it is one of his most evident characteristics, has a natural sympathy and enthusiasm for his own time. " We aren't any longer living in 1870," was the remark which ended one particular discussion on the scheme that issued in the Lateran treaties, and the pope has been heard to thank God who has spared him to live during an age of critical change. A passage from the address he delivered during the celebration of his silver jubilee as a priest in 1904, gives a vivid impression of this side of his character and deserves quotation. " Let us thank God's providence that we are preserved to see such grandeur, such human progress in every direction. For, despite all its abuses and all its faults, we can see in the totality of the result an ascending movement of humanity towards Truth and Goodness, that is to say towards God. . . . And perhaps we can recognise that in these struggles for ideals, for the truth, for the souls of men—in this last most of all—a real pre-occupation with books has an importance all its own, as it has its place of service, even though that importance be only to provide nourishment for the mind. So it is, then, that in our modern way, we come to the care and the administration of what the charming St. Francis of Sales used to call the

---

[1] Cf. especially the Apostolic Letter *Officiorum Omnium* of 1 August, 1922, to the Prefect of the Congregation of Seminaries and Universities, the letter *Quandoquidem* of 25 April, 1922, to the bishops of the U.S.A., the letter *Unigenitus Dei Filius* of 19 March, 1924, to the Superior Generals of the Religious Orders of Men, the Instruction of the Congregation of Religious of 1 December, 1931, addressed to the same, the Encyclical *Studiorum Ducem* of 29 June, 1923, the Apostolic Constitution *Deus Scientiarum Dominus* of 24 May, 1931, the Motu Proprio *Bibliorum Scientia* of 27 April, 1924, the Letter of the Congregation of Seminaries and Universities *Quod Catholicis hominibus* of 28 August, 1929 and the Motu Proprio *Latinarum Litterarum* 20 October, 1924. These are the sources on which what follows is based.

eighth sacrament and the sacrament for priests above all others, the sacrament of learning." [1]

It is not surprising that a man so learned, who yet remained a man of affairs, from whom *nil humani alienum*, should set so high a store on the value of learning to life, and should claim that the priest cannot be too learned. Seventeen years later, on the eve of his election to the papacy, we see him no less concerned for the fullest possible cultivation of the Catholic layman's mind, and insisting that opportunity be given him for a religious formation that is as adequate and as scientific as the secular or professional formation which the university gives him. The quotation is from a letter written by Cardinal Ratti, then Archbishop of Milan, to Father Agostino Gemelli, O.F.M., Rector of the newly established Catholic University of the Sacred Heart. "It is only an institute of higher studies and scientific culture, where the God of Science and the science of God are given the place that Dante and Manzoni desiderated, it is only such an institution that can provide the Christian renaissance of society and of learning with the most useful—indeed the essential—elements of its activities and reactions and the elements too for its direction; that is to say such an institution alone can prepare for that restoration laymen who are enriched with an intellectual formation that is complete, that is, in other words, at one and the same time scientific and Catholic. For such an institute of higher studies will, simultaneously, produce men who are scientifically convinced of the rights of God and the Church, of the needs of society and their country, of the ends at which to aim and of the means they must use in order to serve both the one and the other." [2]

This might be taken as no more than the opinion of a very learned man holding high ecclesiastical office, but in less than twelve months that learned archbishop was Pope Pius XI, and in one of his first administrative acts, within a matter of weeks after his election, he put forth with supreme

[1] Quoted in FONTENELLE, p. 45.
[2] Quoted in FONTENELLE, pp. 44-45.

authority the same ideas to the bishops of the United States, commending and blessing their efforts for the Catholic University of Washington.[1] Not any sort of education, he reminds them, will produce that type of Catholic on whom the Christian renaissance will depend, but only an education where the scientific formation rests on a basis of religion and virtue. The fruits a Catholic university will produce are threefold : the formation of an élite, clerical and lay ; the provision of a steady supply of excellent teachers for the various seminaries, colleges and schools ; the establishment of a certain unity in the whole field of Catholic education throughout the country.

In the fifteen years of the pontificate new Catholic universities have been founded in Poland, Holland and Lithuania.

The chief anxiety, in the matter of clerical education, which occupied the pope at the beginning of his reign, was the losses in personnel brought about by the European war. Thousands of priests, forced into the fighting line by the modern system of conscription, had been killed or crippled. Everywhere the tale was the same of parishes without pastors and seminaries without students. The first remedy to which the pope turned was prayer and a reminder to all the priests of the world of their duty to look out for and to encourage signs of a vocation to the priesthood wherever they showed. Bishops were exhorted to found guilds and associations to provide the necessary funds to educate the less wealthy candidates. Seminaries, it was recalled, exist for one purpose only, the formation of a good clergy, and to this end their whole life and custom must be strictly subordinated. The pope insists on greater care being taken to give the boys in the preparatory seminaries a really good grasp of Latin—a tongue which is a marvellous gift of God to the service of the Church, providentially designed to

[1] Letter *Quandoquidem*, 25 April, 1922.

serve the glory of the Roman Primacy to which the very capital of the ancient empire has, by a kind of inheritance, devolved.

If in the Catholic layman who makes even a pretence of being educated, indifference to Latin is a sign of slackness where his religion is concerned, what can be said of the priest who lacks a mastery of that language ? There is something truly Catholic about the cult of Latin letters, and the pope goes on to demand that this branch of study be given the greatest possible attention. He points out the serious consequences of a half-knowledge of Latin in the ecclesiastical student, an inability to penetrate to the heart of the problems discussed in his philosophical and theological studies, and the ultimate despairing abandonment of the classic fathers and doctors of the Church for more modern authors who, only too often, not only are wanting in literary beauty and logical ordonnance but, even, in the exact enunciation of the truths which occupy them. This wretched state of affairs, the pope's candour confesses, obtains only too frequently.[1]

Even more does Pius XI show himself as the humanist and man of letters—and these always at the service of his priestly mission—in the Motu Proprio *Latinarum Litterarum* of 20 October, 1924, which established a special course of Latin Letters in the Gregorian University, open to all comers, lay students amongst them, and a special invitation to attend which was made to the young priests beginning their life's work in the different offices of the Roman Curia. In this brilliantly written little document the pope speaks of the traditional pride of the Roman See in the latinity of its officials, and the care of the popes always to have at their service secretaries *latinæ scriptionis haud mediocriter peritis*. He insists again that it is one of his chief ambitions that the clergy generally shall have a better practical knowledge of what an English scholar once aptly called " The Holy Latin Tongue,"[2] *ut laus illa, quæ antehac in utroque clero*

[1] Apostolic Letter *Officiorum Omnium*, 1 August, 1922.
[2] The late Mgr. William Barry.

eluxit, perfectioris latinitatis, ne omnino depereat, immo etiam, quoad fieri poterit, feliciter augescat. Another passage of the letter lifts the veil of the pope's own intellectual formation and gives him the chance to quote two of the authors he best loves. He is urging the well-known truth that the more diligently the student cultivates his Latin style, the more surely does he increase his command of his mother tongue. Both Bossuet and Segneri have admitted their debt to Cicero. *Quo in genere memoriæ proditum est, Iacobum Bossuet et Paulum Segneri, qui inter oratores suæ quisque gentis principem locum obtinent, fuisse dicere, si quid dignitatis et virtutis in suis orationibus esset, id se in primis Marci Tullii studio acceptum referre.*

After this demand for improvements in the study of the Church's official language the pope passes to the matter of the young cleric's professional studies. He calls for a scrupulous observance of what the Canon Law here lays down.[1] This is absolutely necessary if the future priest is to be equal to his task. At least two years must be spent in the study of scholastic philosophy, and by this the pope explicitly declares that what he means is the philosophical teaching of St. Thomas Aquinas, Leo XIII's restoration of which to its rightful place in the Church was " the greatest of all the services his long pontificate rendered to the Church and civilisation, a service so great that, had he done nothing else, this alone would rightly have made his name immortal." The same great doctor's teaching is to be followed in the later lectures on theology, and the pope quotes his great predecessor of the sixteenth century, Sixtus V (1585–1590), to the effect that it is St. Thomas's use of philosophy in theological discussion that has made of theology a true science, a victorious defence of the truth revealed by God and " as complete an explanation of it as the human reason is capable of."

This scholastic theology is the most important of all, and while positive theology, the history of Dogma and its development, must be given its place, it must never be

[1] *Officiorum Omnium;* Code of Canon Law, cc. 1365–1366.

allowed to take the place of the more important science. After all, says the pope, to study in their chronological order the different heresies and the dogmas they contradicted is to study not so much theology as ecclesiastical history.

The final point in the matter of studies to which the pope draws the attention of the bishops is the provision in all seminaries of a good course of pastoral theology. This is to be given a more important place than has hitherto been the custom, for it deals with the immediate means by which the salvation of souls is brought to pass. "The lecturer in this science shall not merely occupy himself with a demonstration of how necessary holiness is in the priest who is called to handle holy things. He must show in detail how these holy matters may be so used as to be of the greatest service to men. In this he will most diligently take into account the special needs of our own time. For the course of time has brought into the customs of life many things unknown to earlier generations of Christian people, and with these the priest must be familiar if he is to find in the strength of Jesus Christ new remedies for the new ills, and to bring the saving force of religion to every part of social life."

In conclusion the pope urges the bishops who, for lack of resources or of priests fitted to undertake the work, are unable to organise seminaries for their own dioceses, to follow the repeated instructions of the Holy See and combine to form interdiocesan seminaries, as has so largely been done in Italy.

The next papal action to be chronicled with regard to this important matter of the provision of well-trained clergy, is contained in the Apostolic Letter *Unigenitus Dei Filius* of 19 March, 1924. This time it is to the regular clergy, the canons regular, the monks, the friars, the clerks regular of the modern congregations, the numerous orders of brothers that Pius XI speaks. This is a vast army indeed, its regiments as numerous as the different good works to promote which they were founded, and which, from the variety of its uniforms, contributes even in our own dull day, something of mediæval colour and beauty to the daily life of Catholicism. Augustinians, Benedictines, Carthusians, Trappists, Dominicans, Franciscans, Carmelites, Jesuits, Passionists, Redemptorists, Christian Brothers, Brothers of Mercy and the innumerable rest, these form the congregation to which this letter is addressed. It interests us here, however, for what it has to say about the formation of the priest-members of these great families, for what, once more, it reveals as the pope's idea of the kind of priest the Church needs to-day and of the means by which Pius XI proposes to form such priests. Never surely, it may be said at the outset, has study, especially the study of sacred sciences, been so eloquently praised as a way to spiritual perfection, never has the case for learning as a priestly habit been so authoritatively proposed.

The letter recalls the instructions sent to the bishops about the formation of the secular clergy and declares that they bind the regular clergy also. The chief object of this present letter is, in fact, to exhort those religious who are priests, or are preparing for ordination, to a whole-hearted enthusiasm for the study of the sacred sciences. If they are lacking in the necessary mastery of these they cannot possibly carry out in worthy fashion the duties to which they have vowed themselves. For since it is the chief, if not the only, object of the life of those vowed to God to pray and to contemplate divine things, how can they carry out this purpose if they lack a deep and clear knowledge of the teachings of the faith ? Contemplatives must ever bear this in mind. They make a serious mistake if they imagine they can easily ascend to the heights of prayer and be borne to an interior union with God whether or no they have neglected to study, or to continue to study, the data of theology, and, because of their neglect, are lacking that full knowledge of God and the mysteries of the faith which is the fruit of such study.

Religious whose vocation is the active one of teaching, preaching, hearing confessions, giving missions, must realise that the value of their work, their general effectiveness in fact, is proportionate to their learning and culture. It is not for nothing that the Holy Ghost has said " The lips of the priest shall guard knowledge " (Mal. II, 7). How can those who are the legates of the Lord of all knowledge, and upon whom the faithful depend for the message of salvation, dare to be lacking in learning ? If ever there was a time when it behoved a priest not to be ignorant that time is surely this our own. For to-day a knowledge of the sciences is so bound up with the art of living, and is so closely connected with everyday life, that the most ordinary of mankind continually turn to the sciences in justification of all they say or do. We must therefore make every effort that the faith may be assisted by all that human learning, of every kind, has to offer. The pope quotes Tertullian to remark that Catholicism has only one thing to ask, that it be not condemned before it is known,[1] and St. Jerome to condemn the notion that ignorance does not matter if only the ignorant man is pious.[2]

As far as the religious life is concerned study is a moral and ascetic discipline. To study is to undertake a task that entails hard work, constant sacrifices, and inconvenience of every kind. It is the great enemy of that laziness and indolence which is the mother of every trouble. The habit of study, by the very intensity of thought it induces, trains a man not to make hasty decisions, and to restrain more easily his vagrant emotions. More than this, the study of theology supplies the best of all nourishment for the development of the interior life, and is therefore a very sure road to perfection. It is in the religious who shuns this sacred task that laxity of observance most often shows itself, and the beginnings of that deterioration which may even go as far as the ultimate treason to his vows.

The pope speaks of the religious who studies theology, daily occupied with the thought of God's gifts to man,

[1] " Unum gestit interdum, ne ignorata damnetur," Apol. I.
[2] "Uninformed holiness profits only its possessor, and whatever the service his merits render the Church of Christ, he does it just as much harm when he is unable to throw back the enemy. . . . To give an answer whenever he is questioned on God's law is the priest's office . . ." (Epis. LIII).

through nature and through grace, and the new religious quality given to his intellectual speculation, and how all this, through the spirit of faith, unites the soul most closely to God. `` What man is closer and more like to Jesus Christ than the man who has assimilated into his own substance the divinely brought teaching on faith and conduct ? '' Experience teaches that the religious who have given themselves with the greatest love to the study of theology, have reached often to the very heights of sanctity.

Superiors are to be careful not to extend too ready a welcome to young recruits. They are to see that, along with their religious formation, these young candidates receive a sound secondary education. No one is to be admitted as a novice until this secondary education is completed. To provide this education is not a matter of charity but of justice to the youths concerned, so that if any particular province of an order cannot, for lack of funds, see to it, the youths are to be sent for the purpose to another province.

The study of religion, which is to be one of the principal matters of this secondary education, is not to be wholly interrupted when the young religious comes to study philosophy. The pope suggests that a systematic study of the Roman Catechism [1] may very profitably occupy these years, giving the student not only an admirable model of Latin style but the practice of expressing himself in a way suited to popular instruction and the defence of the faith.

Superiors are warned against any limitation of the studies of their young subjects—a later decree provides that if, for some good reason, they are ordained before the completion of their course, the studies omitted are to be made good before the new priest exercises any pastoral office such as preaching or hearing confessions. Everyone knows, says the pope, that studies gone through hurriedly or in any but their own due order, are scarcely ever brought up to the required standard, if indeed at all. Good masters are essential and the pope insists that those chosen to teach shall

---

[1] Sometimes called the Catechism of the Council of Trent.

be not only models of religious observance but scholars of undoubted competence in the matters they are to profess. There is to be, as the Canon Law requires, a separate lecturer for each of the following subjects at least, Sacred Scripture, Dogmatic Theology, Moral Theology, and Church History.

Again, as in the instructions for the secular clergy, Pius XI insists that it is on the thought of St. Thomas Aquinas that the student shall be bred. This is a sacred and inflexible rule. Again he quotes Leo XIII,[1] and with special reference to his auditory "All who really wish to occupy themselves with philosophy—and religious above all cannot but wish to be philosophers—will look to Thomas Aquinas for the elements and foundations." A competent knowledge of sound philosophy is the *sine qua non* of theological understanding, just as truly as that a total ignorance of divine things is a bar to real competence in philosophy.

Finally, the pope deals with the danger that learning can become if it is divorced from faith and piety. This danger is best met by the practice of faith and humility and the realisation that human knowledge is at its best only human and therefore finite. With an opportune quotation from St. Augustine,[2] the pope concludes the survey of the ideal priest-religious and of the formation that alone can produce the type. " ' Knowledge,' says the Apostle, ' puffeth up.' [3] What then ? Must you run away from knowledge ? are you going to choose to be ignorant rather than be puffed up ? If ignorance were better than knowledge what business should I have addressing you now ? . . . Love knowledge, but give the higher place to charity. Knowledge puffeth up, when knowledge stands alone. But charity, because its work is constructive, will not allow a man to be puffed up by knowledge. Knowledge puffeth up there only where charity is not building : where charity builds there is, not inflation, but knowledge truly solid."

---

[1] Letter *Nostra Erga* of 25 November, 1898.
[2] Sermons cccliv, c. vi.
[3] 1 Cor. viii. 1.

The idea that the spiritual health of the Catholic is conditioned by his knowledge of the teachings of his faith recurs time and again in the direction and instruction of Pius XI.

Thus, in 1929,[1] it was the subject of a special instruction, sent through the Congregation of Religious, to the heads of all the orders of brothers and all the superiors of the orders of nuns. The pope here says expressly that an accurate and really serious training in Christian doctrine is the condition of a lively faith, and that without such a training it is impossible to live a Christian life. To neglect this study is to menace one's own spiritual life and to sterilise one's efforts for the spiritual good of others. Everywhere, to-day, men take up readily all kinds of erroneous theories about God, religion, the rational soul, the nature of society, man's final destiny, and the duty of making a profound study of these matters is greater than ever in the case of men and women consecrated to God for the work of instructing others. The instruction goes on to lay down that, for the future, in all noviciates, of men and women, the novices shall receive a thorough grounding in all these matters—not, says the document, mere memory knowledge —and not be allowed to pronounce their vows until they have satisfied an examiner as to their competence.

Again, to return for the moment to the great letter *Unigenitus Dei Filius*, the pope speaks of the grave duty of all superiors of those orders that have priests among their members to care for the spiritual welfare of the lay brothers, especially by giving them a continuous, systematic instruction in the truths of faith. If a man really knows these, says the letter, whether he be a religious or live in the world, he

---

[1] Instruction of 25 November, 1929. With regard to the study of Christian Doctrine the Motu Proprio *Orbem Catholicum* of 29 June, 1923, should be read which establishes a new special department in the Curia to watch over the execution of all the laws for the improvement of religious instruction throughout the Church. In this document Pius XI says also : "We also greatly desire to see founded in all the principal houses of the religious orders devoted to education special schools to form an élite of young people, with special courses of lectures. There should be examinations and an official diploma certifying the competency of these students to teach Christian Doctrine, Sacred History and the History of the Church."

has only to reflect on them faithfully to find in them every encouragement his virtue needs.

Pius XI has not confined himself to such exhortation as these different letters contain. To say nothing of the Motu Proprio that raises the qualifications required of lecturers in Sacred Scripture,[1] there are the new regulations [2] that order each bishop to send in to Rome a detailed report on his seminary every three years, and the appointment of a new officer whose title Visitor Apostolic of Seminaries describes his office. The life of every seminary, in its minutest detail, is thus to be set down by the local bishop and sent for the Roman See's inspection and comment.[3]

Two other *Instructions* [4]—the one from the Congrega-tion for the Discipline of the Sacraments, the other from the Congregation of Religious—introduce a new procedure into the old business of examining the character, motives, sincerity, and general suitability of clerics to receive the subdiaconate (with its entailed obligation of perpetual chastity) and òf novices about to make their vows of poverty, chastity and obedience. No secret is made of the fact that there have been grave cases of desertion, not only from the life to which religious are pledged but also from those sacred ranks to which the reception of Holy Orders admits a man.[5] Naturally enough the devil leaves no stone unturned to bring such losses to pass. All the more careful then must bishops and religious superiors be to ensure that the candidate is really naturally suitable, that he understands perfectly what he is about to do and that he is acting with full freedom. At each subsequent step the matter must be carefully gone into anew. The candidate is to file an application in writing in which he states his desire, his

---

[1] *Bibliorum Scientia* of 27 April, 1924.

[2] Issued by the Congregation of Seminaries and Universities, 2 February 1924.

[3] Motu Proprio of 24 April, 1931. So far this regulation affects only the seminaries of Italy, but an extension of the Visitor's powers seems likely from the text of the document. (A.A.S., xxiii, p. 151, *The Clergy Review*, July, 1931.)

[4] The Instructions are dated 27 December, 1930 (A.A.S., xxiii, p. 120) from the S.C. of the Sacraments and 1 December, 1931 (A.A.S., xxiv, p. 74) from the S.C. for Religious.

[5] As always Pius XI is nothing if not candid.

understanding of the annexed obligation, his freedom from any kind of pressure whatever and he is to confirm the truth of his statement with an oath. The opinion of the superiors of the seminary, the other officials, the candidate's parish priest, and any other likely suitable person, clerical or lay, is to be sought. Finally the bishop is to interview the aspirant either personally or through some specially delegated priest. This decree is to be read out publicly to all the clerics or novices every year, and superiors are warned of their duty to place the newly ordained priests in posts where to some extent they will be sheltered and have time to adjust themselves to their new life.

The crowning act of all this new effort to raise the standard of clerical life and priestly competence is the constitution *Deus Scientiarum Dominus* [1] which reorganises, on uniform lines, the various Catholic Universities and Institutes of Higher Studies throughout the world. The pope takes the opportunity to recall the Church's continuous care for learning and the establishment of schools since the days of Clement of Alexandria. He notes how, had it not been for the monasteries, the very elements of our culture would, during the darkest ages of our civilisation, have disappeared altogether. He recalls that it was the Church that invented the university, and that of the fifty-two universities founded by the year 1400, twenty-nine were purely papal foundations and that, of the rest, ten owed their origin in part at least to the different popes. Even in our own time the popes have managed to found a score of such institutions. Once again Pius XI cites a phrase of Tertullian to sum up the spiritual justification for this interest in learning. The Church has only one enemy she need fear, ignorance of the truth. *Desinunt odisse qui desinunt ignorare* says the African apologist.[2]

Then comes the grandiose scheme of re-organisation, the general result of which is to increase the requirements for degrees in all the various branches of study. Three degrees

[1] Apostolic Constitution of 24 May, 1931.
[2] Ad Nationies, i, 1. "They leave off hating who leave off not knowing."

are to be offered, the baccalaureate, the licentiate, the doctorate. The final degree is to be taken, in Theology, after five years study, in Canon Law after three years, in Philosophy after four years, at the Biblical Institute after three years, and the same holds good of the Institute for Oriental Studies and the Institute of Christian Archæology. At the Institute for the Study of Canon and Civil Law the period is four years and at the Institute for Sacred Music three years for the degree in Plain Chant, five years for Composition and four years for the Organ. No candidate may be entered for Theology who has not read at least a two years' course in Philosophy and passed the required examination. For the Biblical Institute he must also be at least a Licentiate in Theology, *i.e.*, have studied Theology for four years in a university and passed the required examination. For the special faculties of Canon Law, Oriental Studies, the Institute of Canon and Civil Law, of Christian Archæology, and Sacred Music the candidate must, if he is a cleric, have completed the seminary course of two years Philosophy and four years Theology.

To complete, in a few brief lines, the tale of the pope's practical interest in learning and the arts, he has provided new buildings for the Gregorian University of Rome (the famous Collegio Romano of the Jesuits) the Dominican University called the Angelicum, the Oriental Institute and the Institute of Christian Archæology. He has built a new observatory at the papal villa of Castel Gandolfo, and a new picture gallery for the masterpieces in the Vatican, employing for this his old associate of Ambrosian days, Luca Beltrami. The Lateran palace now houses the great Ethnological and Missionary museum which Pius XI has collected to illustrate the life and habits of all the primitive people of the world. In the Press Exhibition of 1933 he brought together all the literary productions of his 300,000,000 spiritual subjects. The Vatican Library is in process of reorganisation and, as a formal gesture to the importance of learning, at the last creation of cardinals, Pius XI gave the red hat to both the prefect of the Vaticana,

Mgr. Giovanni Mercati and to the pro-prefect, Mgr. Eugène Tisserant.[1]

"To know in order to act" the pope once read on the cover of a report of the *Semaines Sociales* of France. "That is almost my motto," he remarked, "what I like to say is ' To know in order to live '." [2]

The fifteen years of the reign of Pius XI have seen scores of decisions which, slowly but surely, in one way or another, are modifying the ordinary way of Catholic life, adapting the old discipline to the needs of a new age, securing that Catholicism shall form for the new age the character it calls for, helping to form the "new people." The general ideal of Catholic Action has been described and the principles that inspire it. Some details must now be added.

First there should be noted and read three great encyclicals that bear directly on the spiritual life of the individual, namely *Rerum Omnium* (26 January, 1923) pleading for a return to St. Francis of Sales as a spiritual direction most suitable to the new age, *Mens Nostra* (20 December, 1929) on the more frequent use of retreats and *Ad Catholici Sacerdotii*[3] (20 December, 1935) on the Catholic Priesthood. The pope here provides ample material for the spiritual betterment of whoever will read, showing himself not so much the ruler of the Universal Church, as a guide and director paternally anxious for the welfare of every Catholic's intimate, personal life with God.

One of the most useful aids to foster that life, and one of the most characteristically Catholic of all practices is devotion to the saints. In the encouragement of this,

[1] Add also (1) the reorganisation of the commission for the revision of the text of the Vulgate and the creation of the new Benedictine Abbey of St. Jerome to be its home (15 June, 1933, A.A.S., Vol. XXVI, pp. 85, 290) ; (2) the reorganisation of the Pontifical Academy of Science by the Motu Proprio *In Multis Solaciis*, 28 October, 1936.

[2] FONTENELLE, p. 35.

[3] Translation, *The Catholic Priesthood*, 69 pp. Catholic Truth Society London ; N.C.W.C., Washington, D.C.

Pius XI has set a new standard for pontifical action. For centenary celebrations connected with St. Thomas Aquinas,[1] St. Francis of Assisi [2] and St. Augustine [3] he wrote three magnificent panegyrics, that express in a really remarkable way all that these three great personalities did for the Church of their own day, and their effect on the Church ever since. To these should be added, a document of like value, the bull [4] which on 16 December, 1931, canonised Albertus Magnus, the master of St. Thomas Aquinas and declared him Doctor of the Church. It is impossible to exaggerate the value of these four letters as scholarly summaries of important chapters in the history of the Church and as expositions of features of the Catholic tradition still vital to every Catholic.

These are only the principal reminders in a series that embraces over thirty saints.

In another way too, Pius XI has played his part in procuring for the Church all the help that the cultus of the saints can give to the spiritual life of the individual, namely, by the canonisations he has decreed, no fewer than thirty-one in all. The roll of the new saints and the dates of their canonisation is as follows :

17 May, 1925.	St. Teresa of the Child Jesus.
21 May, 1925.	St. Peter Canisius, S.J.
24 May, 1925.	St. Marie-Madeleine Postel.
	St. Madeleine-Sophie Barat.
31 May, 1925.	St. John Eudes.
	St. John Mary Vianney, Curé of Ars.
22 June, 1930.	St. Catherine Thomas.
	St. Lucia Filippini.
29 June, 1930.	St. Robert Bellarmine, S.J.
	St. Theophilus of Corte.

[1] *Studiorum Ducem*, 29 June, 1923 : translation in *St. Thomas Aquinas* by Jacques Maritain, App. iii.
[2] *Rite Expiatis*, 30 April, 1926 : translation published by N.C.W.C., Washington, D.C.
[3] *Ad Salutem Humani*, 20 April, 1930 : translation published by N.C.W.C., Washington, D.C.
[4] *In Thesauris Sapientiæ.*

	St. John de Bréboeuf, S.J. and Seven Companions.
16 December, 1931.	St. Albert the Great, O.P.
4 June, 1933.	St. André-Hubert Fournet.
8 December, 1933.	St. Marie-Bernard (Bernadette) Soubirous.
14 January, 1934.	St. Jeanne-Antide Thouret.
4 March, 1934.	St. Mary Michael of the Blessed Sacrament.
11 March, 1934.	St. Louise de Marillac.
19 March, 1934.	St. Pompilius-Marie Pirotti.
	St. Joseph Benedict-Cottolengo.
	St. Teresa-Margaret Redi.
1 April, 1934.	St. John Bosco.
20 May, 1934.	St. Conrad Birndorfer de Parzham, O. Min. Cap.
19 May, 1935.	St. John Fisher.
	St. Thomas More.

The list reveals an astonishing number of saints contemporaneous with our own generation. Of the new saints three, St. Albert the Great, St. Peter Canisius and St. Robert Bellarmine have been declared Doctors of the Church, as also the famous Carmelite, St. John of the Cross. St. Teresa of the Child Jesus has been, one might not unfairly say, the patron saint of the whole pontificate, and the pope's own personal devotion played a great part in hastening the termination of the cause of St. John Fisher and St. Thomas More.

The beatifications of the reign are too numerous to detail; they number 531 in all. Among them may be noted three great groups of martyrs, the thirty-two French nuns put to death at Orange in 1794; the seventy-nine martyrs of Corea (natives all, except the bishop and two missionaries who, again, were French); the 191 bishops, priests and others martyred at Paris in September 1792; the 136 English martyrs of the sixteenth and seventeenth centuries. Also among this crowd of new *beati* we may note the Scottish martyr, John Ogilvie, S.J., and his fellow Jesuit, Claude de la Colombière, the director of St. Margaret Mary Alacoque and one of the pioneers in the spread of the modern devotion to the Sacred Heart of Jesus.

In matters of discipline the law of the eucharistic fast has been notably mitigated for priests who need to say two masses on the same day and for whom the need to fast would make this impossible. At Rome itself the Cardinal Vicar has effected such reforms in the appearance of the churches as the Duce has done in the city itself, abolishing much that used to cause comment the reverse of pious, abuses of ornamentation and of popular devotion too. One notable change is the disappearance of the votive candles, the decree noting that " this [practice] may in fact easily become, or appear to be a superstition and it fosters the impression that it is done for the sake of gain. . . . This practice must therefore cease." The clergy are to remind the faithful that " a single mass well heard, or a single Holy Communion received with the right dispositions has greater power to obtain heavenly graces and favours than thousands of candles lit even for the longest series of days." [1]

In the matter of ecclesiastical music Pius XI has shown himself the continuator as well as the successor of Pius X. In the lengthy Apostolic Constitution *Divini Cultus* (20 December, 1928) he has supplied the Church with a detailed code for its conduct in this respect. It is well known how long a time it took for the famous Motu Proprio of Pius X to produce any effect, and indeed how little effect in many places it has ever produced at all. The indifference to the papal directions of those responsible for their execution is not unknown to the pope. In a letter to the Abbot-Coadjutor of that great liturgical centre, the abbey of Mont-César (Louvain), defending the Church from the charge that its musical outlook is narrow, Pius XI refers to his own Constitution, and then goes on to say : " Here there is a matter we must lament. In some places the rules of the Motu Proprio have not been fully put into

[1] *Osservatore Romano*, 23 June, 1932 : *Clergy Review*, iv, p. 164.

practice. And of course the expected advantages have not been realised. We know perfectly well that there are people who allege that these rules, so solemnly promulgated, have no force where they are concerned, and there are others, who, after a first submission to them, have, little by little, shown themselves favourable to a style of music that, at all costs, must be banished from the Church . . . " [1]

An interesting example of the care taken to protect the faithful from the evil of superstition is to be found in the joint decree of the Congregations of the Council and of Religious (7 June, 1932) which concerns the indiscriminate, uncontrolled accounts of " miracles " at famous shrines. These are often, the decree fears, published for devotional purposes, with, usually, some mention of offerings made. These reports are often mere gossip, unsubstantiated by any authentic proof. Sometimes, even, the suggestion is made that the result of one's prayers depends on the offering. For the future, therefore, every account of what is alleged to be a miracle at such places is to be submitted to a special censorship, and without this the bishop of the place concerned is not to give permission for the account to be printed.[2] Along with this, another specimen of the same kind of vigilance, we might place the decree of the Holy Office (18 June, 1934) declaring that the alleged apparition of Our Lady at Ezquioga is a phenomenon destitute of all supernatural character.[3]

In the Roman Curia itself the important tribunal called the Sacred Penitentiary has been reorganised,[4] and, to give an example of a reform that affects the Church throughout the world in a local way, bishops who are unable to organise a competent *curia* for what relates to matrimonial causes are bidden refer their difficulties to the Congregation for the Discipline of the Sacraments which will make what provision may be necessary.

[1] Quoted by G. Villiers in the *Revue Saint-Chrodégang* of Metz for Carême, 1937.
[2] *Clergy Review*, November, 1932, p. 425, quoting A.A.S., xxiv, p. 420.
[3] *Ib.*, September, 1934, p. 248, quoting A.A.S., xxvi, p. 433.
[4] Apostolic Constitution *Quæ Divinitus*, of 25 March, 1935.

Of more general interest, perhaps, is the very first change Pius XI made after his election, namely, the extension of the interval which, by Canon Law, must elapse between the obsequies of the dead pope and the opening of the conclave. This used to be ten days. But it has happened more than once that cardinals from the New World have arrived to find the conclave over and the new pope elected. This was the case in 1922. The new regulation [1] extends the interval to fifteen days, and gives the Sacred College power to extend it for yet another three in any particular case.

A word at least must be spoken on one special mark of the pope's care to keep ever before the Church that we are but sojourners in this world, that we have not here a lasting habitation, and to provide, ever more generously, opportunities of grace ; this is to mention the three great jubilees of the reign, in 1925 the usual Holy Year that marks each quarter of the century, in 1929 on the occasion of the golden jubilee of the pope's own priestly ordination, and in 1933 to commemorate the nineteenth centenary of the traditional date of the Crucifixion. There were thus six years in all of special prayer and penitential exercises throughout the Church, and in the last jubilee a great world-wide crusade to remind mankind that the Redemption is the source of all we have, are, or can be, the source even of our civil culture. In the Allocution to the cardinals in which the announcement of this last jubilee was made, the pope spoke about its aim, how it would serve to distract men's minds—to their own great gain—from the chronic preoccupation with " conflicts and differences, suspicion and distrust, armaments and disarmament, damages and reparations, debts, payments, moratoriums, insolvency, economic and financial interests." The year would be given up to a public recall of all the great cycle of events associated with the Redemption of mankind. This jubilee of the Redemption, extended in 1934 to the whole world, came to a close with a new kind of solemnity, the three days of continuous

[1] Motu Proprio *Cum Proxime*, 1 March, 1922.

masses offered at Lourdes, whose special intention was peace, concord and true prosperity, the enlightenment of all who have strayed from the truth and the abandonment of neo-pagan practices and devotions.

CHAPTER VII

(i) *The Foreign Missions*

THERE is no more striking fact in the whole history of the Church than the constant pre-occupation of its rulers to evangelise the non-Catholic races. From the first moments when the divine obligation was laid upon the Apostles to go forth and teach all nations until our own time this work of religious propaganda has never ceased.

" In this work men of noted holiness laboured with great fruit. Among these Gregory the Illuminator joined Armenia to the Church of Christ ; Styria was converted by Victorinus, Ethiopia by Frumentius ; next, the Irish were born to Christ by Patrick, the English by Augustine, the Scots by Columba and Palladius ; then Holland received the light of the gospel while Boniface and Anscar brought the peoples of Germany to the Catholic Faith, and Cyril and Methodius the Slavonic nations. Thenceforward a yet wider field opened out to apostolic men ; William Rubruck brought the light of the Faith to the Mongols, and B. Gregory X sent the first missionaries to China ; these were followed by the sons of Francis of Assisi, who founded there no mean Church of believers, though it was soon afterwards dispersed by the storm of persecution. After the discovery of America, a band of apostolic men, among whom Bartholomew Las Casas, a glory and light of the Dominican Order, is especially to be commemorated, took up the duty both of protecting the wretched natives from the infamous tyranny of men and of delivering them from the cruel slavery of demons. Meanwhile Francis Xavier, who is worthy to be compared with the Apostles themselves, laboured with marvellous success for the glory

of Christ and the salvation of souls in the East Indies and
in Japan, dying on the very threshold of the Chinese
Empire, which he was about to enter, thus by his death
opening the door, as it were, for the first preaching of the
gospel in these immense regions, where thenceforward the
missionaries of so many famous Religious Orders and
Missionary Congregations, in their zeal for the propagation
of the Faith, have exercised the apostleship amid many
anxieties of times and conditions. Finally, Australia, the
latest of the continents to be discovered, and also the
interior wilds of Africa, explored by the daring and perseverance of modern explorers, have received the message
of the Christian faith ; and there is now scarce an island so
remote in the vast Pacific Ocean, that it has not been
reached by the energy of our missionaries. Of these, there
have been very many who like the Apostles, whilst seeking
the salvation of their brethren, have attained the heights of
sanctity ; and not a few, adding the glory of martyrdom
to their apostolate, have established the faith in their
blood." [1]

The reign of Pius XI has seen such far-reaching developments in missionary activity and so great an extension of
this apostolic work that it has often been suggested that
here will lie his chief claim to the gratitude of the Church
of the future. Mere statistics show that where in 1922 there
were under the jurisdiction of the Sacred Congregation for
the Propagation of the Faith—the Church's Ministry for
Foreign Missions—something like 12,000,000 native
Catholics, in 1933 the number had grown to 18,000,000.
Where there were 330 missionary districts of one kind or
another, there are now 512, of which thirty-two are in full
charge of native clergy. To say nothing in detail of the
104 new Apostolic Prefectures established in the course of
the pontificate, there are eighty-eight new missionary
bishoprics—not diocesan sees but apostolic vicariates ruled

[1] Benedict XV, encyclical *Maximum Illud* of 30 November, 1919. Translation published by the Catholic Truth Society, London. *The Missions*, by
H.H. Pope Benedict XV.

by a bishop. Of these new bishoprics thirty-seven are in Africa and another thirty-seven in China. This increase is more than remarkable, especially if the huge losses of property and personnel due to the war be borne in mind and the nineteen years of continuous distress and strain which have followed the war.

Before the missionary policy of the pope is described, however, another less picturesque and more routine kind of church expansion ought to be noticed. This is the creation of new diocesan sees in the countries that have been evangelised now for centuries, the so-called civilised world. These new sees number 99 in all. It is instructive to note their national and geographical distribution. Fifty-three are in South America ; Brazil 19, the Argentine 10, Chili 9, Venezuela 4, Bolivia 3, Mexico and Paraguay 2 each, and 1 new see in each of the republics of Columbia, Nicaragua, Porto Rico and Guatemala. There are 15 new sees in India, 3 in the Philippine Islands and 1 each in Japan, Siberia, Arabia and Transjordania. The new European sees total 19; 4 in Poland, 4 in Lithuania, 2 each in Germany, Italy and Roumania, 1 each in England, Portugal, Latvia, Turkey and at Danzig. Canada has 4 new bishoprics and the United States 4 too. Finally there are 2 new sees in Australia.

As a missionary pope Pius XI is undoubtedly, and in the first place by his own frequent declaration, the heir and the faithful continuator of his immediate predecessor Benedict XV, and in the great encyclical *Maximum Illud* of the pope of the war years, the germs of much of the later growth can be easily discerned. Pope Benedict's sudden death found him in the midst of preparations to celebrate the third centenary of the foundation of the great centre of modern missionary activity, the Congregation of Propaganda. It fell to his successor to preside over the commemoration, and Pius XI's sermon at the mass of thanksgiving on Whit-Sunday, 1922 was, in fact, the new pope's first pronouncement to the Catholic world.

The missionary policy of Pius XI is set forth, with

unusual warmth and feeling, in the encyclical *Rerum Ecclesiæ*, but before we consider this it will be better to recall the great administrative changes which preceded the encyclical, changes little less than revolutionary.

The first of these [1] was the transfer to Rome from its century-old home at Lyons of the Association for the Propagation of the Faith.

Pius XI made up his mind that there should be one single common fund for all the missions. The smallest donation, the little child's halfpenny, should go to this new fund from which the Sacred Congregation of Propaganda would pay out grants to all the missions as they needed. He could not be ignorant that in the splendid creation of Lyons the machinery for this work was already to hand. Hence his determination to transfer its headquarters to Rome, so that it would be not merely the greatest of private good works for the missions but the official agent of the Holy See, with an authoritative place in every diocese of the Catholic world. The greatest glory of modern French Catholicism was to become, not a model for the Church in general to imitate, but the Church's own means to collect the alms of her children for this holy purpose.) " Instead of founding any new organ it seemed better to transfer the headquarters of the Association to the capital of the Catholic world, to adapt it to the new needs of our own time, to give it something of Our own authority and make of it the Pope's own instrument." The directors of the Association generously entered into the pope's plan, and consented to be but assistants in a work where they had so long commanded in chief, their own work, the great society their efforts had built up. Undoubtedly they made a great sacrifice. Pius XI acknowledged it, thanked them for it publicly and congratulated them on the generous faith that prompted it. This French willingness to surrender a national glory for the general good of the Church should be remembered against the common notion that in religion as in all else the French are chauvinist. The pope

[1] Motu Proprio *Romanorum Pontificum*, 3 May, 1922.

held them up as an example to the whole Catholic world.

For the future then Rome is the headquarters of a new missionary organisation of world-wide extent. Its work is to collect money for the missions. Its seat is the office of the Congregation *De Propaganda Fide*. At its head is an international council, whose members are chosen by the pope. France has the special privilege of an extra seat in this council, as a recognition of her unique generosity in the service of the missions. With the work and the methods of the council all the different local missionary activities have to be brought into line. To be a member of the Association all that is necessary is to pay a halfpenny a week to the funds and to say daily one Our Father, one Hail Mary and the invocation *St. Francis Xavier pray for us*, for the blessing of God on the missions. At the head of it is the Secretary of the Congregation of Propaganda. The Association is to be established in every diocese. Its establishment is no longer left to the piety or interest of the local bishop. It is a command which all must obey. The moneys collected are distributed in March every year, and an annual balance sheet is published showing the details of the amount collected and of the distribution. In all the different countries an official monthly magazine is published to interest the faithful in the work of the missions.

There are three other auxiliary societies which Pius XI has done much to favour. There is the Society of the Holy Childhood which enlists the piety and the enthusiasm of Catholic children to provide means for the rescue from death and the baptism of babies in those countries where child life is still held at low value. There is the Missionary Union of the Clergy and there is the Society of St. Peter the Apostle whose end is to provide the means for the formation of a native priesthood in all missionary countries.

This last matter has from the very beginning of the reign had a foremost place in the policy of Pius XI. Already in 1919 his predecessor had spoken, in vehement terms, of the lack of the missions to produce a native clergy. " It is

clear," he wrote, " that there has been something wanting
and unsuitable in the method up to now employed in some
places for the education of clergy for the missions, and for
the removal of this unfortunate state of things." [1] Then in
the sermon of Whit-Sunday, 1922, the new pope went out
of his way to ask for prayers for the native clergy who were
the first fruits of the new policy. His readiness to take over
and transform into an official activity this new Society of
St. Peter was then but natural. In 1929 [2] it became attached
to the Congregation of Propaganda and thereby acquired
the freedom of every diocese in the Catholic world. Its
members pray for an increase in the number of native
clergy, pray for the native seminarists and priests, and
collect money to found burses for their education. This
society, like the A.P.F. itself, has the Secretary of Propaganda for its president, and a system has been devised by
which, through their officials and councils, the two societies
interlock, though they remain separate and individual.[3]

The organisation and conduct of missions to the heathen
is, nowadays, an extremely complex business, as may be
seen from Propaganda's instructions to the superiors of the
missions. The superior, it is laid down,[4] must establish
missionary posts and stations, open schools—elementary
schools and secondary schools—found orphanages,
hospitals and dispensaries, provide all these with the
appropriate staff, build chapels and churches and train up a
body of competent lay catechists. Here is a development
of pastoral theology that makes of it a new thing altogether.

In the encyclical letter *Rerum Ecclesiæ* Pius XI has
written its Magna Carta. As in every other instance where
this pope is developing the schemes of his predecessors he
does so with a breadth of vision, and with an optimism as
to future development that is remarkable in a man of his
years.

The main need of the missions is twofold—more

[1] Encyclical *Maximum Illud*, p. 11.
[2] Motu Proprio *Vix ad summi*, 24 June, 1929.
[3] Motu Proprio *Decessor Noster*, 24 June, 1929.
[4] Instruction of 8 December, 1929.

missionaries and a greater interest in the work on the part of individual Catholics " at home." To arouse and excite this last to the highest possible level the pope organised in 1923 a splendid missionary exhibition held in his own palace of the Vatican. All the " native " countries of the world were put under contribution, and the result was a vast tableau of native life and culture in all its aspects and of the extraordinary variety of missionary efforts in the field of general civilisation no less than in that of the direct work for souls. A further reason for the exhibition, so the pope declared,[1] was the desire to find out the best possible missionary " technique " and to form the missionaries accordingly, so that they may become daily " more intelligent and more useful ministers of grace and holiness." This exhibition, too wonderful a thing to be dispersed after a few months, the pope has since had transferred to a permanent site in the palace of the Lateran.

Care for the missions is not a kind of spiritual luxury or the hobby of those whose fancy is that way inclined. It is " the greatest and the holiest of all Catholic undertakings," and the missionaries themselves the pope cannot praise too highly " fortissimis magnanimisque viris." [2] The pope tells the bishops of the world that the thought of the thousand million pagans is ever before his mind, and that to do something for them is, for all of us, an elementary duty. True it is that upon the pope as the successor of Peter that duty falls first and principally. But the bishops are no less truly the successors of the apostles and in a matter of such grave importance God will exact from them a rigorous account of their duty. What is needed is of course prayer—the habit of prayer for the missions, says the pope, prayer that goes on continuously. A missionary does well to sweat his very life away for the heathen. If prayer be lacking his effort will be sterile. Therefore a campaign to establish the habit of prayer for the missions.

[1] Allocution of 23 May, 1923.
[2] Allocution of 23 May, 1923.

With regard to the shortage of missionaries—in this respect the effect of the war was a real crisis, missionaries having been withdrawn to fight in the different armies and many of them killed or maimed for life, missionaries expelled after the war because of their nationality—the bishops must everywhere encourage and foster vocations for the foreign missions. They must not be fearful lest good men leave their home diocese. For every priest the diocese gives to the missions God will not fail to provide a substitute. In order to foster a real zeal for the missions among their clergy the bishops should establish everywhere that Missionary Union of the clergy which the Holy See has so encouraged and blessed. Its members pledge themselves to special prayer for the missions, to preach the missions whenever possible, and to encourage the seeds of vocations to the missions whenever they find them.

Nor must the bishops be ashamed themselves to become beggars for Christ and the souls dear to Him.

The letter then turns to consider the different problems of the mission itself. The most important of these is the provision of a native clergy. Seven years have gone by since the pronouncement of Benedict XV on this subject, and the progress is still far from satisfactory. We must remember that native clergy are the natural and the traditional agents for the salvation of souls. To provide them, and for them to be the principal agents, has been the Church's practice since the days of the Apostles themselves. How foolish, then, the idea that the only way in which native clergy can function is as the assistants to the missionaries in works of minor importance. To rule and govern, in spiritual matters, their own people is, of course, the native clergy's right. As Benedict XV wisely pointed out —and it is the common sense of the matter—the native priest by his birth, his mentality, his natural feelings, his interests is one with his people, and better than any other he can speak to their hearts. At their best missionaries from outside run the risk of giving an inadequate exposition of Catholicism, thanks to the fact that they are foreigners with an incomplete grasp of the native speech. And because they are foreigners there is always the danger that a native government will identify Catholicism with the nation whence the missionaries come. The native races are not so patient as formerly of their subjection to European tutelage. They are developing a mastery of European ways of life. The day may come when they are in a position to throw off that tutelage, and in that day, if there are none but Europeans among the Catholic clergy, Catholicism may be expelled too.

Already the missionaries have been warned [1] that it is for the Kingdom of Christ that they go forth, and that if any missionaries should think of their own country's interests, anxious to widen these above all else, it would be a very plague in the Apostolate. There is also the new danger, not that the local church may be too French or too Italian, but that it may not be sufficiently Indian or Chinese. The pope insists that this danger be met and in the only possible way by hastening the time when the supply of native bishops and priests will be sufficient to run the mission and the European may then retire to begin again at the foundations of some other new Catholicism.

Everywhere then the missionary bishops must be prepared to build seminaries for the formation of this native clergy. So far such colleges have been exceptional, they must now be the rule. The students received must be trained in all the virtues that befit a priest, and an apostolic spirit developed in them. At the same time it must not be thought that because they are " natives " a less thorough professional training will suffice. They must be put through the whole course of studies prescribed for the education of the priest, without any shortening of it whatever.

Here the pope digresses to make an indignant defence of the intelligence and the capacity of the native races. His own words deserve quotation : " It would be a wholly erroneous judgment to class these native races as made up of a lower and weakened kind of humanity. Long experi-

[1] *Maximum Illud*, p. 12 ; *cf.* also *Decessor Noster*, 24 June, 1929.

ence teaches us that the peoples of the Far East and of the southern hemisphere at times yield nothing to ourselves, and even show themselves worthy rivals in the matter of mental acuteness." [1]

Has not the pope, indeed, evidence of this before his own eyes ? in the students of the many colleges for native races established for centuries in Rome ?

There must then be no distinction between priests because some are Europeans and the rest only " natives." Is it not the same priesthood that they have received ?

Another need of the mission is the foundation of special orders of native nuns for the special work these alone can do, with a rule and customs suitable to the place and to these races' character. And the pope warns the European missionary nuns not to let an exaggerated zeal for their own particular order blind them to the fact that such new orders as he speaks of may be needed and promising vocations be destined really for these by God.

The last section of the encyclical deals with a still more revolutionary notion, the establishment and the encouragement of establishments of contemplative religious in the Far East. In his letter to the Carthusian order [2] Pius XI lauded the contemplative life as, indeed, every pope must. Now he proposes it as a means of apostolate, recalling how many of these oriental races are drawn naturally to solitude, prayer and contemplation. He sees a striking instance of the attraction of this life for the eastern mind in the success of the great monastery near Pekin which holds nearly a hundred Chinese Trappists.

It is perhaps in China above all that the new spirit inspired by Pius XI into the work of the missions has shown itself. The thought of the ancient civilisation and culture of the Chinese no doubt inspired one indignant passage of his letter at least. " He should indeed show himself a rash judge who regarded these native races as beings of an

[1] *Rerum Ecclesiæ.*
[2] Apostolic Constitution *Umbratilem* of 8 July, 1924 (A.A.S., 15 October, 1924, Vol. XVI, p. 383) : text and translation " *The Power of Contemplation,*" Burns Oates and Washbourne, London, 1933.

inferior kind of humanity, and of lower mental calibre. Long experience teaches us that the very contrary is true." Of all these pagan peoples the peoples of the Far East are nearest the heart of Pius XI, the immensity of their numbers, their intellectual and moral qualities, their ancient civilisation make them an object of intense interest and expectation to him. To this must be added the recollection of the hundreds of these people who, in our own time, have gladly given their life rather than deny the faith.

The task of the missionary in China is made much more difficult from the fact that nineteenth-century Europe saw in China just so much raw material for commercial exploitation. The young Chinese of to-day cannot but hate the white oppression and resent the insult to Chinese ideals implied in the numerous concessions, political no less than commercial, that the nineteenth century wrung from China. The danger undoubtedly exists that Catholicism, since it has always been preached in China by Europeans, may come to be hated as a western, European thing. Wherefore the pope has multiplied, for China, his frequent reminder to the missionaries that they are not to be French, Italian or even European, but simply Catholic priests. In a special letter to the Chinese bishops [1] he stresses the point that to the national aspirations of China Catholicism is in no way an enemy. What missionaries there are who have used their spiritual office as a cloak for political and economic manœuvres in the interests of their own country, the Church has always condemned and severely punished. The emphasis of Pius XI and the way in which his ideas are translated into acts—the wonderful event of his personal consecration of six Chinese bishops at the tomb of St. Peter in 1926 for example—seem to have worked a great change in non-Catholic public opinion in China. Less spectacular, but of the greatest importance, was the decision to appoint for China a Delegate Apostolic, that is to say, a resident personal representative of the pope with a kind of general appeal jurisdiction over the whole organisation of the

[1] *Ab Ipsis*, 15 June, 1926.

Church in that country. Though these high officials are appointed for purely ecclesiastical purposes and though they have no commission to treat with the civil government —it is in this point that they differ from papal nuncios, who are diplomatic agents—it is not strange that the civil government should consider them as the local head of the Catholic Church, and, if not in an official way, in an officious way, treat with them whenever necessity arises. Whence the popular interpretation of the appointment of Archbishop Constantini, the first Delegate Apostolic, as meaning that for the future the Holy See would treat with the government of China directly, and not through the French diplomatic service in China, France being the traditional " protector " of Catholicism in that country. Whence also a certain coldness, for a time, in certain French Catholic circles.

Pius XI has also been most insistent that Catholicism shall be so presented to the Chinese that " it is understood in a truly Catholic spirit and not as an occidental importation " and directions have gone out that in the architecture of the different Catholic buildings, in the statues and the pictures and the general furnishing of Catholicism, the servile copying of western models is to cease and the Catholicism of the country find its expression through the native artistic tradition.[1]

Finally, as evidence of Pius XI's special interest in the affairs of China, we must recall his energetic support of *The National Anti-Opium Association of China*,[2] the latest act in the war against the opium traffic which the popes were among the first to wage. Special instructions have for years now been given in all the mission schools, at the direction of the Holy See, to prevent the beginnings of this terrible habit amongst the youth of China.

" When the present Pontiff consecrated beneath the

[1] *Cf.* the Letter of S. Congregation of Propaganda to Mgr. Constantini, congratulating him on what he has achieved in this matter : *Osservatore Romano*, 19 October, 1932, summary in *The Clergy Review*, January, 1933, p. 74.

[2] *Cf.* Cardinal Pacelli's letter of 10 January, 1931, to Dom Celestine Lou Tseng Tsiang, O.S.B.

dome of Michael Angelo six Chinese bishops and a Japanese bishop, he gave a turn to the wheel of the ship of Peter which threw it among the billows of the Pacific. There is now a Chinese, Japanese and Indian Catholic Church, just as there is an English, American, French and Italian Catholicism. This fact contains the germs of a true revolution. . . . The world widens and the Church of Rome takes into account the new realities. She is the West and the East. She is the Mediterranean, the Atlantic and the Pacific at one and the same time." [1]

The pope has ever been insistent that the missionary must show his love for the races to whom he goes in a practical way, for often enough, normally, in fact, the heathen's first attraction to the gospel is the sight of Christian charity in practical application. Hence the direction to the missionaries to establish orphanages and hospitals, and the training in the elements of medicine and nursing now given in most of the colleges where foreign missionaries are educated. The latest step in this direction is the Instruction of Propaganda (16 February, 1935) on Maternity Training for Nuns. Mothers and their newly-born children die only too frequently from lack of proper attention at birth, the Sacred Congregation points out. Whole tribes are threatened with extinction for lack of proper knowledge and of trained help. The different governments and the non-Catholic sects are alive to this problem and surely Catholics cannot afford to be behind them in whatever interests a work of such charity. The great *desideratum* is the foundation of new orders for this special work. Meanwhile special groups must be formed within the existing orders. No nun will be obliged to take up midwifery, but nuns who volunteer must be trained and obtain the official state certificates. They should, if possible, be trained in Catholic hospitals and universities, but where this cannot be arranged they must go to what hospitals and universities are available.

[1] An unnamed "high dignitary of the Church," quoted CIVIS ROMANUS, p. 178.

(ii) *The Eastern Churches*

Akin to the question of the missions for the conversion of the heathen is that other question of the return to the Church of the hundreds of millions of Christians whose ancestors indeed were Catholics, but who are now organised in different independent religious bodies of one kind and another. This vast army of non-Catholic Christians falls into two natural divisions and presents itself to the charity of Pius XI as a double problem.

First of all, there are the peoples organised in the different schismatic churches of the Near East, the descendants of those Catholics to whom the gospel was first preached, and who remained loyal to the faith despite the long centuries when Arianism, Nestorianism and Monophysitism successively assaulted their orthodoxy. Finally their bishops fell victims to the imperial government's control of religion. They rebelled against the supreme jurisdiction of the Holy See, and gradually they fell into schism, their people following them. Twice in the Middle Ages a reunion was arranged, at the General Councils of Lyons (1274) and Florence (1439), but each time it lasted only a few years. From time to time certain sections of these people have come back to their obedience to the Roman See and remained loyal. They form, in great part, the so-called Uniate Churches.

Never, it may be said, has the Holy See been reconciled to accept this division as final and irrevocable. In every generation the popes have appealed to these much tried peoples to return to their ancient place in the Church. In the last twenty years the popes have been especially active in this matter, Benedict XV founding the Oriental Institute, a kind of university for the study of all that relates to the history, theology, liturgy, and canon law of the Eastern Churches, and the Sacred Congregation for the Eastern Church, a special department of the College of Cardinals to deal with all that concerns those Easterns who are Catholics and to form the beginnings of a policy towards those yet in schism.

M 2

As the real first cause of the schism was the activity of the state so, in modern times, one of the greatest obstacles to reunion, to the beginnings of any practical hope of reunion, was—so most people considered—the power and prestige of the Tsar of Russia. The hundreds of millions of his subjects constituted a good half of the dissident Easterns and, beyond his own people, his policies counted for very much indeed in the different Balkan States which were the next most important stronghold of what is loosely called Greek Orthodoxy. Not unnaturally the overthrow of the Tsar, in March 1917, seemed to promise the beginnings of new hope for the reunion of East with West. But, as everyone knows, the " liberal " republic then set up speedily made way for the Communist state which declared war on religion as such, and turned Religious Russia into a vast shambles, making away indifferently with Catholics and Orthodox alike who stood firm in their loyalty to God.

To this famine-stricken, plague-swept Russia of Lenin, Pius XI sent for the relief of the sufferers all the money he could gather, sums whose total must have reached nearly a million pounds, organising one commission after another for the purpose of administration and help. He saw his priests murdered, churches destroyed, his commissions and his charitable advances repelled.

" In Asiatic Russia—a whole continent—not a single Catholic church now exists." [1] " According to the Soviet Press," writes Mgr. d'Herbigny,[2] " it is certain that the order to close, desecrate, and demolish places of religious worship between December 15th, 1929, and January 25th, has affected more than 2,000 churches which, till then, were open." As to the numbers of those put to death for religion, the figures are astronomical. Waldemar Gurian is quoted by Mgr. d'Herbigny as saying " The emigrants . . . reckon the number of persons put to death at 1,860,000 —among them 28 bishops, 1,200 priests." [3] The last priest

[1] *Soviet Atheism*, p. 28—a useful, documented pamphlet by CYRIL C. CLUMP, S.J.   Catholic Truth Society, London.
[2] *La Guerre Anti-religeuse en Russie Sovietique*, p. 13, quoted CLUMP, p. 28.
[3] CLUMP, p. 28.

in Podolia—which has a Catholic population of a million—was arrested in October, 1935, the last in Odessa thrown into prison on 10 January, 1936.

Pius XI has never ceased to protest and to urge the Catholic world to make reparation by prayer and penance for the blasphemy and the sacrilege that have been among the principal occupations of the rulers of Russia during his reign.[1] On St. Joseph's Day—March 19, 1930—there was a great service of reparation in St. Peter's at which the pope himself presided, and recited the prayers. Now, every day, throughout the world, after every mass prayers are said for Russia. A special commission of cardinals for Russian affairs has been set up and a special seminary founded in Rome to train priests for the heroic work of saving Russia for God.[2]

As far as Russia is concerned, the prospects of religion are black indeed. But the work of which the Oriental Institute is a sign continues to go forward. To gather its great library Pius XI despatched Cardinal Tisserant and Fr. Karaclewski with full powers and all the money he could spare for the purpose—showing himself a second Federico Borromeo. The new edition of eastern writers goes forward steadily, the collection *Orientalia Christiana*, and a new commission is at work codifying the Canon Law of the Oriental Churches.

Another sign of the times is the pope's care to celebrate with all possible pomp the centenaries of the great councils in which the Eastern Church played such a magnificent part, Nicea in 1925 and Ephesus in 1931. On both of these occasions special encyclicals were written so that the whole Church should recall the ancient glory of the East and, celebrating the great events, pray for its return to unity. At the Nicene centenary there was a whole week of ceremonies, each of the different eastern liturgies being celebrated in turn before the famous picture of Our Lady called the

---

[1] *Cf. e.g., The Soviet Campaign against God* (Pius XI's letter *Ci Commuomono* to Cardinal Pompili, 2 February, 1930). Catholic Truth Society, London.
[2] Apostolic Constitution *Quam Curam*, 15 August, 1929.

Acheropita,[1] a week which closed with the solemn liturgy
of St. John Chrysostom celebrated in St. Peter's by twenty-
one Catholic Greek bishops and priests, in the presence of
the pope.   The whole Church is to be interested in the
reunion of East with West, and to this end Pius XI has
decreed that in all seminaries there shall be special courses
" to help to do away with the mutual ignorance and scorn "
that too long have helped to perpetuate the schism, and to
develop a deeper knowledge of the history, doctrines and
theology of the Easterns.[2]

Finally mention must be made of the encyclical *Rerum
Orientalium* [3] of 8 September, 1928, which gives the whole
policy of the Holy See in this matter a new, and more
powerful, and more definite direction.   This document
bears all the characteristic marks of Pius XI's personal
action, candour, that is to say, a direct examination of the
roots of the problem, boldness in expression and explanation, and a wide courageous sweep in the planning for the
future.

What brought about the breach was largely the mutual
ignorance and scorn of the two halves of the Church about
and for each other, the pope admits.   Nevertheless the popes
themselves have always done all they could to prove their
affection for the eastern churches and their appreciation of
them.   Pius XI shows this from the history of their relations
with Rome, beginning with Adrian II and SS. Cyril and
Methodius and going on with the long catalogue down to
our own times.   He recalls all that has been done since the
war, and notes, with praise, how the Catholic universities
of the world have come forward in obedience to his directions, and have furthered this matter of the study of the
Eastern Church.   He describes the latest development in
the Pontifical Oriental Institute at Rome, its new buildings
and its new library.   He explains the programme that the
Institute sets out to realise and he makes, once more, a great

---

[1] " Painted without hands."

[2] Instruction of the Congregation of Seminaries and Universities to the bishops
of the Catholic world, 28 August, 1928.

[3] " On the furtherance of the study of what concerns the Eastern Church."

appeal to Catholics throughout the world to second these
efforts of the Roman Pontiff to win back to the Church
these other guests invited likewise to the wedding feast,
" for now all things are ready." [1]

(iii) Reunion

The conditions of those other non-Catholic Christians
whom a common usage calls, in a not too accurate fashion
perhaps, Protestants is very different from that of the
dissident Churches of the East. These western dissidents
originated not in a mere rebellion against Church discipline
but in a doctrinal revolution that declared the Church as it
existed to be a corruption of the true scheme of Christ and
that set up wholly new organisations which claimed to
renew primitive Christianity after it had been obscured for
centuries by Catholicism. The question of the return of
these bodies is a more complex thing, for in their origin they
do not so much represent the schism of organised parts
from the whole to which they belong, as the rebellion or
uprising against it of thousands of individuals whose sole
organisation lies in this fact of their common rejection and
repudiation of Catholicism.

Of late years, in all these various bodies of Protestants,
there have been frequent signs of a desire to lessen the many
inconveniences that result from a division among men who,
whatever their actual differences of opinion or belief, are
all striving to serve God and, each in his own measure and
way, to promote the reign of God in the world. Whence
the numerous " Reunion " schemes and the congresses to
discuss and to further them. Catholics cannot be indifferent
to such a movement, either to the goodwill and energy
shown in it, or to the high aims that inspire it. And yet—a
matter of frequent embarrassment when they have to
explain this to a world which has lost their point of view,
and a matter that causes heart burnings in that world—
Catholics cannot join in reunion movements whose basis
is the tacit acceptance of the principle that all the so-called

[1] Luke, xiv. 17.

Christian religions are equally Christian, or the tacit denial that there is only one Church which is truly the Church of Christ and that to this all others must, necessarily, submit.

This important question also has come before Pius XI's attention.

In August, 1927, a Reunion Congress was held at Lausanne, and Rome was asked whether " Catholics could take part in or give any help to non-Catholic congresses, meetings, lectures, or societies which had for their object that all who in any way claimed the name of Christian, should be united in one bond of religion." The reply of the Holy Office to the question thus stated was in the negative.[1] Some months later than this decree, Pius XI reviewed the whole matter in an encyclical letter.[2]

The pope, in this letter, shows a complete understanding of the aims of all these schemes and of the attractiveness of what they propose, the " hope that all nations, while differing indeed in religious matters, may yet without great difficulty be brought to fraternal agreement on certain points of doctrine which will form a common basis of the spiritual life."

How obvious this seems ! And how unanswerable the arguments with which the schemes are recommended ! " Is it not right, they ask, is it not the obvious duty of all who invoke the name of Christ to refrain from mutual reproaches and at last to be united in charity ? . . . If only all Christians were ' one ' . . . "

These " fair and alluring words " however, cloak a most grave error. They presuppose the erroneous view that all religions are more or less good and praiseworthy, and they distort the true idea of religion. To favour such an opinion is tantamount to abandoning the religion revealed by God.

What the Catholic view of religion is the pope now

---

[1] " An liceat catholicis interesse vel favere acatholicorum conventibus, cœtibus, concionibus, aut societatibus quæ eo spectant ut omnes christianum nomen utcumque sibi vindicantes uno religionis fœdere consocientur ? "

[2] " *Mortalium Animos*, 6 January, 1928 : translation *True Religious Unity*, Catholic Truth Society, London, pp. 9–23 ; N.C.W.C., Washington, D.C. The official title is *De Vera Religionis Unitate Fovenda, i.e.,* On the fostering of True Unity of Religion.

explains. However God might have acted, the fact is that
He acted in one certain specific way. "God, Who at
sundry times and in divers manners spoke in times past to
the fathers by the prophets, last of all in these days hath
spoken to us by His Son (Heb. i. 1)." No religion can be
true but that which rests upon the revelation of God.
Jesus Christ, the only-begotten Son of God founded a
Church, one sole Church. What the nature of this Church,
in its Founder's intention, is a matter about which many
who claim to be Christians do not agree.

In contrast to their various theories Pius XI recalls,
briefly and with almost geometrical simplicity, the traditional Catholic teaching. Our Lord founded His Church
as a "perfect society," external, perceptible to the senses,
under one head, with a living teaching authority. This
Church could not cease to exist, nor could it ever lack the
necessary strength for its task, seeing that Christ promised
ever to be with it. Unless we say—which God forbid—
that Christ had failed in His purpose or that He erred, that
Church is to-day still in existence, exactly the same thing
that it was when He founded it. The Church of Christ is
one—*i.e.*, possesses a unity of faith and government—and
has always been one. This unity, for which Our Lord
prayed, is not a desire or prayer which so far has not been
granted.

Granted that this is its belief what can the Apostolic See
possibly do, when invited to take part in congresses for
which this belief is mere theory and matter of discussion,
except refuse? Nor can individual Catholics give such
enterprises their encouragement or support. To do so
would be to give countenance to a false Christianity, to
allow that the truth revealed by God may be matter for compromise. Our Lord commissioned the Apostles to teach,
and willed that the Holy Ghost should first teach them.
Has this teaching disappeared from the world? or become
obscured in the Church? Our Lord declared that His
gospel was for all ages. It cannot then have become so dim
and uncertain that to-day we must be content to put up

with and make do all kinds of contradictory opinions. Or else we must admit that the coming of the Holy Ghost, the indwelling of the Holy Ghost in the Church, the very preaching of Our Lord have, centuries ago, lost their efficacy. And this would be blasphemy. Nor can we admit that, though this truth does exist, it is only to be found with such laborious effort that a man's life is hardly long enough for its discovery and attainment. This would be tantamount to saying that God sent His Son merely that a small minority, " and those advanced in years," might learn what He had revealed.

As for charity among men, " the foundation of charity is faith pure and inviolate." Unity can only arise from a single teaching authority, one law of belief, one faith of Christians. " There is but one way in which the unity of Christians may be fostered, and that is by furthering the return to the one true Church of Christ of those who are separated from it ; for from that one true Church they have in the past fallen away."

The Church's position is clear, her claims now are what they have always been. Catholics cannot do anything which would be implicitly in conflict with that position, or those claims ; they cannot act with others as though those claims were matters yet to be decided. As for the men of goodwill who makes these overtures, send these invitations, the pope can only invite them—and Pius XI does this in very moving terms—to " draw nigh to the Apostolic See . . . and submit themselves to its teaching and government." For this happy termination of the present divisions all must pray, and particularly the pope invokes " the Blessed Virgin Mary, Mother of divine grace, Help of Christians, victorious over all heresies, that she may entreat for us the speedy coming of that longed-for day, when all men shall be ' careful to keep the unity of the Spirit in the bond of peace '." [1]

[1] Eph. iv. 3.

CHAPTER VIII

THE CATHOLIC RESTORATION IN CENTRAL AND EASTERN EUROPE

THE most spectacular action of the whole pontificate in the eyes of the non-Catholic world, has been—it seems safe to say—the Treaty of the Lateran by which, in 1929, the long-standing differences between the Holy See and the kingdom of Italy were finally arranged. On that eventful eleventh of February there were signed in the papal palace of the Lateran two documents. The one regulated the relations between the two sovereignties—the Lateran Treaty proper—and the other regulated the relations between the Catholic Church in Italy and the Italian state. This is the Italian concordat, and, as will be explained in its place, it is, in the mind of the pope, much the more important document of the two. For the concordat restores religious freedom in Italy, it is an emancipation.

Now this concordat with Italy, though the type of the concordat at its best, the model and the most perfect of all concordats in a world where the best is necessarily imperfect, is only one of eighteen concordats which Pius XI has negotiated, the crown of a whole policy of religious restoration, and this deserves detailed notice. Concordats are negotiated between sovereignties, and through diplomatic procedure. The question of the restoration of religious freedom in Eastern and Central Europe raises, then, the whole question of the Vatican diplomacy.[1]

[1] It may be useful here to quote the least " worldly " of all the popes, Pius X. " We know well that it will be displeasing to some that We also intend to occupy Ourselves with political affairs. However, whoever judges things dispassionately will realise that the Sovereign Pontiff cannot separate politics from the magisterium that he exercises in faith and morals. Moreover, because he is the chief

Why does the Holy See retain its diplomatic service, by what right and for what purposes ? One of the best summary expositions of the matter is that of the late Cardinal Ceretti, one of the most brilliant of the modern ecclesiastical diplomatists, whose last post in the service carried the high responsibility of restoring the good relations between the Holy See and France as the first nuncio at Paris after the long fifteen years breach of intercourse. His remark that the basis and principle of it all is the idea that the will of Jesus Christ shall everywhere be sovereign, accords with that illuminating reply of another famous ecclesiastical statesman, the late Cardinal Merry del Val. To Mr. Algernon Cecil [1] who asked the one time Secretary of State what were the guiding principles of the Vatican diplomacy the cardinal said, "The New Testament." There is a somewhat disconcerting simplicity about the answer, but if one is to frame any coherent explanation for oneself of the work of these innumerable nuncios and other agents of the service it is as well to take this statement literally. It is a key that solves all the difficulties. Without it, or, using other principles, one raises more difficulties than one solves.

We begin then with what Cardinal Ceretti calls " this exquisitely delicate supernatural point of view." The diplomatic action of the Holy See looks to ends that lie far beyond the scope of human diplomacy. Its aim is to ensure that the spirit of Christian truth informs the legislation of the different peoples. It strives to persuade them to give the Church juridical recognition as a spiritual sovereign power—a power that is by its nature international, or better supra-national, and is, like the state, a perfect society, but a society of a higher order than the state, because of the special perfection of its origin, of the

and the director of what is a perfect society, the Church that is to say, the pope must be willing to enter into relation with the rulers of states and the governors of the republic, for, lacking such relation, he would not be in a position to assure Catholics, everywhere and in all places, security and freedom." (Allocution of 9 November, 1903, quoted PERNOT, p. 21.)

[1] *Thomas More* (1937), p. 227, note 4.

objects for which it was founded and of the means it employs
to attain these objects.

Here the cardinal is echoing the language of Pius XI,
" the Church belongs to all nations and is superior to all
nations." [1] The claims of the Church and the rights of the
Church cannot be a matter of indifference to any state
because, by its nature, the Church works for the welfare of
civil society too.[2]

The Church is a sovereign power if sovereignty means
the recognised right to give final judgment, and since states
are sovereign too there must be, between the two powers,
some system of ordered relations.[3] But the sovereignty of
the Church, a spiritual sovereignty, with hundreds of
millions of subjects, has this peculiar quality that it is a
sovereignty independent of, unattached to, and, so to speak,
innocent of any national entity. The relations between it
and the other sovereignties are not international relations
but intersovereign. To no nation then is the Holy See
foreign, and the state that makes a diplomatic accord with
the pope treats with a co-sovereign who is not a foreigner
since he does not belong to, represent, or sum up in his
person any foreign nation.[4] " For French Catholics he is
a Catholic and a French head : he is German for German
Catholics and Austrian for Austrian Catholics." [5]

Whenever a treaty is made between two states the aim
and the effect is to secure favours for the nationals of each
in the territory of the other, to create in each state a place
of privilege for certain foreigners. But the diplomatic
accords of the state and the Holy See have for the object of
their benevolence not individuals who are to the contracting
state foreigners, but the contracting state's own citizens and
nationals. Man owes political allegiance to his country, and
he owes a spiritual allegiance to the Church of Christ. It

[1] " institutum . . . et ad nationes omnes pertinens et nationibus supereminens
omnibus." Encyclical *Ubi Arcano*, 23 December, 1922.
[2] " in bonum quoque ipsius civilis hominum societatis." Allocution of 23
May, 1923.
[3] Leo XIII, *Immortale Dei*, 1885.
[4] *Cf.* RIVET, pp. 41 and following.
[5] Briand, speech in 1906, quoted in CIVIS ROMANUS, p. 157.

is to the interest of the state, no less than to that of the Church, that in the life of the citizen this double duty should work with the minimum of friction. To ensure its easy working is, humanly speaking, the end of the papal diplomacy and the object of all the concordats.

" By its diplomatic relations with the different states the Church sees acknowledged the position designed for it by its divine Founder, Who is the author of both civil and religious society, Who indeed instituted the distinction between these societies in order that they might each attain their noble ends. In this way both powers peacefully exercise their authority on the citizen who is its visible object." [1]

The word " concordat " has, it must be admitted, some very unpleasant associations for all who know anything of the history of the Church in modern times. *Historia concordatorum historia dolorum* is an expression that has become a proverb. Only too often these treaties have marked a surrender by the Church of privileges, property, even of jurisdiction, as the price paid for the continuance of her elementary and primary functions. The Church's first concern always is the good of souls, that the mass should be offered and Catholics be free to assist at it, that the sacraments should be freely administered, and that the Catholic child should be trained in the knowledge about God and about the means to come to God. No sacrifice has been too great to safeguard these elemental necessities. Pius XI has even gone so far as to say that he would negotiate with the devil himself if the good of souls demanded it.[2] The urgency of this matter of men's salvation has placed the Church, to some extent, at the mercy of the state. So long as this great object is really secured, or the means of securing it guaranteed, then the Church must be ready to lose all else. In the past, as has been said, she has yielded much. It is a sign of changed times and of a healthier public life that the concordats of the

---

[1] Cardinal Ceretti in FONTENELLE, p. 307.
[2] Address to the students of the College of Mondragone, 14 May, 1929.

twentieth century do not make the bullying demand on Catholicism such as the Catholic monarchs of the old *régime* were wont to make, and that Pius XI has been able to carry out his pledge never to assent to a concordat that would shackle religious liberty.[1] An examination of the various concordats concluded since 1922, noting the features common to all of them, shows with most encouraging completeness, how real is the recognition of the rights of religion in the post-war world.

If we leave aside concordats for the settlement of particular questions—for example that of 15 April, 1928, with Portugal which regulated certain details of the religious organisation of the East Indies—we can reckon a series of eleven concordats signed in the last fifteen years.[2] The following are the details of the states with which general concordats have been negotiated and the dates of their ratification :

(1) Latvia, 30 May, 1922.
(2) Bavaria, 24 January, 1925.
(3) Poland, 10 February, 1925.
(4) Roumania, 7 July, 1927.
(5) Lithuania, 22 September, 1927.
(6) Italy, 7 June, 1929.

[1] After remarking on the new and altogether unexpected development that, one by one, all the nations of the world have come to renew their friendship with the Holy See (there are now, 1937, thirty-seven governments diplomatically represented at the Vatican), " a development not everyone views with favour," Pius XI repeats that though pure politics are no business of the Church, statesmen must not, under pretence of politics, invade the Church's rights. He then proceeds : " We therefore make our own the determination and the words of our much regretted predecessor Benedict XV . . . the solemn declaration he made in his very last allocution (21 November, 1921) whose subject was the relations of Church and State. What he then said we repeat and confirm namely, ' In treaties of this kind we shall not, for any consideration, consent to any stipulation hurtful to the prestige or the liberty of the Church '." *Ubi Arcano Dei*, 23 December, 1922.
[2] The pontificate of the last pope to reign before the loss of the old papal states, Pius IX (1846–1878) was marked by some fifteen concordats. Leo XIII's reign saw the papal diplomacy forced to be content with less definite arrangements in its great work of restoring good relations between the Holy See and the Catholic powers. Pius X (1903–1914) negotiated one concordat only—that with Serbia, signed on 24 June, 1914, just a few days before the crime at Serajevo which was to wipe out the Europe of the old diplomacy.

(7) Prussia, 14 June, 1929.

(8) Baden, 12 December, 1932.

(9) Germany, 18 September, 1933.

(10) Austria, 2 May, 1934.

(11) Jugoslavia, 25 July, 1935.[1] To these must be added

(12) the Modus Vivendi with Czechoslovakia, 2 February, 1928.

Of these different states some (1, 3, 5 and 12) are new states, the product of the war, others (2, 6, 7, 8, 9 and 10) are pre-war states, while others again are old states but so enlarged by the events of 1918–1919 that they might almost be called new. Such are Roumania and Jugoslavia.

If we consider the religions of the populations in these states, in Czechoslovakia there is an influential anti-Catholic minority, Prussia is definitely non-Catholic, in Latvia a third of the population is Catholic, in Jugoslavia about 40 per cent., in Roumania rather less, in the German Reich, as a whole, less than a half. The remaining states— Bavaria, Poland, Lithuania, Italy, Baden and Austria—are Catholic.

Before we examine the text of these concordats and disengage therefrom something of the aims of the papal diplomacy at the present day, it will perhaps be of service to recall something of the vast problem that confronted the papacy at the end of the war.

Three great empires had been defeated, two of them were in ruins and a crop of new states springing into life where they had been. One of those fallen empires was the power which, of all others, had been most continuously friendly, in its diplomatic relations, with the modern papacy. This was the Austro-Hungarian empire. Now, of her overwhelmingly Catholic population, a great part had passed to the new state of Czechoslovakia where a masonic-inspired government ruled, a second great body had gone to form part of the new kingdom of Jugoslavia where the ruling forces were Greek Orthodox and by no

---

[1] Not yet (*i.e.*, October, 1937) ratified : the date given is that of the signing of the concordat.

means friendly to Catholicism.   Prague and Belgrade would be, for some years yet, centres of much anxious negotiation.

Everywhere there was confusion between ecclesiastical frontiers and the new national boundaries.   Hungarian bishops found that half their people were now in Czechoslovakia, and other Czech Catholics were still under the rule of sees in Austria.   Like Jugoslavia, Roumania, which had had but a small Catholic population in 1914, found itself possessed now of millions of Catholic subjects, thanks to the cession of Transylvania.   Alsace-Lorraine had been restored to France, but to a France which had long since repudiated the *régime* of the Napoleonic concordat, and this still governed the relation of these provinces with Rome. Ireland was beginning its fight for independence, and the Vatican had a further anxiety regarding England in the matter of the political *régime* to be adopted in the Holy Land, and the fate of the Holy Places.

The reigning pope, Benedict XV, a man who has passed into an oblivion as unintelligent as was his war-time unpopularity, set himself to organise the general Catholic restoration.   The complexity of the situation called out every particle of his great diplomatic talent, his long experience of European affairs and every ounce of his energy.   He only survived the peace treaties a matter of two years, but he lived long enough to see the relations between the Holy See and the new Germany saved and saved, too, its relations with Austria.   The Irish question also he saw resolved without any anti-Catholic reaction in England.   France, after years of bitter separation, was once more friendly and its ambassador in his place among the diplomatists at the Vatican.   The relations with the new states of Central Europe—that had been begun through the nunciature at Vienna in the first weeks of the new *régime*— were friendly, even cordial, and the nascent schism in Czechoslovakia was definitely halted.   The eternal Roman Question itself was so much less bitter that it might seem, by comparison with the situation ten years earlier, to be hardly more than a matter of form.   Benedict XV died on

22 January, 1922. No pope, it may be safely said, succeeded to the heavy heritage in more anxious times than Pius XI, and yet, thanks to his predecessor, there was none to whom it came with omens more propitious.

The first aim of all concordats would seem, necessarily, to be that which underlies the words written, many years ago, by a one-time nuncio to the Cardinal Secretary of State : " [The Church's] legal and social life must be prolonged as much as possible, so as to continue till the nations return to healthier ideas." [1] The ultimate means towards the restoration of civil society to the reign of Christ is the state's recognition of the religion of Christ as a public thing, not as the mere private assent of a million individual personalities to certain truths and ideals of life, but as a supernatural polity expressing itself through a visibly organised society, a second State with a supernatural end in view, promoting solely supernatural objects, and yet, since its components are human beings, organised in the way common to all natural states. The recognition of the Church's status is naturally clearest in the concordats with the Catholic powers, and the fact of such clear recognition on their part is a welcome evidence that with the old pre-war world there died also the bad old tradition that too often enslaved the Church to its imperial and royal protectors.

Austria recognises the Church as "societa di diritto publico." Poland and Lithuania, in almost identical terms, " guarantee . . . the full exercise of its spiritual power and of its ecclesiastical jurisdiction, as also the free administration of its affairs and property in conformity with the laws of God and the Canon Law." An Italian jurist sees in this " a full and complete recognition on the part of the state of the Church's organisation and its autonomy." [2]

[1] Mgr. Czacki from Paris, 28 March, 1882, in SODERINI, *Leo XIII, Italy and France*, p. 179.
[2] Amadeo Giannini, *I Concordati Postbellici*, Milan, 1929, p. 123.

In Bavaria there is recognised " the right of the Church to promulgate, in the domain of its own competence, laws and decrees binding on its own members. The state will not hinder nor make difficult the exercise of this right." Baden, the remaining Catholic state among the various contractants, contents itself with a pledge of legal protection for the free profession and exercise of the Catholic religion. This is almost identical with the words of the Prussian concordat. Latvia, a Lutheran state, recognises, to the Catholic Church in Latvia, juridical personality with all the rights accorded to such by the civil code of Latvia ; and Roumania, promising the free practice and exercise of Catholicism throughout the kingdom, also " recognises the juridical personality of the Catholic Church represented by its lawful, hierarchical authorities according to the common law of the country."

The Austrian concordat promises freedom in the exercise of spiritual powers, as of public worship, and the state guarantees that it will put no hindrance to the Church's power of making laws in its own sphere. All Catholic societies or organisations in Austria to which the code of Canon Law attributes juridical personality are given it also by the state.

The Holy See meets the demands of the new nationalism by a specific pledge, in every concordat except that with Latvia, that no part of the national territory shall form part of a foreign see, that no change shall be made in the present division of the country into dioceses without consultation of the government and that all the bishops shall be of the nationality of the country.

The thorny question of the appointment of bishops, the pivot on which the fortunes of the Church have turned all through history, is differently solved in different places. Everywhere the state recognises that to appoint Catholic bishops rests solely and absolutely with the Holy See. Everywhere the Holy See pledges itself, before publishing its nomination, to advise the government of the person of its choice, in case the government has any objection of a political nature against his appointment. In two of the concordats a precision is added to explain further the meaning of this political objection. In the Czechoslovakian it is any " reasons that regard the security of the state as, for example, that the candidate chosen might have incurred the guilt of political activity of an *irredentiste* or separatist kind, or directed against the constitution or the public order of the country." The second case is the concordat with Baden where it is specified that " political does not mean political in the sense of party politics " such, for example, that a Liberal government would be entitled to object that the proposed bishop was Conservative in his sympathies. The newly-appointed bishop, before entering on his functions, is moreover to swear a special oath of allegiance to the state—in Latvia, Poland, Lithuania, Czechoslovakia, Roumania and in all the states of the German Reich. Austria is the only country not to demand this. The text of these various oaths varies somewhat, but they are substantially the same, and in the case of the first three of the countries named the bishop is pledged " to see that my clergy respect the government established by the constitution." In Poland and in Lithuania the bishop also promises " I will not allow my clergy to have any share in [activities that may endanger the state.]"

The well-being of Catholicism, and the full fruition of its beneficent mission in the state, require imperatively that it should be in constant communication with Rome. It was Rome that, in the greatest century of the Middle Ages, freed the sees of western Europe from the tyranny of the local Catholic rulers and it was the breakdown of this active Roman supervision that led first to the losses of the Reformation and then, in the centuries that followed, to the devitalising of Catholicism's spiritual power in the lands that still remained faithful. In all these countries the popes, for centuries, could only communicate with the bishops at the good pleasure of the Catholic sovereign. All correspondence with Rome was subject to state censure. The modern concordats—Poland, Lithuania, Austria and the

German Reich—give a specific guarantee that the fullest freedom is allowed to the Holy See to communicate with bishops, clergy and the Catholic laity, and *vice-versâ*. Also the bishops enjoy a like freedom with regard to their own clergy and people.

The freedom of the bishop to nominate his parochial clergy according to the provision of the code of Canon Law is expressly recognised. But again it is everywhere required that these be nationals and, in the case of the Austrian and German concordats, that they shall have been educated in German universities or institutes or in one of the Pontifical institutes at Rome. The old rights of patronage have been entirely abolished in Roumania, left intact in Bavaria, and left intact for the present in Poland and Lithuania. In Prussia a special arrangement is to be negotiated about this matter. In Baden the state's right of patronage is abolished, but the right of private patronage remains. In all cases the code of Canon Law is to govern the exercise of these rights.

A favourite field for the interference of the Catholic state in the bad old times was the regulation of the recruiting of the different religious orders. In the *régime* of liberty to which the concordats unanimously testify, there are no longer any state restrictions on the foundation of religious houses, the number of religious, or the social classes from which they may recruit new members. The religious orders enjoy juridical personality in Poland, Lithuania, Bavaria, Roumania, Baden and Austria, Lithuania also granting explicit recognition to whatever the code of Canon Law enacts as to their rights of buying, selling and administering property. Again, in the matter of religious superiors, the Holy See recognises, and makes concessions to, the sharpened sense of nationality. If there are sufficient religious to form a province the provincial superior must be a national; this universally. If the religious are not so numerous then, in Czechoslovakia, they are to be immediately subject to the General of the order, all the local superiors being native. In Austria it is only superiors of houses in orders with *stabilitas loci* who, like the provincials, must be nationals. As to the introduction of new orders, in Poland there is no restriction provided that the foundation involves no expense to the state ; in Lithuania the special permission of the Holy See must be obtained, in Roumania, the special consent of both the Holy See and the government.

The Canon Law strives to maintain the ideal of the clergy's spirituality by forbidding the clergy certain contacts with ordinary life. The concordats recognise the usefulness of this to the state in various ways. Latvia, Poland and Lithuania declare the cleric in holy orders exempt from military service. The same countries, Austria also and the German Reich exempt him from jury service. Austria recognises his obligation not to reveal, for any purpose whatsoever, admission of guilt made to him in the confessional. There is another clerical exemption, recognised everywhere except in Czechoslovakia and Roumania, that has a more novel sound. This concerns the clergy who may be convicted of crime. It is provided that the bishop shall be informed of the accusation and the proceedings, that he shall have the right to a place at the trial and that, if the accused is convicted, he shall either purge his crime segregated in a special prison or monastery, or, if the matter be sufficiently serious, be first unfrocked by the ecclesiastical authorities before suffering, be it death or penal servitude, with the ordinary criminals.

As far as taxation goes clerics enjoy in Poland and Lithuania the same treatment as state officials. Churches, seminaries and presbyteries are exempt from taxation in Latvia, and in Poland and Lithuania also. In these last two countries a distinction is drawn between the revenues destined for the personal use of the beneficiary and those destined for religious uses. Also all novitiates and the houses of religious bound by a vow of poverty are exempt from taxation.

A last point that most of the concordats deal with, in this matter of clerical life, is the education of the clergy.

That to control this is the right and duty of the bishop is a truth that needs no proof. The code of Canon Law lays down in great detail the procedure to be observed, the ideal of life that seminaries must adopt, the discipline, the studies, the religious observance. On the other hand there have not been lacking in the past princes and states to thrust them-selves into this peculiarly ecclesiastical business, sometimes in the hope of bettering the clergy, sometimes in the interests of bureaucratic tyranny. In the territories which were once the Holy Roman Empire it has long been traditional that the clergy should be educated in the national universities. The provisions of the different concordats show a wise recognition of local traditions while providing for the Church's right to have the final word in the forma-tion of her clergy.

There is no mention of this matter in the concordats with Poland, Lithuania, and Czechoslovakia. In that with Latvia it is simply provided that the Archbishop of Riga shall found a diocesan seminary, that it shall be under his authority, and that (except for the lectures in theology and philosophy) the national language shall be used. This concordat also looks to the foundation of a Latvian college at Rome. In Roumania the right of each bishop to found a diocesan seminary is recognised and also the absolute dependence of the seminary on the bishops. There is to be a course of Roumanian Literature and of the national history and the state is to be notified of the programme of studies.

It is in the German concordats that this matter begins to be really important, those with Bavaria, Prussia, Baden, Austria and the German Reich.

The Bavarian concordat speaks of seminaries to which the government pays a subsidy, of establishments of higher instruction in philosophy and theology and of the theo-logical faculties of the Universities of Munich and Wurz-burg. In Prussia " the faculty of Catholic theology in the Universities of Breslau, Bonn, Münster and in the Academy of Braunsberg will continue for the scientific formation of

ecclesiastics." Seminaries may be founded by the Archbishop of Breslau, and by the bishops of Treves, Fulda,
Limburg, Hildesheim and Osnabrück. The state is to be
notified of the programme of studies in these seminaries,
and of the appointment of professors. The standard of
studies is to be that of the state universities. In Baden, too,
a seminary is authorised for the archdiocese of Freiburg-
im-Breisgau and a house of residence for ecclesiastical
students. In the university there is a faculty of Catholic
theology and the state is pledged to found chairs of philosophy and of history to suit the needs of students for the
priesthood. The same kind of provisions are to found in
the concordat with Austria, permission to found seminaries
and houses of residence (Konvicte) which depend entirely
on the bishops, provision for the scientific formation of the
future clergy through faculties of Catholic theology in the
state university and also in the Catholic university of Inns-
bruck. It is the state which, in all these cases, nominates
the professors in these Catholic faculties of the state
university, but always after consultation with the Catholic
bishop. The name of the proposed professor is submitted
to him and if he has any serious objection, whether on the
score of the man's faith or morals, the nomination does not
go into effect. If, later on, the bishop has any objection to
make on either of these grounds to one of these professors
the state will see to his removal. The programme of
studies, it is agreed, shall accord with the prescriptions of
the Canon Law. In Baden it is expressly provided that the
archbishop shall be consulted and in Austria that the
regulations shall be those of the papal constitution *Deus
Scientiarum Dominus*.

Nowhere, perhaps, have the concordats rendered such
service to the states concerned as in the field of education.
The modern state, the state of the last sixty years, has come
to be intensely interested in this matter of the training of its
future citizens. Hundreds of millions are gladly spent every
year out of the public monies to found and maintain schools,
high schools and universities, sums surpassing the total

revenue of the state a hundred years ago. The state's object is social, that the child may be more amenable to the discipline of the common life, that it may be a profitable citizen because it is a trained citizen, that it may not fail when circumstances bring it into competition with the citizens of other states. This matter of education is related to the most sensitive of all modern forces, the instinctive nationalist patriotism of the state. No domestic question is felt to touch the life of the state so intimately. On no point can the feeling of a whole country be so easily stirred and excited against the critic, the reformer or the propagandist of what appears to be a non-national ideal. More and more is it coming to be felt that in all but its private life—and perhaps even in this too—the child belongs to the state and that it is the state's future welfare that should determine the details of the child's education. The general acceptance of this concept of the state as bound to train the children of its citizens after a national pattern for national ends is so modern in origin that we might fairly call it a contemporary product. It is not anything like a hundred years old and yet the tendencies deriving from it influence life to-day almost universally.

This theory is not one to which a Catholic can subscribe. Catholicism exists to educate man, not for natural ends and therefore not with natural truths merely, but for the attainment of his supernatural destiny, that he may ultimately come to union with God, his last end and destiny, or, to put the matter more popularly still, that he may save his soul. The first consideration in education is that a man shall know the divine truths and the divine law of life. Religious education is the most important of all, and should be the centre around which all the rest of the curriculum is built. The Catholic point of view, its justification and its practical application are the subject of one of the three most important pronouncements of the present pontificate.[1] Here we are concerned merely to note the latent possibilities of conflict between this Catholic conception and the current nationalist

[1] The encyclical *Divini Illius Magistri* which is discussed in a later chapter.

secular ideal, and to see how the various concordats face the grave difficulty and what the lines are on which they offer to solve it.

A brief summary of the Canon Law relevant to schools will throw light once more on the value of the concordats as instruments by which the Canon Law—in the twentieth century as in the thirteenth—is showing itself possessed of sufficient vitality to make its way into the contemporary social structure.

Catholics are to be so educated that from the very beginning their religious and moral training has the chief place in their formation. This is what the Church means by a Christian education. In every elementary school there should be this systematic religious instruction. Catholic children are not to frequent schools which are open to non-Catholic children too. So serious is this matter that only the bishop of the diocese can judge where leave to frequent these other schools may be safely given. The Church has the right therefore to establish schools, not only elementary schools but also high schools and universities. If Catholic schools are lacking it is the duty of bishops to establish them. If the universities of a country are not imbued with Catholic doctrine, or Catholic in sense, it is desirable that a Catholic university should be founded. The matter of Catholic religious instruction in all schools is subject to the authority of the Church and the teaching to inspection by that authority. Bishops have the right and the duty of inspecting all schools in their territory to satisfy themselves that all is well from the point of view of faith and morals. Likewise it is for them to see—it is their right and their duty—to the approbation of those who teach religion and the books they use. Should the circumstances call for it— i.e., some failing in faith or morals—they must work for the removal of the offending teacher.[1]

Latvia and Roumania expressly declare the right of the Church to found Catholic schools. The first state promises to respect the religious character of the schools, and the

[1] Code of Canon Law, Canons 1372–1383.

Church agrees to respect the laws of the state regarding private schools. In Roumania these schools, founded at the Church's expense, are open to state inspection and control. The Church has also the right to open training colleges.

The concordat with Poland has but a single article dealing with education. Religious instruction is obligatory in all the public schools. Those who teach it are appointed by the state from a list of teachers drawn up by the bishops. This religious teaching is supervised by the bishop and he is granted a supervision in what concerns the faith and morals of the teacher of religion. If the bishop withdraws his authorisation from a teacher, the teacher loses all right to teach religion. This applies through the whole system of education, even to the lecturers in the faculty of Catholic theology in the state universities.

There is no mention in the concordat with Poland of Catholic schools founded by the Church. But provision is made for such schools in the Lithuanian concordat where it is laid down that schools maintained by the bishop which comply with the education programme of the state shall have their diplomas recognised as equal to those of the state schools of the same kind. But, again, it is with the public state schools that the concordat is chiefly concerned. In all these, and in all schools assisted by the state, religious instruction is obligatory. The curriculum is fixed by the bishop and the text-books too. As in Poland he has a decisive say in the appointment of the teachers of religion and in their supervision " in accordance with the Canon Law." [1] The bishop's decision as to suitability, whether in matter of faith or morals, is, here also, decisive. Those from whom, on these grounds, he withdraws his authorisation lose all right to teach religion. Moreover, the state promises to assist the bishop to see that pupils have facilities for their religious duties and it expressly recognises the duties and rights of the bishops

[1] Article XIII, 1.

as expressed in Canon 381 of the code of Canon Law.[1]

In Roumania too, where we have seen the recognition accorded to the purely Catholic schools established by the Church at its own expense, the right of the Church to instruct in the public and private schools of the kingdom the Catholics who frequent them is expressly recognised. In schools—secondary and elementary—where the majority of the pupils are Catholic, religious instruction is to be given by Catholic teachers nominated jointly by the bishops and the state, and paid by the state. The bishop's objection, on the score of faith or morals, to such teachers of religion will be upheld. The programme of religious instruction in state schools is to be drawn up by the bishop and communicated by him to the government. The bishop's approbation is needed for the text-books used for religious teaching and he has the right to superintend that religious teaching.

Of the concordats with the different German-speaking states, that with Prussia does not so much as mention the question of education. In the remaining four it is one of the chief matters dealt with. In Austria there is the provision that religious instruction is obligatory in all the schools. The teachers of religion and the text-books used are to be approved by the bishop. It is the bishop who draws up the programme of instruction and who supervises and controls the teaching. In this concordat, too, we find the clearest and most explicit recognition of the Church's right in these matters : " To the Church belongs the right to give religious instruction." The state is moreover greatly concerned that the quality of that instruction be improved and a strong hint to that effect is given by the concordat to the bishops. " The diocesan ordinaries shall enter into consultation with the competent supreme authority in educational matters in order to introduce a

---

[1] Canon 381 declares that the religious instruction of youth *in all schools* is subject to the authority and inspection of the Church and also that it is the bishop's right and duty to preserve the faith and good morals of *all* the schools in his territory.

more ample scheme of religious instruction than that which now obtains."

In Bavaria there are Catholic public elementary schools, and in these none but Catholic-trained teachers are to be employed. They must have the licence of the bishop, who is represented on the commission that issues the diploma to teach, and for such Catholic teachers the government will provide appropriate courses in the state training colleges. Such Catholic elementary schools will be founded by the state wherever there is a sufficient number of pupils and the parents demand the school. Religious instruction is an " ordinary " subject in all the high schools and in most of the elementary schools. In those elementary schools where it is not, it will be allowed to be given privately, the state paying costs of lighting and heating the school during the time it is given. The inspection and control of religious instruction in all schools is in the hands of the bishop. If circumstances arise which are unfavourable to the religious or moral life of the Catholic students, or which menace their faith, the bishop has a right of appeal to the education authority. The state promises to help in the provision of facilities for religious duties.

Private schools may be founded in Bavaria by the religious orders, so long as these conform to the state's laws, and the private training colleges established by the orders for their own members are recognised in this sense that their students are allowed to sit for the state examinations.

The concordat with Baden is less detailed, but the sum of its provisions is much the same as in these other cases. Religious instruction ranks as an " ordinary " subject in the schools. All the rights at present enjoyed by the Church—to give religious instruction, to control such teaching and to protect it from danger—are guaranteed for the future.

One last point dealt with by several of the concordats is Catholic Action. This, says a famous allocution of the reigning pope,[1] " is a function of the pastoral ministry and

----

[1] 23 May, 1923.

therefore so bound up with Christian life that whatever assists it or hinders it is a definite assistance to or a violation of the rights of the Church and of souls." In Latvia the state " will put no hindrance to the activity of Catholic associations controlled by the Archbishop of Riga. They shall enjoy all the rights that other associations recognised by the state enjoy." Lithuania, more explicitly, grants " full liberty to organise and to work associations whose end is principally religious and which form part of Catholic Action and which are, as such, under the jurisdiction of the bishop." In Austria full liberty and encouragement is promised to all associations of Catholic youth and a special clause grants the Catholic press all possible freedom in the defence of Catholic truth.

The concordat with the German Reich has been the subject of so much controversy in recent months that it will be useful to consider it separately.[1]

This concordat, signed 20 July, 1933, and ratified 10 September of the same year, does not abolish the earlier concordats with Bavaria, Prussia and Baden. These remain in force in all their detail in the states that made them. The new concordat obliges all the rest of the German Reich for all its provisions and obliges the three states mentioned wherever it treats of matters not dealt with in their own special concordats.

The concordat guarantees in the usual terms the freedom to profess and publicly practise the Catholic religion. It recognises the right of the Church, within the limit of existing laws, to regulate and administer its own affairs and to enact laws for its members within the field of its own competence. There is the pledge we have met in other concordats that the Holy See shall enjoy the fullest liberty to communicate and correspond with the bishops, the clergy

[1] Text (Italian and German) in A.A.S., 10 September, 1933, vol. XXV, pp. 389–413.

and all who belong to the Catholic Church in Germany. Bishops and other diocesan authorities enjoy the same rights *vis-à-vis* their own subjects in all that belongs to their pastoral office. Here there follows a detailed explanation that instructions, ordinances, pastoral letters, official diocesan magazines, and all other acts that have to do with the spiritual government of the faithful and that derive from ecclesiastical authority in the field of its own competence, may be freely published and brought to the notice of the faithful in the way hitherto customary. Ecclesiastics are made equal to state officials in so far as the law protects them in the execution of their office. Insults offered to them or to their office will be punished, and also any disturbance of their exercise of the ministry. The protection of the civil power in all this is specially guaranteed. Clerics and religious are exempted from all those obligations of civil life which Canon Law declares incompatible with their office and particularly from acting as jurors, magistrates and assessors of taxes. No ecclesiastic will be appointed to any public employment under the state without his bishop's *nihil obstat*. The secret of the confessional is respected.

The present division into dioceses is to hold good for the future. Any new arrangement will only be made after consultation with the civil authority. This matter of new sees apart, ecclesiastical authority may make what changes it will, provided they do not involve any expense to the state. What aid the state shall give in the foundation of new parishes shall be fixed by conference between the state and the diocesan bishops.

Parishes and other similar religious bodies, parish associations, diocesan associations, the episcopal sees, the dioceses and chapters, the religious orders and the congregations, and all endowed foundations administered by ecclesiastical authority, are accorded juridical personality.

With the exceptions provided for in the three concordats with Bavaria, Prussia and Baden, the Church is absolutely free in appointments to ecclesiastical offices. Priests appointed to any post must, however, be of German citizenship, educated in some German institute of higher learning, and have passed three years at least in the philosophy-theology course of some German university or academical institute or in one of the Pontifical institutes at Rome. The state will be consulted, before the publication of ecclesiastical nominations to sees, in order that no one shall be appointed against whom there are objections of a general political nature. The bishop, before taking possession of his see swears a special oath of loyalty.

Full freedom is given to all the religious orders, to establish themselves, to administer their property and to carry out the work for which they were founded. But superiors resident in Germany must be German citizens, and when those resident in Germany do not form a German province, the Holy See will secure that, if possible, they are not subject to a foreign provincial.

The right of the Church to found schools of philosophy and theology for the education of the clergy is expressly recognised and also the entire dependence of such schools on the bishops, so long as no subsidy for them is sought from the state.

Instruction in the Catholic religion is an " ordinary " subject in the elementary, professional, middle and higher schools of the state. In this instruction—a novel clause by no means without interest—particular care will be taken to educate the conscience of the pupil in all that relates to his duty to the state, according to the maxims of the faith and of the Christian moral law—matters that will also receive due attention in the other parts of the school curriculum. The programme of religious study, and the text-books to be used will be settled in agreement with the bishops. The bishop will be given opportunity to examine, in agreement with the education authority, whether the instruction given is in accordance with the doctrine and the regulations of the Church. In the appointment of teachers of religion there is to be an understanding between the state and the bishop. Teachers to whom the bishop raises an objection on doctrinal or moral grounds will not be employed to teach religion so long as the objection endures. All existing Catholic schools will be preserved and the state guarantees that new ones may be founded in time to come. Wherever the parents demand a Catholic elementary school and the number of children makes this feasible, the state will build such schools. In all Catholic elementary schools Catholic teachers only will be appointed. Special provision for the training of such teachers will be made in the schools for training teachers.

The religious orders are authorised to found private schools, so long as they fulfil the requirements of the law. If they adopt the state programme of education their diplomas have equal value with those of the state schools. Religious may be appointed to teach in the various kinds of state school, if they possess the ordinary qualification for the post.

Catholic Action is the subject of a very long article.[1] Associations whose end is exclusively religious or cultural or charitable and which as such are subject to ecclesiastical authority, are protected by law. Other associations which have in addition a social or professional objective enjoy the same protection so long as they can guarantee that their activity is independent of any political party ; this without prejudice to their ultimate absorption in the state associations. The German episcopate and the Reich government will together draw up a list that shall classify the different Catholic societies for the purpose of this article.

In so far as concerns associations of young people, formed for sport or other purposes, by the Reich or by particular states, care will be taken that their members are given facilities, on Sundays and other feast days, for the performance of their religious duties. They shall not be obliged to do anything incompatible with their convictions or with their religious and moral duties.

The Church will instruct all its priests and religious that

[1] No. 31.

they are to take no part whatever in party politics. This does not mean that they lose their right to do their duty in explaining publicly the doctrine of the Church, and this not only in dogmatic matters but in morals also. All matters that concern ecclesiastics and ecclesiastical things and that are not treated of in this concordat, are to be regulated, as far as they concern the ecclesiastical sphere, according to the Canon Law.

CHAPTER IX

ITALY. I. TO THE LATERAN TREATIES

THROUGHOUT this book the reader will no doubt be as conscious as the writer that the presentation of contemporary history is an all but impossible task except for those who are themselves making it. Documents, which are the chief basis of historical reconstruction, are in great part not yet accessible. The verbal testimony of those who "know," it is rarely allowed to cite. The historian can do little more than recall the published acts, the known events, and group them in an order that has something organic about it. In no matter is this chronic difficulty more evident than in all that relates to the diplomatic activity of the Vatican. It meets us once more, though to a less degree here, in the reconstruction of the events that led to the "final and irrevocable" solution of the Roman Question in the treaty of 11 February, 1929.

More than any other act of the pontificate this was the personal will of Pius XI.[1] It was, also, equally, the personal act of Benito Mussolini. To understand the magnitude of what the Lateran Treaties accomplished and the spirit in which the high contracting parties put their signatures to the accords, the whole story of the relations between the Vatican and the Quirinal since the end of the war must be

---

[1] "Principally, not to say solely and wholly, it was through Our responsibility—a heavy and terrifying responsibility truly enough—that the whole thing came to pass and will for the future work. Nor could it be otherwise than in this way, for if in the critical moments of a voyage, the captain has need, more than ever, of faithful and devoted assistance (and this aid was given with touching devotion and faith and with unbelievable generosity), less than ever can he, in those moments, yield his post to others and with his post the dangers and the responsibility of high command. We can truthfully say that there is not a line, not an expression of the accords in question, that has not been during thirty months, the special object of Our study, Our meditation, and still more of Our prayer. . . . " (Pius XI, *Address to the Parish Priests of Rome*, 11 *February*, 1929.)

borne in mind and also the circumstances which brought
to the direction of the Italian national problem the author
of the solution we have come to know as Fascism.

Something has already been said of the long misery of
the forty years which separated the fall of the Temporal
Power from the outbreak of the European War. Poverty,
discontent, disappointment, chronic political inefficiency
and corruption, a paralysing sense of national inferiority,
these seemed to be the settled destiny of the new Italian
kingdom. Then came the war. Italy, partially allied to
Germany and Austria, was won over to the side of the
Allied Powers and in the Treaty of London of 1915
rewarded for her change of view with promises of truly
magnificent territorial expansion. The war dragged on.
Caporetto came and then Vittorio Veneto to avenge it.
Italy lost 632,000 men killed and 2,000,000 more wounded,
a country whose total population was less than 40,000,000.
At Versailles the manœuvres of superior minds worked the
luckless Italians once more into the jackal's place that had
been Cavour's after the Crimean War and his country's,
so far as diplomacy was concerned, ever since. The Treaty
of London was ignored, in the name of ideals, and Italy was
given but scraps where an empire had been promised.

In the next three years the Italian kingdom touched the
lowest point of its long degradation, of self-contempt and
of despair. The currency was depreciated by 70 per cent. ;
the cost of living mounted endlessly. In the elections the
Socialists gained on the old Liberal plutocracy. Communism appeared and in the industrial districts seized the
factories and in several northern cities, the local government, too. There were strikes, riots, a miniature civil war,
and on the part of the authorities universal irresolution and
timidity. Anarchy seemed to have become the normal
state of affairs.

Mussolini, one-time school teacher, one-time Socialist,
expelled his party for his nationalism, a journalist of wide
experience and great power, wounded badly in the war, had
formed, in 1919, his union of ex-service men to fight

Socialism and Communism. As the months went by the movement grew increasingly nationalistic. Its local branches grew more numerous, and everywhere it was established it challenged and fought, with all possible violence, the Socialist and the Communist. In November 1921 it definitely proclaimed itself a political party and, wherever it could, laid hands on the local government, everywhere treating its opponents as brutally as it had need to, or as local personal animosity required. The Fascists, as they were now everywhere known, broke the general strike of August 1922, and during the summer there were bloody scenes in Cremona, Pavia, Bergamo, Ravenna and elsewhere. In September, Mussolini made it clear that the new movement was not republican. At the party congress at Naples a month later he declared that if the government would not hand over to Fascism he would march his bands on Rome and take possession. On 29 October he marched. The king refused the petition of his cabinet to proclaim martial law, and on 30 October the Fascists marched into a Rome that watched in anxious, impressed silence the progress through its streets of so much hard, disciplined resolution. The cabinet resigned and, at the king's invitation, Mussolini stepped into its place. Italian history, and the history of Europe, had entered on a new era.

The task before the new *régime* was colossal. To mention one element alone of the complex problem, the budget deficit was forty times what it had been four years earlier, 40 milliards of lire. But the most noticeable and the most advertised features of the first two years of the new government were the acts of violence committed in its name and to further its ends. Everywhere the supporters of the old *régime*, and the critics of the new, were violently suppressed, banished, exiled, imprisoned, beaten up and even murdered. The old officials were everywhere displaced and successors appointed, to rule as absolutely as their master, in carrying out the new plan of national salvation.

Of the regeneration of Italy, the renaissance of national self-respect and of civic virtue, the new energy in every department of life that followed on this drastic revolution there is no need to speak. Whatever may be thought of the price at which this has been bought, it seems simple fact that what was bought was the country's very existence. Could anything else at that moment have saved Italy from becoming in 1922 what Spain is in 1937 ? If it was Fascism which brought such salvation to Italy, and there is much ground for believing this to be the case, then, though its crimes be not by any means thereby justified, much is explained of the general acceptance of the *régime*, and of its acceptance as a working system of government, even by those who cannot subscribe to its political and social doctrines. For these, too, even Fascism, if they have ever glimpsed the alternative, cannot but be tolerable.

The terror having done its work, Mussolini turned to make himself really master of the great force he had called into being and to make Fascist and Italian synonymous. From about 1925 there began a general suppression of all organisations of any kind, and for any object, that were rivals to kindred Fascist organisations, and an assimilation of everything by and into the Fascist party.

One fact deserves mention apart. Mussolini suppressed the Freemasons, as he also hunted down and wholly destroyed the Mafia, the terrible secret society that had blighted the life of southern Italy for generations.

Such is the nature, such the spirit and the methods that brought to the direction of Italian affairs the power with which the Holy See consented to treat and from which it won the Lateran Treaty. Without spending any time in speculative comparison between the natural genius of the two leading personalities concerned, something ought to be said of the spirit which informed the relations of the

Vatican with the Quirinal at the moment when Mussolini came into power.

As the first year of the twentieth century passed, the relations between the two powers began to lose their bitterness. The fear that had haunted Italy ever since 1870, the fear that the Vatican would seize any chance that came to destroy the new state by violence, gradually disappeared. The other side also became aware, likewise, that Europe, Catholic Europe, too, had accepted the Italian kingdom as one of the facts of the situation. The Catholic sovereigns might, in deference to the feelings of the Holy Father, refuse to meet the King of Italy in the capital of the popes, but this was precisely an act of personal consideration rather than an act with any political significance. Whatever solution of the Roman Question time would bring, it would, apparently, not be a solution from outside Italy. For if the old fears and the old suspicions on the part of the Italian government were dying down, the old *amour propre* was as strong as ever on this point, and in the generation born since 1870, with the most devoted Catholics no less than with the sectaries, there was a passionate attachment to Italian unity and a feeling of gratitude to the House of Savoy under which it had been realised.

"The temporal power," Cardinal Manning had said in 1879 to Mgr. Bonomelli, Bishop of Cremona, "is a matter that Providence has settled. The faith of the people gave it to the pope, the faith has gone and has taken the papal power with it. God will provide for the liberty of the Church in the future in a better way. Meanwhile, be careful not to put men in the position that they must choose between national sentiment and religious sentiment. If to-day they were faced with this alternative they would choose the first and not the second." [1] It was these words that set the bishop on the difficult task that occupied him

[1] GALLARATI-SCOTTI, p. 208.

for the next thirty years, of reconciling Italian Catholicism to the *fait accompli* lest there befall the worse fate of a national schism.

Manning oversimplified the matter, and, it may be thought, Mgr. Bonomelli and the earnest, devoted men who followed him oversimplified it too. They were, first and foremost, Italian. Their chief preoccupation, naturally, was the fate of Catholicism in Italy. The popes, too, had this anxiety, but in addition an anxiety for the Church as a whole, anxiety in particular that the world should know and believe that the exercise of their *magisterium* was free from Italian manipulation or pressure. Italian though they might be—loyally as Pius X, passionately even as Benedict XV, who wept bitterly at the news of Caporetto—they could only be Italian in the second place. If need be, Italian Catholicism must suffer for the sake of Catholicism in general. This was often not understood in Catholic Italy, enthusiastic patriotic Catholics were more than once disappointed, and in their disappointment bitter. To this day Leo XIII has never received his due from many of them.

The Roman Question could not have been settled before the accession of Pius X (1903) at all events. This seems a safe statement to make. But during the years that preceded that event and during all the years that followed, whatever might be the chance of the Roman Question being solved, a daily problem of practical politics demanded an answer. Italy was a democratic country, with a two-chamber Parliament and a wide franchise. If Catholics used the electoral system, were nominated, stood for election and were elected, or even if they only voted at the elections, would they not, tacitly, seem to accept the *fait accompli* of 1870? And if so, would not the Holy See's protestations appear gradually to be toning off into an acquiescence too? And with this disappear all the evidence that the Holy See was *not* a part or partner in United Italy? The matter was solved very simply, as in the crisis it could only be solved, by a decree of the Holy Office forbidding Catholics to participate in any way in the parliamentary elections. They could not be candidates nor could they even vote. *Nè eletti nè elettori* was the formula.

Once the generation of crisis was passed, and the danger with it that any Catholic participation in political life would compromise the independence of the Holy See's action in the Universal Church, the prohibition was gradually relaxed. Pius X left it to the discretion of the local bishop to suspend the decree wherever the participation of Catholics might be beneficial to the cause of religion. Benedict XV abolished it altogether and even allowed Catholics to form a political party—a party for which, however, the Church took no responsibility. It was not a Catholic party, but rather a party formed by Catholics whose programme was the translation into political action of the Catholic principles of social justice. This was the famous Partito Popolare Italiano, organised by the brilliant Sicilian priest, Don Luigi Sturzo. In 1921 it held over a hundred seats in the chamber of deputies, and was the second most numerous body there.

Italian Catholicism now had its place in the national life and the chance to do something to catholicise that life, left for fifty years to the mercy of anti-Catholics, liberals and masons. But the Roman Question still remained.

During the war the Italian government and the Holy See had come through a period of grave embarrassment by means of mutual acts of courtesy and confidence, none the less real and effective for all their lack of official character. The Quirinal had assured the Vatican that it made no objection to the diplomats of powers with whom it was at war continuing to reside in Rome, nor to their free communication with their respective governments. The Vatican had been grateful, but had requested the ambassadors to move to Switzerland for as long as the war lasted. Every facility had been offered, and gratefully accepted, for the spiritual welfare of the Italian armies. The Vatican passports were allowed as valid by the Italian authorities, and the great bureau established by Benedict XV, for the exchange of wounded prisoners and for the discovery of the missing, again received whatever favour the Italian government could extend to it. When the war ended, Pope Benedict, as a practical gesture of peace on the part of the Holy See, withdrew the prohibition that kept Catholic sovereigns from visiting the King of Italy in Rome. When, shortly afterwards, the pope died, the Italian flag was flown at half mast over all the government buildings of Rome, cabinet ministers entered the Vatican on a quasi-official visit of sympathy, and, but for a sudden crisis that dissolved the government, there would have been in the Italian Parliament an *éloge* of the dead pope by the Prime Minister.

Sixteen days later Pius XI was elected, and, the first act of his reign, broke the tradition of fifty years and appeared in public to bless the world in the manner once traditional and to receive the prescribed royal salute from the Italian troops massed in the square below.

Was not the Roman Question settled ? So much good-will, such practical harmony, even co-operation ? A contemporary French observer [1] writing about this time gave a suggestive reply to such queries : " To-day the Vatican is more favourable than ever to an official *rapproche-ment* with the kingdom of Italy, a tacit *rapprochement* having been a *fait accompli* for a long time already. But if the reconciliation of the powers that dwell in Rome would have for its consequence the absorption of the one by the other, or the subordination of the one to the other, if the Italian government aimed at using the Holy See and the Catholic Church as instruments to promote its own policies, whether in Italy or abroad, the Vatican would not for a moment hesitate. To an alliance so compromising it would prefer hostility. The Papacy would never, in order to gain the support of Italy, risk the loss of that independence and universality which make it the greatest moral force in the world." Wise words these, the common sense of the matter, the fruit of experience and long observation and of a know-ledge of human nature.

[1] PERNOT, p. 116 (1924).

Despite the mutual goodwill, the harmony in a hundred practical arrangements, there still was lacking any evident, incontestable, unmistakable assurance, of an objective nature, that for the Italian government the Holy See was an independent, self-sufficing sovereign thing, there was not yet the one thing that mattered, namely, " the public acknowledgment of the sovereignty of the Roman Pontiff."[1] Despite the progress in mutual understanding, and admitting a new sympathy on both sides, it was still true that the pope was possessed of neither territory nor subjects. He simply, as in 1870, retained his hold on the Vatican from which Italy had never, so far, sought to expel him. The pope's retention of the external trappings of sovereignty had still the same precarious and contingent character as at any time during those past fifty years which had so often seen the threat to put an end to these too.

In one sense the difficulties of the Holy See were growing. The basis of the papal guarantee to the world that the papacy remained a free agent despite 1870 had been the pope's repeated protestation, the chronic *malentendu* between Vatican and Quirinal. But this, if the new age of good relations continued and the participation of Catholics in the national life of Italy, would ultimately come to seem a mere matter of form. Rights not claimed effectively cease to be rights in the common understanding of things.

From this point of view it was more than ever urgent that the order of things in practice and fact should correspond to the theory that the Holy See is sovereign in spiritual matters. To make the situation of the Holy See sovereign in spiritual matters there was now, as always, from the nature of the case, one sole means, granted that it is on men that this spiritual sovereignty is exercised and that it must therefore be exercised through visible acts. The pope must be free to place those acts with the freedom acknowledged in the man who commands, without there being anywhere anyone with the right to command him.

---

[1] Words in which Pius XI described what the treaty ultimately effected : " *agnito publice Romani Pontificis principatu.*" Allocution of 16 December, 1929.

The pope's final competence in all his own affairs must be publicly acknowledged by the power that, in appearance and in fact, itself claims sovereign jurisdiction over the territory where the pope is lodged. The visible sign of sovereignty in the pope is the acknowledgment of his sovereignty over a territory. This is everywhere the sign and proof of sovereign independence, and it is the only sign. For the sake of the Church, the world being what it is to-day, and men's notions of these things being universally what they are, the pope must be able to show this proof that he is master absolutely and is subject to none.

On the papal side the need for a solution was then a fact no less urgent in 1922 than in 1870 and, following the example of all his predecessors in the same situation,[1] Pius XI made his public declaration to this effect. "It is scarcely necessary to say with what deep sorrow of mind We note that Italy is not among the number of the nations that have bound themselves to the Apostolic See in links of friendship, Italy Our own most dear fatherland, the country which God, in His providence, has chosen to be the land where His vicar should fix his see. From that day, in effect, this august city, once the capital of an empire, vast indeed, but yet limited, became the capital of the whole world. As the see of that divine principate which transcends all boundaries of nations and races, Rome gathers to itself all the peoples of the world. Now the origin and the divine nature of this sovereignty, the sacred right of the universality of the Christian people throughout the world, both these demand that this sacred sovereignty be seen not to be subject to any human power, or to any laws (even though these profess to surround the freedom of the papacy with certain guarantees or safeguards). On the contrary that sacred sovereignty must visibly appear, and must actually

---

[1] The list of the chief protestations is as follows : (1) the Cardinal Secretary of State (Antonelli) to the Diplomatic Corps, 20 September, 1870. (2) Pius IX, encyclical *Respicientes* of 1 November, 1870, and the next three popes in their first encyclical letters, viz., Leo XIII, 21 April, 1878, *Inscrutabili;* Pius X, 4 October, 1903, *E Supremi Apostolatus;* Benedict XV, 1 November, 1914, *Ad Beatissimi.* The quotation is Pius XI 22 December, 1922, *Ubi Arcano Dei.*

be, absolutely its own master in law and in power. The one safeguard with which God's providence had for centuries provided the authority of the popes has gone, trodden under foot by hostile violence. That divine providence has not made known any other, nor has the ingenuity of man devised any that would suitably take its place. The papacy is necessarily in a position that compromises its prestige and which must continue to fill Christian hearts everywhere with deep distress. Wherefore heir to Our predecessors, of their ideas as of their obligations, vested with that same authority, to whom alone it falls to decide a matter of such vast moment, not led by any empty desire for an earthly kingdom—the very thought of such desire would fill Us with shame—but with Our mind fully fixed on Our own last hours of life, and recalling that most strict account We must render to God Our Judge, We therefore, as a duty imposed by Our holy office, make the protestations which Our predecessors made for the defence of the rights and the prestige of the Apostolic See: We make all these Our own and in this place We renew them."

For all the deliberate vigour of this protestation it is distinctly not hostile either to Italy or to Italian pretensions. The very use of the name "Italy" is new in pontifical documents. For the first time a pope has given the state that despoiled him and is the cause of his embarrassment the name it gives itself. The protestation is followed by an explicit pledge that " never will Italy have any loss to fear from this Apostolic See, for the pope, whoever he may chance to be, will always be the one to say ' I think the thoughts of peace and not of affliction '(Jer. xxix. 11) " ; and in the same encyclical Pius XI has yet another affectionate reference to the race from which he springs.

Pius XI came to his high office unembarrassed by any associations, official associations, of his past career. In this, from the point of view of the Roman Question and its solution, he was better placed than either of his immediate predecessors. Pius X, though personally not at all hostile to the House of Savoy, had had his appointment as Patriarch of Venice held up for months by the hostility of the government, and in his career as Bishop of Mantua he had known by experience all that an anti-Catholic bureaucracy could do to harass the spiritual work of the Church. Benedict XV, as the right-hand man of Leo XIII's Secretary of State for sixteen years, had known from the inside all the bitterness of the very worst days of the *malentendu*. But his successor's career had brought him, through nearly forty years, into daily contact, on neutral grounds, with all the various classes of the Quirinal's supporters. He had friends, personal friends, in the different high places of the civil administration and, on his mission to Poland, he had not hesitated to fraternise with his compatriots who fulfilled the like services for the Italian state.

That the milieu in which he lived at Milan, the scholarly ecclesiastical circles in which he moved, and the chief personages there—Ceriani for example—were less than sympathetic to the official attitude that in those days obtained at the Vatican, has been asserted. How far this is true one cannot say. Certainly there has never been any bar on a man's thoughts in this matter, nor on his conversation nor his private endeavours. As far as public life went, good Catholics did their best not to embarrass the Holy See by any action that did not accord with its known directions. We do possess, however, an important public statement on the Roman Question by the pope in the days before he was pope. It occurs in the address he gave when on 8 September, 1921, in the cathedral of Milan, he took possession of his see and was solemnly enthroned. It is not difficult to see in its vivid actualities an effect of his residence abroad. Rarely has it happened that an ex-ambassador of the papal service has received on his promotion one of the great Italian sees. This circumstance sharpened the phrases used by Cardinal Ratti and gave the reference a special importance.

What he said was this : " The pope is, for us who are Italians, above all things the most loyal and the most sincere of all our country's friends. Only recently he gave proof

of this again, praying for Italy and hailing her as the cradle
of all culture. It is when one lives abroad that one sees,
better perhaps than in other circumstances, how true it is
that the pope is Italy's greatest glory. It is because of the
pope that millions of Catholics throughout the world turn
to Italy as to a second fatherland. Rome, because the pope
dwells in Rome, is truly the capital of the world. A man
must have his eyes closed to the evidence of the facts who
cannot see—and especially to-day when one state after
another is turning to the papacy—the prestige and the
advantages that must accrue to our country from his
presence within it, taking account of the pope's international
status, and his supranational sovereignty, which the
Catholics of the whole world recognise as a thing divinely
instituted. Upon us Catholics who are Italians, to whom
the Providence of God has committed the guardianship of
the pope, there lies a responsibility to the Catholics of the
world that is a great honour." [1]

"Especially to-day when one state after another is
turning to the papacy." These words recall a matter which
was beginning to influence Italian public opinion. When
the Temporal Power came to an end in 1870 there were at
the papal court twenty-two diplomatic representatives of
foreign powers.[2] In 1914 these had shrunk to a bare half-
dozen, but with the war the understanding of the papacy's
importance in world affairs had been too much for old
prejudices (or old feuds) and in 1921 thirty-five states were
represented at the Vatican.

Italy began to feel its isolation, and to be anxious as to
the consequences of a situation where every power in the
world except itself was on good terms with the Vatican,
and linked with this vast repertoire of information by
diplomatic appointments. When in the summer of 1921

[1] Cardinal Ratti—Sermon upon enthronement as Archbishop of Milan,
NOVELLI, p. 192.

[2] The four ambassadors of Austria, Spain, France and Portugal, the fourteen
Ministers-Plenipotentiary of Bavaria, Belgium, Bolivia, Brazil, Ecuador, Costa
Rica, Chili, Guatemala, the Sovereign Order of Malta, Monaco, Nicaragua, Peru,
the Argentine and San Salvador, the chargé d'affaires of Prussia.

France renewed its representation, after an interval of sixteen years, the anxiety developed into alarm and there was a heated debate in the Italian Parliament. "It does not seem to be impossible," said one deputy,[1] " to find a formula which shall reconcile the demands of the Holy See in what regards its full independence with the needs, internal and external, of the Italian state." Another speaker in the debate was Mussolini—still a year and a half away from his revolutionary success. He spoke more clearly still : " I say that the Latin and imperial tradition of Rome is to-day represented by Catholicism. If it is true, as Mommsen declared, that without some mark of universality nothing survives at Rome, it is my opinion and I make it known, that the only mark of universality in the Rome of to-day is that which is possessed by the Vatican. . . . The development of Catholicism throughout the world, the fact that four hundred million men, from every country under the sun, have their eyes fixed on Rome, there is a thing that must interest us who are Italians and should fill us with pride." [2] The almost literal coincidence of the last sentence with the address of Cardinal Ratti delivered just three months later is very striking.

The relations between the Holy See and the Quirinal under the new pope, Pius XI, and the new head of the state continued in much the same strain as during the last years of Benedict XV. The Catholic kings began to pay their official visits to Rome, Albert of Belgium and Alphonso XIII of Spain. King George V appeared there, too, in 1923. Mussolini presented to the pope the great Chigi library [3] when the Italian state bought it, with the palace, from the

---

[1] Rocco, 21 June, 1921, quoted MOLLAT, p. 414.

[2] Quoted in PERNOT, p. 89.

[3] The importance of this collection to the Holy See may be judged from the fact that it contains the as yet unstudied despatches and papers of Cardinal Fabio Chigi (later Pope Alexander VII, 1655–1667) who was the papal nuncio at the imperial court and played a great r le in the conferences of Westphalia that brought to an end the Thirty Years' War. If a personal reminiscence be allowed, I remember well hearing, when this gift to the Holy See was announced, that Mussolini had said to one who congratulated him, " When the time comes I shall make such an offer to the Holy Father [in the matter of the Roman Question] that he will not be able not to treat."

Cardinal Achilles Ratti, Archbishop of Milan

prince of that name. The Fascist Commissary-Royal for Rome paid an official visit to the Cardinal-Vicar and this was duly returned. The crucifix was replaced in all the public schools, the seminarists dispensed from their military service. Archbishops, and cardinals too, were heard to praise the *régime* in public speeches, even cardinals of the curia speaking in Rome. Then the pope, when the King of Italy's eldest daughter married, lifted the interdict that for fifty years and more had lain on the Pauline Chapel of the Quirinal Palace.

All went peacefully forward. Occasionally the rash pen of some enthusiastic journalist interpreted this progress as a hint that the Vatican was tacitly surrendering to 1870. A dry correction in the *Osservatore Romano* would restate the facts of the spoliation. The reconciliation *de iure*, when the moment for this came, would find the papacy unembarrassed by the recollection of any equivocation or ambiguity.

Meanwhile the Holy See had before it the fact of the civil disorders, the violence and the bloodshed in Italy of these critical years (1922–1924). More than once it intervened, four times in fact in the eight months August 1922–April 1923. "The disorders that in these last few weeks have filled Italy with desolation have caused the most grievous sorrow and a very genuine anxiety for the future in the hearts of all those who sincerely love their fatherland," the new pope wrote.[1] The writer's sincere concern for his race and his native country is evident and this undisguised expression of it a novelty in a pontifical document. Pius XI goes on openly to declare that his natural patriotism, far from being stifled by his new responsibility to the whole Church, has thereby been transmuted into something higher. The disorders are described with plain, blunt truth, in that realistic spirit that was to characterise all the new pope's criticisms of the less pleasing features of contemporary life. Factions, partisans, bloody struggles, reprisals, the natural instinctive shrinking from blood almost killed by the years of bloody indulgence in war, and

[1] Letter *I Disordine* to the bishops of Italy, 6 August, 1922.

in consequence, the whole fabric of the state so shaken that it barely holds together. Who can estimate the loss of international prestige all this has brought, the economic and monetary loss in the nation itself, the decay in moral and religious observance and, what is bound to follow, if the evil be not arrested, the coming decay of intellectual life. The pope urges on the bishops the preaching of a great return to prayer and religious living, a return to Jesus in whose blood all men are brothers. In a brief anticipation of the coming encyclical *Ubi Arcano Dei*, Pius XI shows how if God be given His place in human life all the other necessary subordinations will function peacefully. He quotes Leo XIII to the effect that to bring about a return of civil prosperity and happiness by reconciling man and God is the very function of the Church in human society.

During the critical days of the Congress of Naples, two days only before the Blackshirts marched on Rome, the pope renewed his appeal for " il nostro diletto Paese." " In the name of the brotherly spirit that unites all Italians in a love of this land that God has so blessed, in the name of a more noble brotherhood still, that supernatural brotherhood which gathers into one family all Italy's children, the religion of Our Lord Jesus Christ, we cry in the words of St. Stephen: ' Men, ye are brethren, why hurt you one another ? ' " [1] The bishops must redouble their efforts, persuading all whom they can influence not to push party spirit so far that the national interests are sacrificed to it. Rather shall they show themselves true patriots by giving up their own desires where the public good requires it, and by practising the Christian virtues of charity, kindliness and forgiveness.[2]

A more private letter had gone to each of the bishops, from the Cardinal Secretary of State, a few weeks before this.[3] It defended the Holy See from the latest attacks of the

[1] Acts vii. 26.
[2] Letter to the bishops of Italy, *Ora sono*, 28 October, 1922.
[3] Letter *E noto*, 2 October, 1922.

hostile political Press. This time it was the Liberals who maintained that the Partito Popolare was the pope's instrument to achieve his will in the Italian state. The cardinal recalls how, from the days of Leo XIII, in every country in Europe, in Bohemia, in Belgium, in Poland and elsewhere, the popes have continuously striven to keep the clergy out of political life. This has been the known settled policy of the Holy See and to all parties as such it is impartial and indifferent, ready to blame and to protest wherever any one of them conflicts with the interests of religion. In practice it is not always easy, the cardinal admits, to fix the limits between the cleric's rights as a man to think for himself politically and his duty as a cleric to steer clear of any association with party politics. In case of doubt the safer course must be followed. At all costs the priest's *rôle* must be preserved from any suspicion of political influence or aims. Eight months later the cardinal returned to the matter with a still more urgently worded note.[1] The clergy cannot be too prudent in avoiding even the appearance of favouring any particular political party.

The Partito Popolare now could not but lose its clerical leaders and directors. The events had their importance in regard to the Roman Question too. Once again the Holy See had fought, and Catholic Italy had made sacrifices, this time in order that the question of the Holy See's independence should never be bound up with the activities of party politics. When the time came the Holy See's action would not be tied by any previous compromise or political association.

The time came swiftly. In 1925 the Fascist government, in its task of overhauling the whole structure of Italian life, came to the vast collection of laws regulating different religious activities. To study these and to report on the necessary changes it set up a commission, and seats upon this commission were offered to, and accepted by, several Catholic prelates. The report was delivered on the last day of the year. The minister in charge of the matter

[1] Letter *Il Sottoscritto* of 25 April, 1923.

explained the proposed changes and made much of the fact that among the commission were these three prelates. He recommended the acceptance of the proposals in a phrase that, immediately, set many forces moving, " We wish to change the state of war for a state of quasi-concordat."

The different newspapers were filled with commentaries and controversies after this report, and were especially interested to discuss the significance of the co-operation of the three prelates. What was the position of the Holy See in the matter ?

They were not left long in doubt. On 18 February, 1926, Pius XI wrote a public letter [1] to Cardinal Gasparri that made the whole thing crystal clear. The pope notes, gratefully, the improvements the new proposals contain. The co-operation of the three prelates was merely allowed by their respective bishops for the sake of the matter in hand. It was not, in any sense, an official collaboration. They simply placed their expert knowledge at the service of the state as private individuals, and the bishops allowed them to do so. The projected new laws still contain many things that need correction. Ultimately no change can effectively be made in this matter of ecclesiastical legislation without the sanction of the Holy See. The pope cannot allow that any other has the right or power to make such laws " unless by virtue of appropriate negotiations and a lawful understanding with this Holy See and our-selves." [2]

Surely the Catholic does not exist, the pope continues, who actually proposes to make regulations for the Catholic Church in Rome itself and to give it a new legal standing without some such previous understanding with the Holy See ! How the pope would greet such measures of reform he has already declared in the allocution of 14 December, 1925.[3] " But no such appropriate negotiations, no such lawful accord has taken place nor can it ever take place so

[1] *Si è annunciato.*

[2] " Se non previe le convenienti trattative ed i legittimi accordi con questa Santa Sede e con Noi."

[3] *I.e.,* just two months before this present letter.

long as there endures the evil status in which the Holy See and the pope have been placed."

Italy wanted some kind of concordat.   Very well, but concordats are only made between independent, mutually recognised sovereignties.   The official reply to the letter *Si è annunciato* was the speech of Signor Rocco declaring that the matter would be discussed anew " on a broader basis " (14 May, 1926).   That very evening the Vatican commissioned a well-known priest-journalist, Mgr. Pucci, to find out what this promising phrase really meant.   He was told, formally, that the Fascist government had in view the settlement of the Roman Question.   " Then let Mussolini," said Cardinal Gasparri, " name someone with whom we can talk and accredit him formally."   The Italians hesitated.   Would the Vatican really receive their man ? They were assured that a discussion would be welcome, and the thing was on.

The two negotiators were, for the Holy See, Signor Francesco Pacelli, brother of the then nuncio at Berlin who is to-day the papal Secretary of State, and, for the Italians, Signor Domenico Barone, both jurists of the very first rank and of proved capacity.   Their conferences began in August 1926.   Both parties had a condition *sine qua non* to ask at the outset.   The Italians could hold out no hope of restoration of the old papal states.   It was made clear that there was no question of this.   On the other hand the pope asked that the initiative should come from the Italians, and that the Law of Guarantees should play no part in the discussions.   Also that these should be kept absolutely secret. Never, it may be said, was secret better kept.   When Cardinal Gasparri on 7 February, 1929, summoned the diplomatic corps to announce the treaty, the news took them completely by surprise, as more than one of them has testified.

I do not wish to fill this already lengthy chapter with the details—so far as they are known—of the course of these long negotiations.   It will be sufficient for the purpose of a book which is a study of the policy of Pius XI to say simply what from the beginning the pope did not ask, to say what in the end was accorded and accepted, and to point out his own personal share in the long diplomatic discussions.

From the beginning no pope had ever demanded the restitution of the papal states as they were on 1 January, 1859, before the Sardinian adventure began. " Sovereignty in times such as these," said Pius IX in the last days of his power, " is not a thing to be craved. All that I desire is a little corner of the earth where I shall be master. Not that I should refuse my states were they offered to me. But so long as I have not that little corner of earth I cannot exercise my spiritual mission in its amplitude." [1] All manner of schemes had been proposed in the interval to give the pope " sometimes a territory in the environs of Rome with the Vatican as a starting point, sometimes the city of Rome itself, and again a territory round about the Vatican with a narrow corridor to the sea." [2]

During the war offers were several times made from within the Central Empires to the Vatican, but always politely declined. In October, 1914, for example, it was suggested that the pope should be given the Italian part of the Trentino by Austria, which he should then hand over to Italy, receiving in exchange whatever modifications of the existing *régime* he thought proper. In May, 1915, the offer was to bring about an internationalisation of the Law of Guarantees. The pope's independence of Italy would have the joint guarantee of all the states of the world, and he should be possessed of an independent state running from the Vatican to the sea along the right bank of the Tiber. There was talk of establishing the Holy See, with sovereign status, in Elba, in some island of Dalmatia, in Lichtenstein.

On the part of the papacy, if there had been no offer of

[1] To the Comte d'Harcourt, French Ambassador to the Holy See, 2 July, 1871, in MOORE, *Peter's City*, pp. 75–76 and Appendix VII, where there is a documented correction of the usual version of the pope's statement that omits the words " Not that."

[2] RIVET, p. 91.

a plan (and it was hardly the papacy's place to make offers to the state that had despoiled it and on whose power its material being still depended) there had been, during these same years of the war, at least one effort to find a way out. This was the commission of five cardinals [1] charged by Benedict XV to find a *modus vivendi* " even at the cost of a final renunciation of the lost territory." On one point only did they come to an agreement, that whatever arrangement was found satisfactory it must receive the guarantee of an international ratification. This, apparently, was in 1916, and the finding is, at first sight, in curiously flat contradiction to the public declaration of the Cardinal Secretary of State made to an interviewer on 28 June, 1915, that "the Holy See, for the regularisation of the situation, looks to the Italian people's sense of justice." [2] Voices in the Sacred College were strongly divided in 1915–1916 on this question as, apparently, they were to be divided until the very end.

The first care of the negotiators in 1926 was to prepare a draft treaty, and then, after Mgr. Borgongini Duca, Secretary of the Papal Commission for Extraordinary Ecclesiastical Affairs, had been added to their number for the purpose, an outline of a concordat to regulate the future relations of Church and State in the kingdom of Italy. The draft treaty was ready by the end of November, 1926, the draft of the concordat by the following April. How patiently the work was done may be gathered from the details given by Signor Pacelli.[3] He had 110 conversations with Professor Barone, and there were ten meetings at which the three delegates worked together. Each of these meetings took up the whole day, from eight in the morning until six or seven in the evening. The pope controlled the

---

[1] They were the cardinals Vannutelli, de Lai, Merry del Val, Giustini and Pompili; MOLLAT, p. 410.

[2] RIVET, p. 87, quoting *Corriere d'Italia*, 28 June, 1915.

[3] Quoted at length in MOORE, pp. 88–92.

papal end of the business at every stage. Signor Pacelli had no fewer than 129 audiences during the two years or so that the negotiations continued, many of them lasting two and three hours.

The text of the concordat was virtually complete by February 1927 and the treaty by August 1928. All was now ready for the next stage in the business and the Cardinal Secretary of State now officially declared the willingness of the Vatican to negotiate a settlement of the Roman Question along the lines of these drafts. The King of Italy then appointed Mussolini his plenipotentiary, and the pope named Cardinal Gasparri. This was in November 1928. The last stages of the negotiations were the work of these two, though actually it was Signor Pacelli who met Mussolini " sometimes in the afternoon, but more often in the evening, in his private house in the Via Rasella. The conversations began at nine o'clock, sometimes lasting until one the following morning." [1] The whole matter was thus reviewed in every detail, the final consents were given, and then, on 7 February, 1929, the Cardinal Secretary of State summoned the diplomatic corps to tell them officially that on the eleventh the Roman Question would be settled for ever.

The treaties [2] were signed on 11 February and ratified on 7 June, 1929.

[1] Pacelli in MOORE, *op. cit.*
[2] The official text is in A.A.S. XXI, pp. 209–294; translation in MOORE pp. 220–243.

CHAPTER X

WHAT THE LATERAN TREATIES ACCOMPLISHED

THE twenty-one articles of the treaty begin with an acknowledgment by Italy that Catholicism is the sole state religion. Italy explicitly recognises the sovereign status of the Holy See in international affairs and this as an attribute inherent in its nature, conformably with the Holy See's tradition and the needs of its mission in the world. As to the Vatican with all its dependencies, Italy recognises that the Holy See holds it in full proprietorship, with exclusive and absolute power over it and sovereign jurisdiction. The Vatican thus becomes the " City of the Vatican," created by this treaty for the special ends of the treaty. The limits of this jurisdiction are indicated in an annexed plan. In this city of the Vatican the pope is King. The pope, as a sovereign, enjoys the same protection in Italy, as against insult and injury, that is given to the King of Italy. Those who live in the Vatican in a permanent way are citizens of the Vatican state and the ways in which this citizenship is acquired and lost, together with the exposition of the relations of such citizens to the country of their origin, are set out in some of the most interesting articles of the treaty.

The diplomats accredited to the Holy See, even though their residences may be in Italian territory, enjoy the customary diplomatic immunity, and this even though their own state has no diplomatic relations with Italy. The Holy See is guaranteed full freedom of correspondence with the other states, including enemy states of Italy in time of war, and also with the bishops of the whole world. For the future there will be an Italian ambassador at the papal court and a papal nuncio at the Quirinal. Cardinals enjoy the status of princes of the blood royal. Those who reside in Rome are citizens of the Vatican.

Two articles lay down the principles governing the co-operation of the two powers in the punishment of criminals, and all sentences of ecclesiastical authority concerning ecclesiastics or religious persons in spiritual or disciplinary matters have full civil effect once they are officially communicated to the civil authority.

With regard to international affairs, the Holy See declares that it is its will that its sovereignty shall remain a thing outside all the temporal competition of the different powers and the international congresses called for such purposes. The Holy See, however, reserves the right to use its moral and spiritual resources whenever the parties to a dispute unanimously make appeal to its mission of peace. The Vatican shall be always and in all circumstances taken as neutral and inviolable territory.

The financial injury to the Church due to the loss of the ancient papal states and the loss of ecclesiastical property was immense. The Law of Guarantees had pledged the state to pay the pope an annual sum of 3,225,000 lire on this account. This money had never been touched, and considering the needs of the Holy See, its just claims, the never accepted indemnity on the one hand and, on the other, the present financial and economic distress of Italy, the pope limited his demands to what was absolutely necessary. Italy, with a grateful acknowledgment of the pope's fatherly attitude, agrees to pay 750 million lire in cash and 1,000 million lire in 5 per cent. consolidated stock. This wipes out the financial indebtedness of Italy to the Church created by the events of 1870. The Holy See— this by a later arrangement—agreed to receive the money payment in gradual amounts and also not to sell the stock.

Finally, this treaty that opened with Italy's recognition of the sovereignty of the Holy See, closes with the pope's recognition that the sovereignty as here recognised and in these conditions places him " in possession, in a manner that is adequate, of all that he needs to provide with due freedom and independence for the pastoral care of the diocese of Rome, and of the Catholic Church in Italy and throughout the world." Furthermore, he "declares that the ' Roman Question ' is now definitively and irrevocably settled and therefore eliminated, and he recognises the Kingdom of Italy under the House of Savoy with Rome as the capital of the Italian State."

The Law of Guarantees is abolished and all laws contrary to the present treaty.

Such in brief are the details of the great treaty, which, truly enough, has solved a difficulty that for twelve hundred years and more has troubled European life, the difficulty how to contrive that the pope shall not be the subject of any state and that he shall yet be free of the embarrassing complications that sovereignty brings with it.

There is an all-round satisfactoriness about this masterpiece of modern juridical and diplomatic skill. Non-Italian nations are delivered from the objectionable state of things that their nationals are obedient in religious matters to an outsider who is himself regarded as a subject by a foreign power. The newly-recognised territorial independence is a thing less easy to violate than the mere *de facto* liberty of the years since 1870, a liberty that was never recognised as a right. Whatever advantages the situation of those years had are preserved in the new arrangement, the benefits that accrued *de facto* are now benefits *de iure*, and the legal embarrassments inevitable even in the best days of the *régime*—embarrassments due to the mentality that was the consequence of the Law of Guarantees—are now removed and indeed destroyed. The ambiguity is ended and both parties enjoy the immense advantage, from a juridical point of view, that what was merely the way things had happened is now transformed into the way things ought to happen. What before was vague and matter for discussion is now clear and incontestable.[1]

In the long discussions the Holy See did not ask for corridors to the sea, or any large extension of territory. It did ask the Villa Doria-Pamphili, an estate adjacent to the Vatican on which the pope had the idea of building residences for the diplomatic corps. Italy offered it under suzerainty, at the nominal rent of a lira a year. The pope feared future complications and withdrew his request. Later, on the very evening before the treaty was signed, he made a last change, conceding to Italy the territory on which stood the palace of the Holy Office. In the end what was recognised was exactly what the words of Pius IX had described in 1870, " a little corner of the earth," the 108 acres of the Città del Vaticano with 639 citizens, and what Leo XIII had desiderated too, " such a condition of independence that not only would the pope's liberty not be shackled by any power at all, but it would be evident to all the world that this was the case." [2]

What are the guarantees that this happy state of things will endure ? Whatever guarantees had been asked and given there is, ultimately, under all conditions, only one guarantee for the independence of the Holy See—and an independence that these material conditions assist to function but do not create—and that guaranteee is a spiritual thing, the strength of the Holy See's own attitude to the world that surrounds it and its watchfulness in safeguarding its freedom.[3] But this point of the ultimate value of guarantees the pope has himself dealt with.

In two addresses [4] immediately after the signature of the treaty and concordat he dealt with what it may be permitted to call the criticisms from within. With the realism of a true historian he pointed out the failure of the powers

[1] RIVET, p. 188.
[2] Letter to Cardinal Rampolla, 15 June, 1887, quoted RIVET, p. 88.
[3] Cf. RIVET, p. 164.
[4] (1) To the parish priests of Rome and the Lenten preachers, 11 February, 1929. (2) To the students and one-time students of the Catholic University of Milan, 13 February, 1929 ; translated, in part, in How the Roman Question was Settled, Catholic Truth Society, London.

in 1860–1870 to protect the papal states from the brigandage of Sardinia.[1] Why waste time to-day renewing the kind of guarantee that proved so unreliable a safeguard then? As for the future, who can tell? " Of that we know nothing. The future is in God's hands, that is to say in the best of hands." Speaking on 9 March, in reply to the congratulations of the diplomatic corps,[2] the pope again referred to the question of guarantees, and pointed out that there are guarantees that no pope could either desire or accept, namely, juridical guarantees, for juridical guarantees imply an inferiority, a subordination to the guarantor in the one for whom the guarantee is made. The only guarantee possible is the moral guarantee. " We place faith and have placed faith in the loyalty and persevering goodwill of those who have shown themselves so ready and desirous to treat with us." In what other spirit could the pope treat, once he had resolved to treat? Though it be through political machinery—because human machinery—that the papacy must work, the ultimate ends for which it works are spiritual, and that in every century. *Regnum meum non est de hoc mundo*, and it is not without its meaning that the first time the now recognised sovereign of the Vatican manifested his freedom by a public appearance outside his palace, it was in a solemn religious procession where, as priest and bishop, he carried the Blessed Sacrament.

" The Treaty concluded between the Holy See and Italy has need of no other explanation or justification outside itself, for in reality it is itself the clearest and most definitive explanation of all. But, all the same, there is an explanation, a justification of it from outside itself that is no less clear than the Treaty itself and no less definitive. That explanation and justification is the Concordat . . . for the Treaty

---

[1] This phrase is not the pope's nor suggested even remotely by the words he used. It does nevertheless describe the morality of what was done.

[2] Translated in *The Sovereignty of the Holy See*, published by Catholic Truth Society, London.

the Concordat is a condition of very existence and life . . . from the beginning the *sine qua non* of the Treaty . . . " [1] These are the pope's own words describing the relation of the two documents, their necessary relation, for in the Italy of the pre-concordat *régime* the treaty would not have been possible, the Church within the kingdom of Italy being bound to the state as a slave—even a favourite slave —to its tyrant master.

The *Risorgimento* had long since freed Italian life from the degrading yoke of the old absolutist monarchies, but until 1929 the new state had carefully preserved what it could of the no less degrading servitude in which they had held Italian religion. The liberating work of the concordat of 1929 can never be exaggerated. For the first time in centuries Catholicism in Italy is really master in its own spiritual domain. The Italy with whom the treaty has been made is a new Italy that no longer desires to imprison the Church in the trappings of royal patronage.

There is now secured to the Church the free exercise of its spiritual power, the free, public exercise of worship, and of its jurisdiction in ecclesiastical affairs. In all their spiritual functions ecclesiastics are specially protected. The Holy See can freely communicate with bishops, clergy and people, and the bishops likewise with their flocks. Full freedom is guaranteed in the publication of pastoral letters, instructions, decisions and the official diocesan magazines. Where necessary the bishops may issue official translations of the Italian or Latin text. Ecclesiastical students and the novices of the religious orders are exempt from military service, and ecclesiastics and religious are exempt from jury service too. No ecclesiastic, or religious, will be employed in the public service without his bishop's consent, and clerical apostates or those under censure will not be allowed to teach or be employed in such a way that will bring them into immediate contact with the public. The seal of the confessional is respected and convicted delinquent ecclesi-

Address to the students of the Catholic University of Milan, 13 February, 1929.

astics are to receive the special treatment of a prison apart, unless they have been unfrocked. Churches are not at the disposition of the civil authority for other than religious purposes, nor may they, for any reason, be demolished without the bishop's consent. The concessions made by the Holy See in other concordats, of privileges for military chaplains and the spiritual welfare of the army, are repeated here. The dioceses are to be rearranged by a mixed commission and their number considerably reduced. There are, once again, the usual provisions to ensure the coincidence of ecclesiastical and national frontiers. Bishops and all beneficed clergy are to be Italians, and before they take possession of their sees the bishops are to swear an oath of loyalty to the Italian state.[1] This oath in no way differs from that found in the concordats with other states made since 1922. The Italian bishop is not more controlled by Mussolini than the Latvian, Lithuanian, Polish, Roumanian, Czechoslovakian or German bishop by the heads of these different states.

So far the concordat with Italy follows the general lines of all the concordats Pius XI has made. But it proceeds to deliver the Church in Italy from a whole series of special servitudes. In this way. All the sees of the one-time kingdoms of Sardinia and the Two Sicilies, and most of those of central Italy too, were filled of old by royal nomination. Likewise a vast number of canonries. In addition to this " royal patronage," certain sanctuaries and places of pilgrimage—Loreto, for example—were under the " royal protection " and outside the jurisdiction of the bishop of the diocese. Moreover, the crown claimed, by virtue of concordats between the Holy See and the long-destroyed monarchies, the right to present or to nominate to yet other sees. All this had meant in practice, since 1870, that no ecclesiastic could take possession of his benefice until he had obtained the government's consent,

[1] It will be seen that this is not a special concession to Mussolini on the part of the pope—as a recent writer, Mr. William Teeling, implied. The last chapter shows it to be, nowadays, " common form " in concordats.

given in the *exequatur* (for bishops) or the *placet* (for other benefices). Not infrequently the government refused and there have been archbishops of Bologna and Venice who, in the end, weary of the campaign to obtain the *exequatur* from a hostile Minister of Justice, resigned their sees in despair. At one time there were some fifty sees simultaneously vacant in Italy through the operation of this superannuated system—a system which the Holy See never acknowledged, since the *Risorgimento* had swept away the kingdoms in which it had been erected.

This kind of working veto on appointments was but one of the state's instruments to keep the Catholic Church " in order." The ecclesiastical properties confiscated during the revolution were, as has been described earlier, administered for the Church by the state. The revenues, such as they came to be, paid a special tax of 30 per cent. towards a fund for the equalisation of benefices (that never really worked), a tax of mortmain, and a tax that took the place of succession duty. There were taxes on appointments, a professional tax, and others still. Even in 1870 it was recognised that the system was a legal chaos, and the Law of Guarantees pledged the state to a reform of it. From time to time hints were given that the reform was being drafted, but not until 1925 —the commission that has been mentioned—did the state really move in the matter. The chaos worked for the advantage of the state treasury and the state's hold on the Church. Why then hurry to remove it ?

The effect of this tangle of ancient cesaro-papist jurisprudence was to produce the most complicated ecclesiastical organisation Europe has known, a whole army of officials— or rather horde, for army suggests a clarity of division and a simplification of function that this *régime* never knew— administered it, delivering permits, making inventories, giving receipts, collecting dues—including the revenues of vacant benefices—and administering the entire business of not a few religious foundations and charitable societies. Nor is this the end of the tale.

How did such a system work, even for half a century ?

" The Holy See only managed to accommodate itself to it by a truly miraculous flexibility, by an everlasting subtle gymnastic. None, indeed, but Italians could ever have done it." [1]

The supposedly informed critics—Catholics among them—who sigh at the spectacle of the Church enslaved to Mussolini, can know nothing at all of the state of things that obtained during the first seven years of the *régime*, nor of the enormous power in matters ecclesiastical which he has surrendered by the concordat. And if Pius XI is still grateful to " the man whom Providence set in our way " [2] has he not reason to be, and all future generations of Catholics in Italy with him ? For the first time for centuries, let it be repeated, the Church in Italy can really breathe without the permission of the officials of the state. For the concordat has abolished the whole miserable system of these " legal fetiches, which the uglier and the worse shaped they were so much the more were they to be venerated and preserved inviolable." [3]

First of all the state recognises that " the choice of archbishops and bishops belongs to the Holy See." As in every other country where it has made a concordat the Holy See pledges itself to make it known to the government its proposed choice before it is published. The government has a right to make objections of a political nature. All ecclesiastical appointments—with a very few exceptions in the chapels royal—are in the hands of the bishops. Again the government is to be advised beforehand, and may object political reasons against the individual proposed. The *exequatur*, the *placet*, " and all manner of imperial or royal nomination in the matter of appointments " is declared abolished. The state renounces the " royal patronage " and the right to the revenues of vacant benefices. A cleric is now possessed of his benefice immediately the nomination is made by ecclesiastical authority.

---

[1] Pertinax, p. 35.
[2] Address of 13 February, 1929.
[3] Pius XI, address of 13 February, 1929.

There is a generous recognition of juridical personality for ecclesiastical organisations, sees, parishes, religious orders and the like, and the extraordinary taxes just described are abolished. For the future the Church alone will administer Church property, free from all state interference. The Holy See accords full condonation to all those who hold ecclesiastical property through the Italian laws which, years ago, confiscated it.

Two points alone remain to be mentioned in this summary of what has been called " the greatest homage to the Canon Law modern times have seen." [1] These are the dispositions of the Italian concordat relative to marriage and to education.

" Italy considers the teaching of Christian doctrine according to the received form of Catholic tradition to be the foundation and the crown of public education, and therefore consents that the religious instruction now given in the public elementary schools shall receive a further development in the middle schools, according to a programme to be settled between the Holy See and the State." So runs Article XXXVI of the concordat. The teachers who give this instruction are to be approved by the religious authorities, who also determine the text-books to be used. Teachers from whom the bishop withdraws his certificate lose the right to teach. All the state associations for physical training, the Avanguardisti and the Balilla, will so arrange their time-tables that on Sundays and the ten holidays of obligation [2] (which the concordat recognises as public holidays) the young people will not be hindered from their religious duties.

Catholic Action too has its recognition, that is to say, " the organisations depending on the Italian Catholic Action, in so far as these, following the directions of the Holy See, develop their activity independently of any

[1] FONTENELLE, p. 208.
[2] The ten prescribed by the Codex of Canon Law, i.e., Christmas Day, the Circumcision (1 January), the Epiphany (6 January), St. Joseph (19 March), the Ascension, Corpus Christi, SS. Peter and Paul (29 June), the Assumption (15 August), All Saints (1 November) and the Immaculate Conception (8 December).

political party and in immediate dependence on the hierarchy, for the diffusion and the realisation of Catholic principles." The Holy See renews its prohibitions to all ecclesiastics and religious against giving in their names to, or taking an active part with, any political party whatsoever.

The space given to marriage is the long Article XXXIV. Like the article on education it begins with a striking profession of faith on the part of the state. " The Italian State, wishing to restore to the institution of marriage, which is the basis of the family, that dignity which is in keeping with the Catholic traditions of its people, recognises full civil effects to the sacrament of marriage as the Canon Law regulates it." The notification of the marriage is made at the town hall as well as in Church. Within five days of the marriage the priest notifies the civil authority it has taken place by sending in a copy of the certificate. All cases of nullity of marriage, or of the dispensations sought for marriages ratified but not consummated, are reserved to the ecclesiastical courts. Their sentences pass for revision to the supreme Roman ecclesiastical court called the Segnatura, and the decision of this court—which settles the matter—is then notified to the state court of appeal. Cases of personal separation are dealt with by the state courts.

Such is the new charter of Italian Catholicism, the concordat " which from the beginning, we willed to be indissolubly united to the treaty," [1] a concordat " which if not the best that could possibly be made, is certainly among the best made so far, thanks to which we believe, with deep satisfaction, that we have given God back to Italy, and Italy to God." [2]

The pope makes no claim that the work is perfect, nor does he expect that everyone will applaud. "As for Our own share in the matter, We realised from the beginning that We should never reach the point where We pleased

[1] Pius XI : Address of 11 February, 1929.
[2] Address of 13 February, 1929 ; translation of both addresses in *How the " Roman Question " was Settled*, published by Catholic Truth Society, London. These last words are inscribed on the papal medal that commemorates the great event.

everyone. That, usually, is a thing that not God Himself succeeds in doing. We have, even, made Our own the words of the prophet and of Our Lord himself, ' I am in fact prepared for suffering : Ego autem in flagella paratus sum.' As a matter of fact this has become one of the habitual practices of life with Us." [1]

No one who knows what the concordat has accomplished can fail to be thankful for it. " When we see the juridical personality of the Church recognised with all the rights that flow from it, when the sacrament of marriage takes in civil life and legislation the place that is its own, when the juridical personality of the religious orders is recognised too, the Catholic University of the Sacred Heart enjoying the special consideration it merits, when religious instruction is given its due place, the place of honour, when Catholic Action is recognised as bearing a lawful right to its place in life, truly it is easy to understand, one cannot not understand, how we can and must, with full hearts, be really grateful to the Lord." [2]

This would seem to be the last word on the subject.

[1] Address of 11 February, 1929.
[2] Pius XI : Address of 13 February, 1929.

CHAPTER XI

WE have recalled the relation of the pope with Italy in the years preceding the treaties, and at length, because to the public mind it is by this phase of his activity that Pius XI is best known in a general way and is chiefly judged. We have examined in some detail what they achieved for religion. Something must now be said about the relation of the pope to the Italian state in the eight years since the treaties went into operation.

From the very beginning the pope has watched the development of Fascism in Italy with the very closest personal attention. He has noted and remarked on the various phases of the national revival, as he has publicly expressed his joy at the restoration of religion. But the men who have thus restored religion have not so much done this as Catholics, but rather as patriots concerned to draw from an age-long source of Italian vitality all that it holds of value. The Fascist state may be sufficiently aware of the facts of history to understand that Catholicism is necessary to the perfection of the Italian character, and therefore be prepared to make all possible concessions in order that Catholicism may do its good work in the nation. But this is not a Catholic attitude towards Catholicism, it does not derive from a Catholic understanding of Catholicism, and the situation where Catholicism has to ally itself with rulers whom such a spirit inspires—to say nothing of a state where Catholicism would be dependent on them—such a situation is charged with danger. Fascism—the Fascism of Italy—is not a mere collection of national policies, a programme of reform in the different departments of the national life. It is a gospel of national regeneration, a moral and political philosophy whose principles are ascertainable and known. If those principles are identical with the principles of social justice as the Catholic Church, divinely guided, teaches them, then Catholics can, with an easy conscience, should they so choose, ally themselves with Fascism, become whole-hearted apostles of the movement. If the principles of these two things, Fascism and Catholicism, are not identical then, though a Catholic may co-operate in the promotion of particular measures which do not conflict with the true interests of the common good, that is all he may do. He may follow Abraham Lincoln's famous advice and no more, " Stand with anybody that stands right. Stand with him while he is right and part with him when he goes wrong." [1]

From the very beginning of the pontificate Pius XI has, with the utmost clearness, criticised the Fascist conception of the state. After a really warm expression of his gratitude for all that had been done to restore the public recognition of Catholicism in 1923, he went on [2] explicitly to warn parents not, in slothful security, to allow anything of their natural right to watch over their children's education to be taken away from them. There is not anywhere a more serious matter for their consideration than this. The Church is immortal, for God has promised this. But the state has no such gift. The fate of civil society depends on the family, and if the state interfere with the family " the State can only reap what it has sown, truth or error, the true faith of Christ or some perversion of paganism, a humane civilisation or some detestably barbarian arrangement of things—a barbarian disorder, whatever the brilliance of outward show and elegance with which the inventions of modern times allow it to be decked."

Just a year later, [3] while once more appreciating all that the Fascist reorganisation had done to lessen class hatred and to promote national unity, the pope pointed out the

[1] Speech at Peoria, 16 October, 1854, LINCOLN, *Complete Works* (1905), II, 232–233.
[2] Allocution of 24 March, 1924.
[3] Allocution of 14 December, 1925.

serious weakness that none of this social legislation had
been inspired by Catholic teaching. The Church is the
friend of liberty and its rights. Her mission obliges her to
defend them. Hence her hostility to the licence and
anarchy into which the errors of the liberalism and the
socialism she has condemned would plunge human society.
The Church is no less hostile to any and every other theory
of politics which would hold that the state is self-sufficing,
as though it were itself its own final end. Such theories
end, speedily and necessarily, with the state overthrow-
ing and absorbing in itself all the private rights of its
citizens, with consequences as melancholy as they are
cruel.

This solemn warning addressed to the intelligence of
Italy was followed, again twelve months later, by a still
more explicit declaration that the doctrines criticised are not
compatible with the Catholic faith. A man cannot assent
to them and remain a Catholic. " We have recently seen a
new storm breaking over Italy," says the pope to the Sacred
College.[1] " We have seen Catholics attacked and Catholic
institutions. We have seen property damaged and sacked.
The boldness and the impudence of some of these rascals
has broken all the limits, profaning churches and the very
persons of the Catholic episcopate. There has been a blind
attack on Catholics—the most strenuous and loyal supporters the cause of good order knows—as seditious and
rebels. There has been a movement to single out some
most distinguished Catholics for especial opprobrium and
disgrace, their writings and their activities, men whose sole
aim has been the dissemination of good literature, the promotion of the good of religion and of human society in all its
aspects. . . . ." The storm has passed. Orders have been
given that it should cease, that the guilty should be sought
out and punished, that no such atrocities must ever occur
again. The pope's anxiety none the less persists. There is
every sign that sooner or later, somewhere or other, there

[1] Allocution of 20 December, 1926. The date should be noticed. The first
conversations on the Roman Question were just beginning.

will be a new endeavour to destroy the organisations which make up Catholic Action in Italy, " the apple of our eye." One reason for so thinking is the renewed propaganda for that theory of the state " which is in flagrant contradiction with Catholic teaching, namely that the State is its own last end and the citizen not born for anything else than the State's will, that to the State every activity should ultimately turn, that in the State all things should be absorbed."

The new storm which the pope feared was not long in coming. A state decree ordered the disbandment of something like half the troops of the Catholic Boy Scouts. There should be only one association for small boys in Italy, the Balilla, a state organisation in which, from their babyhood almost, these children should be bred up Fascists, trained in the new theory that what mattered, first, most and supremely in life was the Italian state.

Pius XI reacted strongly. In a long letter to the Cardinal Secretary of State [1] he protested and yet once again clearly explained the antagonism of these two conceptions of the nature of the state and of its relation to its citizens. " There is here a question of legislative enactments that prescribe the teaching of a doctrine which, we have reason to fear, is founded or culminates in a conception of the state of such a kind that, in virtue of Our duty of Apostolic vigilance, We have already twice pointed out it is not in conformity with the Catholic conception."

For a little while, after this storm, there was peace. Then came the signing of the Lateran Treaties (11 February, 1929), and the speeches in which Mussolini proposed their ratification in the Italian parliament. He had the delicate task of so presenting them that the remnants of the old Liberalism would not be able to decry the achievement as a surrender of the state to clericalism and, not unnaturally, after stressing the importance of the reconciliation, he preferred to dwell on what the state had not conceded in the concordat, on the powers it still retained where ecclesiastics and ecclesiastical matters were concerned.

[1] Autograph letter *Abbiamo Sotto*, 24 January, 1927.

As luck would have it, a papal audience had been arranged for the day after this speech for the students of the Jesuit college of Mondragone (14 May, 1929). The pope could not but refer to the Duce's interpretation of the concordat, at any rate in its clauses concerning education. A fortnight later, in a long and elaborate letter to the Cardinal Secretary of State [1] he reviewed all that the Duce had had to say and criticised it in language which, if courteous and appreciative even, was direct to the very limits of severity.

" It is not the function of the State," the pope said in the speech to the Mondragone students, " to absorb, to swallow up, to annihilate the individual and the family. This would be absurd, contrary to the nature of things, for the family existed before the State, as it existed before society." The state's *rôle* in education is to collaborate with and to assist the parents, with those means with which, better than anyone, the state is furnished. In the matter of education the prior rights are with the family and the Church. So God and the nature of things require. On this point the pope cannot but be, not unwilling to discuss, but intransigent. Nor is this the pope's fault. " Two and two make four, and it is not our fault that they do not make three, or five, or six, or fifty." The pope is not unwilling to treat. If the salvation of souls demands it, he will find the courage to treat with the devil himself ! [2]

To Cardinal Gasparri, with the treaties still unratified, Pius XI opens his whole soul and with most undiplomatic frankness, corrects the errors of Mussolini's speeches, points out what cannot ever be accepted in Fascism and states the limits of all possible concession. Other reasons apart the pope declares that he could not " in loyalty go any further in the matter of the treaties without giving such

[1] Autograph letter *Ci si è domandato*, 30 May, 1929.
[2] It is a crazy misrepresentation of this to say (as does G. Seldes, *The Vatican*: *Yesterday, To-day, To-morrow*, p. 384), that the pope " referred to Mussolini as the devil ! " : a misrepresentation supported on p. 385 by the insertion of the words " with the devil " into the pope's speech at the words " We negotiated some time ago . . . "

explanations as would dissipate, and make impossible, any ambiguity, any misunderstanding." The Duce is thanked for the goodwill of his personal compliments to the pope, but he is told frankly that his ideas on the origin of Catholicism, the essence of Catholicism, and the *rôle* of the Roman Empire in its fortunes, are "heretical and worse than heretical." [1] The attempt to get round this by distinguishing between the facts of history and the teaching of the Church, is Modernism of the worst type.

The pope notes, and protests against, the many places where Mussolini's language seems to veil the treaty's clear and undoubted recognition of the sovereignty of the Holy See and the all-important fact that the concordat is a thing negotiated between equal sovereignties, and is not a concession of the state to the Church. Mussolini has assured the world that absolute liberty of conscience still remains in Italy. But so long as man is dependent on his Creator this cannot be. There is indeed a certain liberty of conscience which man enjoys, liberty from the state's interference with his conscience. The Church alone—and this because God has so arranged things—has any competence in what relates to conscience. "Liberty of conscience" in a Catholic state must be understood and practised in accordance with Catholic teaching. In this connection logical necessity forces the recognition that it is not to the state but to the Church that the full and perfect mission of education belongs; the recognition, too, that the state cannot hinder or restrain the exercise and the fulfilment of that mission, nor yet again restrict it to the carefully measured teaching of religious truth. The pope will have none of Mussolini's ambiguous compliments—however well intentioned— about the liberal spirit of the Catholic university where, nowadays, books are published on Kantian philosophy. This does not mean, the pope corrects the Duce, that

---

[1] Mussolini had explained that if Christianity was Catholic it was so thanks to its connection with Rome as the capital of the empire. Had it not been for Rome Christianity would never have been more than a Jewish sect.

Catholicism is coming nearer and nearer to Kant. Catholics study Kant to expose and refute him.

" Italy is a Catholic State," the treaties declare, and now it is said, "but a Fascist State also." Pius XI examines this, and allows it to be true since it no doubt means that the Fascist state, in the realm of ideas and theory as in that of practical action, will admit nothing that is not in accord with Catholic teaching and practice : without such loyalty to Catholicism there will not be, there could not be a Catholic state.

Again the pope picks out, and exposes the Italian leader for, the ambiguity with which, continually, he speaks of the state as " conferring " one right after another upon the Church, where, in fact, the treaties distinctly say these rights are " recognised " by the state.

There is a final repudiation of any interpretation of the treaties other than accords with the spirit of this letter, and the pope declares himself willing to see the treaties go unratified, the whole thing scrapped, rather than these ambiguities be tolerated. He has said, and it has been understood, that the treaty and concordat are indissolubly united. The hints that, in the future, the lot of each may be different are not to be borne. By the very pacts as signed, both treaty and concordat are equally irrevocable, henceforward beyond the possibility of discussion, settled once and for ever. " Hence it comes that *simul stabunt* or *simul cadent*, even though as a consequence the ' City of the Vatican ' disappears with the State it constitutes. For Our part, with the help of God *impavidum ferient ruinæ*."

And this is the man whom a writer has recently described as the shivering, fearful tool of Italian policy !

A few days after this *mise au point* the treaties were ratified, 7 June, 1929.

The worst storm of all was, however, yet to come.[1] In

[1] That Pius XI was never under any illusion as to the fact that the world in which he moves is human and imperfect, the following vivid anecdote shows :

the month of April, 1931, more than two years after the signature of the Lateran Treaties, there began to appear in the *Lavoro Fascista* articles that criticised and attacked Catholic Action as anti-Fascist and contrary to the laws of the state. The thing should be suppressed, it was urged. What this Press campaign was leading up to was soon evident. On 19 April the General Secretary of the Fascist party—Signor Giurati—made an important speech at Milan to the General Assembly of the movement. His point of view was that of the *Lavoro Fascista*. Those who made appeal to the concordat as affording legal existence to Catholic Action should remember that the state with which the concordat was negotiated was a totalitarian state, a corporative state, a Fascist state moreover. Fascism, also, means to bring up the children of the nation in the religion of their fathers. Its whole practice since it came into power is witness of its will in this matter. There is no need for these desperate gestures to secure the safety of what is already saved. There is nothing left for Catholic Action to do, the state already doing all.

The speech was insolent in tone, and its substance was the dangerous doctrine that there is a means for Catholics to achieve the fullness of their Catholic stature by other means than the divinely instituted guidance of the Church, the heresy already interwoven in the affair of the condemned Action Française.[1]

The papal reply [2] was immediate, an admirably patient analysis of all that totalitarianism can imply and a Catholic criticism of the notions underlying the speech. The pope wishes, almost at all costs, to find a way of agreement with the chiefs of the state. He is no less definite that they owe

---

" The very next day [after the King of Italy's visit to the pope, 29 December, 1929] I stood with others in the Pope's study and one who spoke for us congratulated His Holiness on this historical happening. The smile with which he was greeting his sons from overseas died on his face and a serious look came into his keen eyes. ' Yes,' he said, ' but it is not finished yet. You must still go on praying '." S. J. Gosling in *Clergy Review*, October, 1932, p. 334.

[1] *Cf.* p. 286 *seq.*

[2] The autograph letter to Cardinal Schuster, Archbishop of Milan, *Dobbiamo Intrattenerla* of 26 April, 1931.

a duty to religion, and that there is a limit to all concessions. In its opening paragraphs, its scarcely veiled rebuke of the Fascist speaker's sins against good form, there is in this letter, as in the Mondragone address, a touch of quite unusual liveliness, a dry, pawky liveliness.[1] Once more it is announced in so many words that to educate Catholic children and young people in Catholicism is the Church's business. Here the *régime* has the duty " not only to follow the Magisterium divinely committed to the Church, but to favour it when in operation." [2] At the moment it is just the contrary of this which obtains, and the practice of their religious duties is made difficult and in a manner impossible for these young people, while they are exposed to every inspiration of hatred and irreverence. For the pope it is not a matter of securing to them just that minimum of Christian, supernatural life which may save them from the flood of neo-paganism. He will leave nothing undone to bring to them that fullness of life to give which Our divine Redeemer came on earth, as He testifies Himself, " I am come that they may have life and may have it more abundantly " (John x. 10). As far as this life and our salvation is concerned we can say of the Church what St. Peter said of Jesus Christ Himself, " there is no other whereby we may be saved " (Acts iv. 12).

The Church alone has the mission to save men, the Church alone has the means, namely, the teachings of the faith, the divine and ecclesiastical law, the divine preaching, the sacraments, prayer, the theological and the infused virtues. It is precisely because Catholic Action is the collaboration of the laity in the Church's work of salvation and sanctification that the pope was so concerned to find a place for it, and guarantees, in the concordat.

And here the objection is made that the state with which

---

[1] Giurati had said there were " some who had appealed to the concordat," " coloro che . . . fanno apello . . . " The pope says sharply " Ora quei ' coloro ' siamo ' Noi '." All through this long controversy one seems to hear steel on steel. Pius XI does not hesitate to venture his person in the melée and he gives as good as he gets.

[2] " non solo di seguirne il Magisterio ad essa divinamente affidato, ma anche di favorirne la pratica."

the concordat is made is totalitarian-Fascist, and corporative-Fascist.[1] But how can this circumstance affect the right of Catholic Action to function according to its nature ?

The *régime* is totalitarian ? This may mean that to the state, in its own sphere, the totality of the citizens is subject and subordinate, a subjective totalitarianism the pope calls it, and this we must allow the state. We cannot say as much for the idea that the state is totalitarian objectively speaking, that is to say for the idea that the totality of its citizens must apply to the state and depend on the state—worse still chiefly depend on the state or depend on it alone—for the totality of all that may be needed for every phase of life, even their individual, domestic, spiritual or supernatural life. To confine ourselves to the matter in hand, is it not too evident that a state totalitarianism that claimed to extend as far as the supernatural life would be absurd as a theory and, as a political system, a monstrosity ?

Now Catholic Action, as has been consistently explained for years, has to do with the supernatural life of man. First of all, under the direction of the bishop, it works for the spiritual betterment of the individuals who are its members, and they then work in a more fruitful and wider apostolate. To the Church and to its hierarchy Catholic Action is a necessary, lawful and indispensable means to form and to spread the supernatural life. It cannot be a political thing ; this follows from its nature. The pope has persistently corrected any endeavours in a political direction that uninstructed zeal may have inspired.

The state is corporative. Is there anything in this fact to make Catholic Action incompatible with loyalty ? That special organisation of the state which makes it a " Corporative " state is an organisation of civil life for natural ends. Catholic Action, whose ends are supernatural, is a thing on another plane altogether. It is of course true that Catholic Action is an *organised* thing, made up of visible human beings. The bishops, it must be allowed them,

---

[1] " col Regime totalitario fascista e con lo Stato corporativo fascista." Giurati's own words.

have the right to choose the form of organisation which is best suited to the particular needs of special localities. It must also be allowed that the field in which Catholic Action functions is a very wide field indeed. It is the whole field in which the Church's own mission lies. Wherever anything can be done for the good of souls, wherever there is a soul in danger, wherever there is question of God's honour or of insults to God, of the observance or the violation of God's law or the laws of the Church, of problems or of interests that are moral—and not purely material, mechanical or economic—and that have an inevitable moral reaction on the individual, the family and society, here is the field for Catholic Action.

This is the reason why the Church and the hierarchy have the right, and the duty too—and Catholic Action with them, in due proportion—to betake themselves also into the domain of what affects the working classes, labour and the social organisations [1] ; not to usurp or to hinder the activities of the trades unions and like societies—this is not their business—but to safeguard, and everywhere promote, the honour of God and the good of souls.

Corporate activity and Catholic Action cannot then but meet continually, given the identity of their human subject matter, man taken individually or collectively. Given good will on both sides there is no reason whatever why there should be any conflict.

There is one element of Signor Giurati's criticism still to be met, that Catholic Action has no place in the state because the state is "Fascist." This objection can be answered, says Pius XI, very briefly indeed. Fascism declares itself to be, and wishes to be, a thing that is Catholic. Well then, to be Catholic in reality and not just in name, not Catholic like children who are a continual affliction and trial to their parents, a bad example to their brothers, there is only one means to be such, one means only. It is a means that is indispensable, and nothing can supply for it if it be lacking. This is to obey the Church

[1] " di portarsi anche sul terreno operaio, lavorativo, sociale."

and its Head, to share the feelings of the Church and its Head ! [1] Now what the Church wills, and what the Church feels about Catholic Action has never been in any doubt, and it has never been so clearly known as in these our own times.

May this letter, God helping, end all the mistrust and banish those unjustifiable suspicions that have worked so much harm in the matter of contacts and co-operation that should be useful to all of us.

Within a few weeks of this letter the annual congress of Italian Catholic Action met in Rome. This was the signal for a new campaign in the *Lavoro Fascista* and the main point of the attack was the Catholic organisation for young people. A prominent leader of the Catholic Action, Mgr. Pizzardo, had urged, so it was now said, that the movement be turned to destroy Fascism and the *régime*. It was time for Catholicism to seize the reins. Catholics must be ready to march. Fascism would shortly be exposed before the public opinion of Italy and the whole world.

These allegations were immediately, and officially, denied in the *Osservatore Romano*. But as the month of May neared its close the anti-Catholic critics passed from words to deeds. There were anti-papal demonstrations in Rome itself and at the university the students burnt publicly the number of the *Osservatore Romano* which printed the pope's protests and denials, to cries of " Death to the Pope." Nor did the authorities take the slightest notice of the insult. Catholic students were set on and " beaten up," papal employees too. In Milan, Pavia, Bari, Benevento, Venice and Trieste there were similar scenes, and everywhere the police remained passive. At Verona the bishop's palace was fired. When the police did intervene it was to order the dissolution of all clubs and associations of young people that were part of Catholic Action. Their property was put under sequestration.

The pope's protest—in an address to the students of the

---

[1] "non c'è che un mezzo, uno solo, ma indispensabile e insurrogabile: ubbidire alla Chiesa ed al Suo Capo e sentire con la Chiesa e col Suo Capo."

Istituto Pio XI—was characteristically clear and vigorous. Mussolini, meanwhile, announced to the world that the dissolution of the societies which were independent of the Fascist party had been decreed and the decrees carried out " without the least incident."

On 31 May the pope summoned an extraordinary meeting of all the cardinals in Rome. It was decided, as a public protest, that " seeing that at Rome itself, that is to say in the very presence of the central authority," there had been these outrages, the mission of the Cardinal Legate to the forthcoming celebrations at Padua [1] should be cancelled. The Diocesan Eucharistic Congress at Rome was suspended and also all the Corpus Christi [2] processions throughout Italy.

Some days later Mussolini broke his silence with a communiqué to his party and a radio-broadcast. Documents were to hand, it was announced, which proved that certain sections of Catholic Action were openly, or sullenly, hostile to Fascism. The *régime* was resolved not to tolerate any anti-Fascist survivals. All the Fascists of Italy should bear this in mind and remember that the blood of the martyrs who died for Fascism demands that Fascism be defended against no matter whom. The charges made by the *Lavoro Fascista* have been confirmed as true, 99 per cent. of them, by the admissions of the *Osservatore Romano* itself. The Vatican's complaints about persecution are ridiculously untrue. In those places where, despite its prohibition, the Corpus Christi procession took place there was perfect order and respect. More bluntly still it was said : " The assertion that Catholic Action has not any political character is completely false. . . . Almost all its leaders were members or leaders of the Partito Popolare, which was one of Fascism's strongest opponents." The destruction of the Catholic associations was then a simple duty of self-defence on the part of the government, for

---

[1] For the seventh centenary of the death of St. Anthony : *cf.* the Apostolic Letter *Antoniana Sollemnia* of 1 March, 1931, to the Bishop of Padua.
[2] The feast of Corpus Christi fell, in 1931, on 4 June.

Catholic Action is " a strong association under the orders of a foreign power, the Vatican."

It is rare, and has always been rare in European history, for one ruler, so bluntly and crudely to give another the lie direct, rarer still for this to be done in circumstances where correction is easy to make. The most likely explanation of this frightful gaffe on the part of Mussolini is his expectation that by now the spirit of his opponent must be broken— the eternal mentality of the bully.

Pius XI was not at the end of his resources, nor of his courage. By 5 July there was circulated to all the bishops of Italy, and there appeared in the *Osservatore Romano* (gone to press four hours in advance of its time to escape any chance of a police raid), one of the major encyclicals of the reign *Non Abbiamo Bisogno*, the final damning reply to the lies and bad faith of the Fascist state. This lengthy document,[1] prepared and written down to its smallest detail by the pope himself, must be read in its entirety if the personality of Pius XI, the ideals, the motives, the vision, the methods of this great leader of men are to be understood at all. Through it all there rumbles the deep indignation of an honest man who feels he has escaped, and only just escaped, the trickery of rogues, and there is the still deeper anxiety and distress that come of the fact that what is seemingly at stake is the future of Italian Catholicism.

No summary can convey the effect of this tremendous philippic, whose spirit and vigour recall the traditional *rôle* of the popes as the guardians of the spiritual world and, indeed of civilisation, against the destructive genius of barbarism.[2] Since, however, the encyclical is the crown of the papal commentary on Fascism, and the condemnation of what errors are bound up with it, something more than these generalities must be set down in order to complete this chapter.

[1] Translation published by N.C.W.C., Washington, D.C., and Catholic Truth Society, London. "*Concerning ' Catholic Action '*" pp. 1–42.
[2] And if anyone can read Italian let him read the encyclical in its native dress. The English translation, accurate indeed, is to this as the Bohn translations are to the text of Vergil and Homer.

The pope publishes now to the world what the *régime* had hoped to stifle, " the disbanding of the Associations of young people and of the University students affiliated to Catholic Action [was] carried out in such a way and by such methods as to give the impression that action was being taken against a vast and dangerous association of criminals . . . even (as it happened) [of] such groups as the little children's clubs and the society of the Children of Mary." Next he turns to " the principal falsehoods and real calumnies scattered by means of the hostile party press, the only press which is free to say and to dare to say anything, and is often ordered or almost ordered what it must say." These calumnies were largely summarised in the broadcast, " a non-official " broadcast (" cleverly chosen word ! " [1]), administered to the public. Rarely in all his experience as a librarian, the pope remarks, " with the most profound bitterness," [2] has he met anything so tendentious and so contrary to truth and to justice as this message. Once more the pope solemnly denies its facile, not to say impudent, assertions. The attacks lead him seriously to doubt whether the former benevolence and favours were indeed prompted by any real love for religion. As for the Corpus Christi processions, as the broadcast described them, the pope does not know of a single instance of such willing compliance. There were places where the Roman decrees did not arrive in time, and there were other places where the utmost violence was used to coerce the clergy ; other places again, where, with the connivance of the authorities, blasphemous parodies of the procession took place.

All the declarations as to the nature of Catholic Action and the repeated prohibitions against the use of its organisations for political purposes are eloquently renewed. The insult that on this point the Régime has allowed the pope publicly to be called a liar, Pius XI merely notes and passes on to show how empty the charge is that Catholic Action is nothing but the Partito Popolare.

[1] " un messagio, sia pure non ufficiale (cauta qualifica)."
[2] " con la più profonda amarezza."

Again—the pope is now answering the grandiloquent
excuse that " defence of the realm " calls for the suppression
of Catholic Action—of the societies suppressed 10,000 were
or are composed of girls and young women with a membership of 500,000. Of these half million only 220,000 are set
down as effective members, more than 100,000 are little
aspirants and 150,000 more are still smaller " Benjamins."
All the papers and the correspondence of the Catholic
Action are in the hands of the government, they are still
intercepting letters, and yet they have not been able to
point to a single individual about whom any one of their
charges of interference in politics is true. To accuse
Catholic Action in Italy of such intervention is real calumny.
But, of course, all this talk about Catholic Action is just an
excuse. The real aim is to take away from the Church the
youth—all the youth of the country.

Our Lord has severely threatened those who put obstacles
in the way of a child's salvation. " Suffer the little children
and forbid them not to come to Me," He has said, and " Woe
to that man who shall scandalise one of these little ones."

The pope proceeds to reveal the especial danger of this
Fascist plan to monopolise the formation of youth. His
words are the most explicit condemnation so far made of
the ideal. He speaks of the undoubted " resolve . . . to
monopolise completely the young, from their tenderest
years up to manhood and womanhood, for the full and
exclusive advantage of a party, of a *régime*, on the basis of
an ideology which openly resolves itself into a true, a real
pagan worship of the State—[which is] no less in full
conflict with the natural rights of the family than with the
supernatural rights of the Church." [1]

----

[1] The English translation published by the Catholic Truth Society differs
slightly from this, and as the passage is really important it will be well to give the
text of the Italian original :

" . . . il proposito—già in tanta parte eseguito—di monopolizzare interamente
la gioventù, dalla primissima fanciullezza fino all'età adulta, a tutto ed esclusivo
vantaggio di un partito, di un regime, sulla base di una ideologia che dichiaramente
si resolve in una vera e propria statolatria pagana non meno in pieno contrasto coi
diritti naturali della famiglia che coi diritti soprannaturali della chiesa." Text in
Actes de S.S. Pie XI, tome vii, p. 207. Paris, Bonne Presse, 1936.

The pope repeats, summarily, all that he has so often had to say about the respective *rôles* of State and Church in the matter of the formation of youth. He recalls that the Church's mandate in all this is divinely given. What then of these Catholics who now proclaim that, Fascism having supplied all that is needed for the Catholic formation of youth, the Church need no longer interfere ? " It is an unjustifiable pretention, irreconcilable with the name and the profession of Catholic, for any of the rank and file of the faithful to come forward to teach the Church and its Head what suffices and what must suffice for the education and Christian formation of souls. . . . " As for what may be done through the religious instruction given in the schools and through the care of the chaplains to the Fascist youth associations, all this, at its best, only gives the Church the chance to put forth the very minimum of her spiritual and supernatural effectiveness.

What kind of Catholicism is this new state production ? Pius XI describes it. " A frame of mind in religious matters that rebels against the directions of higher religious authority, and which enjoins or encourages disobedience to them, a frame of mind that becomes persecution and which tries to destroy all that the Supreme Head of religion notoriously prizes most dearly ; a frame of mind that excels itself in insult and injury against the person of the Father of all the Faithful to the point of crying ' Down with the Pope,' ' Death to the Pope ' ; an apprenticeship truly to parricide. Such a sham of religion cannot in any way be reconciled with Catholic teaching and Catholic conduct."

Again " A conception of the State which makes the rising generations belong to it entirely, without any exception, from the tenderest years up to adult life, cannot be reconciled by a Catholic either with Catholic doctrine or with the natural rights of the family. It is not possible for a Catholic to accept the claim that the Church and the Pope must limit themselves to the external practices of religion (such as Mass and the Sacraments) and that all the rest of education belongs to the State."

These doctrines are false, erroneous. Pius XI has never ceased to point this out. He has never, however, formally and explicitly condemned them, for he has always hoped that they were exaggerated assertions, sporadic, and the work of elements which were not sufficiently representative, assertions sufficiently dealt with if the individual authors of them were censured. In this attitude he has had many critics, some of them worthy of every consideration. The pope himself has now to admit there is no possibility of doubt left. " We must say and declare that no man is a Catholic—except by baptism and in name—who makes his own and develops a programme that adopts doctrines and maxims in such conflict with the rights of the Church of Jesus Christ. . . . "

What then about the oath, which even little boys and girls must take, to carry out without discussion orders which, as has been the case, may run contrary to the Church's rights, and to serve with all their strength, even with their life, this revolution that is robbing the Church of its children ? Only one reply can be given to a question so put. " Such an oath, as it thus stands, is not lawful." [1]

This stern, uncompromising denunciation of the dictator's malice and treachery fell with the force of a thunderbolt. The political aspect of Fascism was left untouched, the pope nowhere makes himself judge in the other disputes of which the movement has been the centre but he solemnly condemned as unacceptable to Catholicism the Fascist claim over the totality of the citizen's life.

What was the immediate effect of the encyclical on the master of Italy no one has ever revealed. Nor do we know in what circumstances, with what words, from what point of view and through whom, a peace was patched up. But after eight weeks of critical silence the decree against the centres of Catholic Action was withdrawn, and a few days later, 2 September, 1931, it was announced that an agreement had been reached.

" Un tale giuramento, così come sta, non è lecito."

The three main articles [1] of this were (1) Catholic Action, in accordance with the religious nature of its aims, does not, in any way whatever, occupy itself with politics, and in its external organisation it abstains from all those practices traditionally proper to political parties.[2] The flag of the local associations will henceforward be the national flag. (2) As regards the Catholic guilds for special classes of members : " It is no part of Catholic Action to found professional guilds in the proper sense of the term,[3] nor does it propose to undertake the functions proper to such guilds. These internal, professional sections are founded for purely religious aims." (3) The Catholic youth associations will refrain from all athletic and sporting activities. They will confine themselves to the exercise of those activities which, while being recreational or educational, have a religious end in view.

If the delicate question " Who won ? " be asked it may be answered that the Church found herself at the end of the struggle with her rights recognised, outside school hours, to " inculcate her principles, in reunions of an educational kind just as intensely as the Fascist principles are inculcated in the Fascist sporting clubs." [4] The main point was gained. On the other hand the Church undertook to make a notable change in the organisation of Catholic Action. Henceforward the local associations are not subject to a diocesan lay committee but to the bishop directly—a concession to the Fascist fear of anything at all that is organised in the spirit of free election and real representation. The bishop is to name all the officials and he must not appoint any one-time political opponent of Fascism. Moreover, the national central committee of the movement has ceased to be.[5]

On 11 February, 1932, the third anniversary of the treaties, Mussolini paid his first official visit to the pope.

[1] FONTENELLE, pp. 267–269.
[2] *I.e.*, the badge, cards of membership, special flags, etc., the use of which by the different Catholic societies had been urged as a proof that they formed a political party.
[3] *I.e.*, for professional purposes.
[4] *The Times*, quoted FONTENELLE, p. 269.
[5] QUERRE, p. 114.

Another chapter in the long history of the Holy See's relation to Italy was at an end. It will not be the last, nor, since human nature continues to be human nature, will it be the last to tell of storms. But the future, as the pope is fond of saying, " is in God's hands and therefore in very good hands."

Since 1932 the chief feature of the relations between the pope and the Italian government to interest the world in general has been the pope's action regarding the invasion and conquest of Abyssinia.

For Pius XI war is the greatest of all evils, sin apart. All war, just or unjust, war of defence as war of aggression, brings in its train such a flood of misery, of suffering, of sin that, almost at all costs, war should be shunned. Moreover, in the state of international tension that for a generation now has been Europe's unhappy lot, any war may loose upon the world just such another scourge as that from whose effects it still suffers. The next European war, it seems universally acknowledged, will be the last act of civilisation, as the west has known civilisation for a thousand years and more. " As for the menace of a new war, while the nations are yet suffering so cruelly from the terrible last war, We do not wish to believe, We cannot possibly believe that there exists to-day a civilised state that would wish to achieve such monstrous murder and, almost certainly, such self-destruction. Were We to conceive so much as a positive doubt that there were such a state, We should have to turn to God with the prayer of the prophet king who, for all that he knew what war was and victory too, cried ' Scatter, O Lord, the nations that wish for war '." [1]

The difficulty before the modern papacy is that which has always afflicted a power whose ultimate resource is moral. No more than its divine Founder can the Church

[1] Address to the cardinals, 24 December, 1930.

act effectively if the will of its subject be turned against it. There have been times when the papacy was in a position to coerce the Catholic peoples. History is witness how limited the success of such methods must be, and inevitably, for it is not the death of the sinner, nor his punishment merely as such, that is the Church's object, but his conversion to a new life. Manning's advice that as far as possible, no man should be asked to choose between his natural patriotism and the claims of the Church was sound. Too many men, good men, are not strong enough for it to be expected that they will always do the better thing. While insisting at every step on the principle involved, Pius XI, we have seen, will go to the very limits of concession to ease the burden on the individual conscience. He will declare the law, clearly, and the good Catholic will obey. For those who disobey or who continue to rebel he possesses sanctions. But even her sanctions the Church prefers to use medicinally. Where is the wisdom, the charity of so using them that they merely harden the sinner, make it—in a natural sense—more than ever impossible for him to change, since now there is involved that question of "honour" that tops all others? And if this is true of individuals, how much more of nations? Sentences doomed from the beginning to be void of effect are what no pope can ever allow himself to pronounce. Had St. Pius V known the condition of things in England when he launched the famous deposition of Queen Elizabeth he would never so have acted. No pope has repeated that once powerful gesture, nor, since Paul V failed with Venice, three hundred years ago, has there been a papal interdict upon a whole people. The day for these things is gone—it may return, but it is no longer with us, and even with a case proved to the hilt, the pope would court disaster and nothing but disaster who should forget the golden rule that proportions the harm one occasions with the evil one cures.

"With a case proved to the hilt," as, of course, the case against Italy, in the matter of Abyssinia, has never been proved to the hilt so far as concerns the papacy. It was proved to the satisfaction of Geneva, no doubt, but not by what Geneva knew from the general talk of informed circles, or from the despatches in the press. Geneva's knowledge was quasi-juridical, through official statements by the parties concerned, made by their accredited representatives in a kind of confrontation before a recognised power. Was all this to be done again at Rome? Not this time on a matter of League of Nations pacts—of which the papacy cannot be cognisant, for it is not a member of the League nor can ever, apparently, become such. Was all this to be done again at Rome to settle, this time, the moral question of right and wrong? And if not, how could Rome decide? And if so, then Abyssinia as well as Italy must plead before the papacy. And can anyone see any single nation of the world so presenting itself to state its case at the pope's invitation? Had the pope been so trusting, would he have been answered? And by what law or principle would he have judged? Let it be supposed that Italy, being Catholic, is subject to the moral law as he declares it. Abyssinia is no more Catholic than England. And if the pope, in a friendly charitable endeavour to preserve peace and England with it, invited England to present its case, to risk condemnation therefore—and presumably a high-sounding spiritual sanction—in the event of her losing, does anyone see even a "thank you" going out to the Holy See for its effort?

As the world is so constituted the Holy See can, in public, do one thing only in the international field on its own initiative. It can, wherever there is danger of war, recall the great moral principles and with all its power strive to obtain a hearing for them before national sentimentalism has drowned the intelligence of the nations concerned in floods of patriotic emotion and considerations of "honour." This the papacy does, and this, in a most remarkable manner, Pius XI did throughout the Abyssinian crisis, even at the grave risk of provoking such another crisis in Italy as the one we have just described. In this the pope continued to act as he has acted throughout his long reign. "Peace at any price" is an immoral saying. But there must always be a relation of sane proportion between the peace we are going to lose and the chance of good in the *régime* to come, and between this last and the price to be paid for it in war.

Throughout the year 1935, as the Italo-Abyssinian situation developed, the pope redoubled his efforts—privately through diplomatic channels, who can doubt it? as well as publicly. In speech after speech he recalled the frightfulness of war and of the crime of war making. More than that he even examined publicly the case put up for Italy that this was really a war of defence against Abyssinian aggression. The pope did not discuss whether this fact was true or not. That lay outside his power, for to settle such questions of fact only juridical inquiries will serve. But, taking the fact as proved, the pope proceeded to instruct the Italians in the nature of this right of self-defence.

"We long for peace and We pray God that We may be spared from war. The mere thought of war is a terror to Us. And now We understand that, abroad, there is talk of a war for conquest, a war of aggression. That is a hypothesis that We do not wish even to consider, a supposition which is truly disconcerting. Any war which is a war of conquest only would be an unjust war, obviously—a thing which routs imagination, something sad beyond words and horrible. We cannot think about an unjust war; We cannot envisage its possibility, and We deliberately turn our mind from it; We do not believe, We do not wish to believe there can be an unjust war.

"On the other hand, in Italy, they are saying that the war of which there is question will be a just war, because it is a war of defence, to make the frontier safe against the continual, the incessant dangers to which it is exposed; that it is a war necessary now by reason of the expansion of the population which is increasing from day to day; that it is a war undertaken to defend or to make certain the country's material security; that such a war justifies itself.

"It is however true, and We cannot but reflect on this truth, that if there is this need for expansion, if there is this need to defend the frontier and make it secure, We can only wish that some other means may be found than war. What is this other means? Obviously it is not easy to say. We do not believe it is impossible to find another means. All the possibilities must be studied. One thing there is which seems to Us beyond all doubt, this namely that if the need for expansion is a fact with which We must reckon, the right of defence has its limits and qualifications, and these must be observed if the defence is to be free from blame."[1]

Throughout the summer English and French ministers had been busy with proposals that would stave off the impending war, and to these pacific efforts Pius XI referred when he said, continuing the address just quoted, "We pray God to second the activity and the industry of those far-sighted men who understand what the true happiness of the nations and social justice demands, men who are doing all in their power, not through threats, which can only aggravate the situation and irritate men's spirits, nor through postponements and delays which are a waste of precious time, but who with a genuinely humane intention are doing their utmost to maintain peace, men sincerely anxious to keep war at a distance."

Of the two claims or excuses put forward by Italy the need of expansion is a fact, but a fact is not the same thing as a right. The defence of the frontier is a right. But to be lawfully exercised the right must be exercised under certain conditions.

At Geneva the long quasi-judicial procedure dragged on slowly if surely. The Abyssinian appeal had been put in on 16 March, 1935. It was not until 4 September that the Council of the League began its examination of it. By then "things had gone too far for any proceedings at Geneva to affect the issue."[2]

On 8 September, speaking to an international pilgrimage

[1] Address to the International Congress of Catholic Nurses, 27 August, 1935.
[2] CARR, p. 225.

of veterans of the last war, Pius XI, at St. Paul's outside-the-walls, made another public appeal for patience until a juridical solution had been sought for and tried which " would satisfy the aspirations and the demands and the needs of a great and good-hearted people, and thus achieve justice together with peace." The French minister, M. Laval, was about the same time declaring publicly at Geneva that there was the chance of an arrangement which would satisfy the legitimate aspirations of Italy without injury to the essential rights of Abyssinian sovereignty.

On 2 October the Italian invasion of Abyssinia began : on 18 November the League decreed against Italy the famous sanctions. The papal diplomacy turned to the most practical need of the moment, the limitation of the war. The question of right and wrong between Italy and Abyssinia was wholly disproportionate to the catastrophe of a general war in Europe, even supposing Italy wholly wrong and that a general war would have saved the Abyssinia that the public opinion of western Europe believed to exist and to have been wronged. To have let loose or encouraged others to let loose a general war for such a purpose would have been an insanity by the side of which Italy's alleged crime is a peccadillo. It has been said—with what degree of accuracy, one cannot say, for the writer who said it is one of those who never give any authority for their assertions—that the pope did his best to induce the Latin American states to vote against sanctions. It may well be that the pope foresaw what actually happened, that the only effect of sanctions would be to unite all Italy in a passionate resolve to go through with the war. The diplomatic history of those anxious months will not be known for a generation or more, but that the nuncios throughout the world worked on a common plan for the restriction of the war to these two combatant nations may be taken for granted. That the motive behind this diplomacy was the safety of civilisation, and that the papacy was sincere and detached from the sole aim of supporting Italian imperialism no one will doubt who has any detailed knowledge of the character of Pius XI as every act of his long pontificate makes it known.

Pius XI replied to his critics in the Allocution of 16 December, 1935. He had for months now made known to the world the fullness of his thoughts on the general question of war, on the general question of such wars as this war claimed to be. Anyone and everyone who really wanted to know what the pope thought had ample documentation at his disposal : "Would that all those would hearken to his admonition who still stand in astonishment, not to say scandal, as though We had not sufficiently fulfilled the duties inherent in the teaching office divinely confided to Us." More than this the pope will not say, for "amid the uncertainty, the human uncertainty and the uncertainty of events, of the present moment, it is to be feared that Our words, whatever words We speak, may either not be well understood or even be openly turned and deformed."

If it be pleaded that the conventions and the forms and the style of the different papal allocutions are a mystery to the general reader, there remains for the student the elucidation given in the commentaries of the *Osservatore Romano*. On this matter that organ of the Holy See said "The Pope has deplored not a particular war, but all wars, wars also that are an excess of defence. He has exalted peace as the supreme good, a blessing worth all possible self-denial and sacrifice. Not only that but he has pointed out the way to peace, and the way to peace can never be a war that will multiply conflicts and massacres. The way to peace lies through an equitable examination of facts and needs, facts and needs which even though they do not confer rights, cannot be left out of consideration." [1]

The war was soon over. On 1 May, 1936, the Emperor Haile Selassie left Abyssinia, Addis Ababa was occupied by Italian troops, and on 9 May King Victor Emmanuel III was proclaimed Emperor of Abyssinia and the country annexed to Italy. "Although economic sanctions had

[1] Quoted FONTENELLE, p. 405.

paralysed Italy's trade and caused a drain on her gold reserve, they had not sufficed to hamper her military operations," says the singularly competent author of the most recent summary of these events. "It was clear that nothing short of war would compel her to release her prize ; and Great Britain was not less firm than France in her resolve not to be drawn into war with Italy." [1] Sanctions were then withdrawn, on Great Britain's motion, in July, 1936, and the different powers began to arrange, each in its own way, for the most dignified method of recognising the *fait accompli* without too much sacrifice of their own self-respect.

So far our own country has managed to keep this impending necessity from unduly disturbing its peace. The Holy See, that had clearly proclaimed the moral issue in the months when Italy was preparing for war, and that had striven to limit the war to Africa, could not but rejoice that the war had in fact gone no further. It had never judged Italy, for it had never been in a position to judge of the facts alleged : its *rôle* was that precisely of judge and not of jury. The war now over it remained to make the best of the situation, to save what could be saved and this the pope proceeded to do. The war over there ended with it the menace of a general war that had darkened Europe for nearly two years. And, whatever the rights and wrongs of the Italian invasion, who could doubt that under its new rulers the lot of the natives would be happier than under the Amhari ? An optimism that never despairs of the future, that is always hopeful that in the future the errors and the losses of the past will be repaired, an optimism that is a personal characteristic of Pius XI, inspired his great address of 12 May, 1936, at the opening of the Catholic International Press Exhibition in the Vatican. It was a masterly review of the thought and life of the day, a critique of the neo-pagan and communist influences, and, being almost coincident with the end of the war, the pope's first public act since then, it was inevitable that he should

[1] CARR, p. 228.

make some reference to it. That reference was as follows :
" May God bless this exhibition, the opening of which
coincides almost exactly with the triumphal joy of a whole
nation of good-hearted people, joy at a peace which they
hope will be an effective element in and a prelude to that
true peace that is European and world wide." Divorce
this sentence from its context in the papal policy of the
previous two years and it can bear any interpretation the
reader chooses. In its setting it is no more than consistent
with all the rest.

As the year 1936 drew to its close the pope, for the first
time in his long life, fell seriously ill. He was past his seventy-
ninth birthday, and it was the whole weight of a life of
continuous hard work and mental application that fell on him
in the sudden collapse. For some weeks he appeared to be
in danger of death. " The fundamental cause of the illness,"
said a communiqué in the *Osservatore Romano*, " is diffused
arterio-sclerosis, with a prevalent myocardic trouble and
consecutive disturbance of the cardiac rhythm." For three
months nearly the trouble continued, with other complications to add to the anxiety of the Church and the suffering
of the patient. Gangrene set in, and there was nephritic
trouble too. The pain began to be and continued to be
unbearable. " Ask God to give me the grace to bear this
as a pope should," he said to his visitors. The pope made
an offering of his sufferings, for the restoration of Spain,
for the success of the Eucharistic Congress about to take
place at Manila, for the welfare of the sick throughout the
world. " Something would be lacking to one's experience
of life," he said in a moment of peace, " however great
one's life had been, if suffering were lacking. So we should
thank God when He sends us this experience."

When, in the spring of 1937, the round of duties was
resumed, it was another man who performed them, a pope
who looked somewhat his great age and, with something

of a shock, those who had for years had to do business with Pius XI realised, for the first time, that he was and had been for a long time old beyond the normal years of human activity. They had had before their eyes all that time, a miracle of intellectual and physical energy—humanly speaking—and till now they had never realised it. From his sick-bed, however, on 24 December, the pope managed to broadcast a message to the Church and to the world. No one who heard it ever will forget the moving contrast between the powerful language and the frail aged voice, that only an iron will sustained, which spoke. Once more the message was a plea for peace, a reminder that the condition of peace is goodwill, that peace is a tranquillity deriving from order, from the due satisfaction of lawful rights. There can be no peace unless there is justice, between individuals and between the nations.

CHAPTER XII

THE TEACHER OF HIS OWN TIME

(i) *Educational Ideals*

THERE are two things which concern closely the very existence of Catholicism and its future, and that are to-day matters of universal discussion. These are the question of the education of young people and the question of marriage, the kind of thing marriage is, its relation to the community and its effects on the individuals who contract it. On both of these questions Pius XI has provided instruction and guidance for his three hundred million people in two masterly encyclicals which restate the Christian ideal in relation to the needs, and the criticisms, of to-day, and recall the rules for practical right conduct in both these fields. These two encyclicals have both been translated into English, they are not hard to understand, and their teaching is readily available for all who wish to know it. There is no need then here to do more than recall, very briefly, the line of argument in both cases—this much at least we must do if we are not to pass over unmentioned two of the major utterances of Pius XI, two of his pronouncements that will effect most surely the generation of that " new people " which he desiderates.

With regard to education [1] the pope notes how naturally this has become one of the most absorbing topics of modern life. Man, everywhere, is realising more and more that the new material prosperity is not making him any happier. He turns to something higher than the merely material, to things of the spirit, to education. " There can be no true

---

[1] *Divini Illius Magistri*, 31 December, 1929; translation *The Christian Education of Youth*, pp. 50, Catholic Truth Society, London; N.C.W.C., Washington, D.C.

education," Pius XI warns him as he sets out on this new quest for happiness, " which is not wholly directed to man's last end, and in the present order of Providence . . . there can be no ideally perfect education except that which is called Christian." [1] This principle laid down, explained, and proved the pope passes on to consider whose business it is to educate youth. It is, he declares, the business of all three of the societies in which man finds himself, the Family, the Church, and the State.

First of all education is the business of the Church, that society founded, for supernatural ends, by God and commissioned by God to teach, in order to realise those supernatural ends. Here the Church shares the divine teaching office of God Himself. She has the right to found schools, of every kind and degree, and to control the entire education of her children, in all institutions, public or private, and this not merely in regard to the religious instruction given there, but with regard to every other branch of learning and to every regulation in so far as these may affect religion and morality. Interference ? Not at all, but the natural exercise of the Church's motherly care for the safety of the souls in her charge.

The Family, also, has received its mission of education directly from God the Creator. Its right to educate its children is inviolable. No earthly power can do away with this right. But the right is not so absolute that it is not subject to divine law.[2] It is in defending the Family's rights here that Pius XI makes his celebrated quotation from a judgment of the Supreme Court of the United States [3] to support the statement that " the child is not the mere creature of the State."

The State is not, however, without rights in the matter. These rights derive from its God-given authority to promote the common welfare in temporal matters—which is, indeed, the whole office, function and *raison d'être* of the

---

[1] " plenam perfectamque educationem dari non posse, nisi eam, quæ christiana vocatur."

[2] And therefore it is that the Family comes second to the Church in the matter.

[3] The Oregon School Case, 1 June, 1925.

State. Its educational duty is twofold : (1) to protect the prior rights of the Church and the Family ; (2) to protect the rights of the child against incompetent parents. The State then assists the schemes of the other two societies— and seconds their initiative and activity. It has also the right to secure that its citizens have the knowledge needed to perform their civil and political duties, and that they reach a certain degree of physical, intellectual and moral culture. In exercising its own just rights the State must not tyrannise. " Any educational or scholastic monopoly which, physically or morally, forces families to make use of government schools, contrary to the dictates of the Christian conscience, or even to their lawful preferences, is unjust and unlawful."

Church and State must co-operate in the work of education and work harmoniously together, and the pope quotes St. Augustine very happily to describe what Catholicism can do here for society in general. " Let those who declare the teaching of Christ to be opposed to the welfare of the State, furnish us with an army of soldiers such as Christ says soldiers ought to be ; let them give us subjects, husbands, wives, parents, children, masters, servants, kings, judges, taxpayers, and tax-gatherers who live up to the teachings of Christ ; and then let them dare assert that Christian doctrine is harmful to the State. Rather let them not hesitate one moment to acknowledge in that doctrine, if it be rightly observed, the greatest safe-guard of the State." [1]

What is it that is to be educated ? Man, says the pope, " man whole and entire, soul united to body in unity of nature, with all his faculties natural and supernatural, man such as right reason and revelation show him to be, man fallen from his original estate but redeemed by Christ and restored to the supernatural condition of adopted sons of God."

[1] Letters, 138.

Any system, therefore, which leaves out of account the fact of original sin and its consequences, which, in other words, relies on the sole powers of human nature is unsound. Any system which excludes or weakens the supernatural Christian formation is false. To-day we can see a fairly general movement to withdraw education from any kind of dependence on the divine law. Such systems do not " emancipate " the child, but make him the slave of his own blind pride and of his disorderly affections.

Two more dangers of the day are noted and condemned. There is the wrong kind of education in sex matters, that ignores the great fact of man's inborn weakness in this particular and also, what experience teaches us, that evil practices are the effect not so much of ignorance as of a weak will. There is also the " false and harmful method " of co-education, which ignores the fact that the sexes are complementary, and educates both boys and girls as though they were in all respects identical.

Where should children be educated? As much as possible in the family, the example of a well-ordered and well-disciplined Christian family being the greatest of all helps. The pope notes in the world of to-day a falling-off in this respect. Few parents will make the sacrifices that this fundamental duty entails, and the tendency that prevails is for the children to be sent away from home " even in their tenderest years." Pius XI is then reminded of Russia, and the unnatural system of communal rearing of children, in a kind of religious atheism and hatred. Fired with sudden passion, he exclaims : " For the love of Our Saviour, Jesus Christ, therefore, we implore pastors of souls by every means in their power, by instruction and catechisms, by word of mouth and written articles widely distributed, to warn Christian parents of their grave obligations."

The Church offers a second setting for education in her sacraments, her ritual, and the churches themselves, to say nothing of the innumerable pious societies of one kind and another.

Finally there is "that social institution the school." It is necessary, but it should never be forgotten it is subsidiary to the settings just described of family and religion. If the school is to succeed it "must form with these a perfect moral union." Hence if the school is what is called "neutral" or "lay"—a school where secular instruction alone is given—it goes contrary to the fundamental principles of education, and, of course, in practice—experience teaches this—it becomes anti-religious. Nor can those schools be considered suitable which are open to non-Catholics and Catholics alike, even though separate religious instruction be given in them to the Catholics.

The Catholic ideal is this : "It is necessary that all the teaching and the whole organisation of the school and its teachers, syllabus and text-books in every branch, be regulated by the Christian spirit, under the direction and maternal supervision of the Church ; so that Religion may be in very truth the foundation and the crown of the youth's entire training ; and this in every grade of school, not only the elementary, but the intermediate and the higher institutions of learning as well. To use the words of Leo XIII : ' It is necessary not only that religious instruction be given to the young at certain fixed times, but also that every other subject taught be permeated with Christian piety. If this is wanting, if this sacred atmosphere does not pervade and warm the hearts of masters and scholars alike, little good can be expected from any kind of learning, and considerable harm will often be the consequence '." [1]

Lastly, perfect schools are the result not so much of good laws as of good teachers. [2]

It will not perhaps be without interest to set down here something of the source of the pope's thought on education, or rather the aids to its formulation that he finds in the literature of the last two thousand years. This encyclical is in its expression what all treatises on education should be,

---

[1] The quotation is from Leo XIII's Encyclical *Militantis Ecclesiæ* of 1 August, 1897.
[2] " non tam rectis legibus quam magistris rectis tribuenda est."

the fruit of a rich general culture. Sacred Scripture is quoted twenty-one times (Deuteronomy, Wisdom, Proverbs (twice), Matthew (four times), Mark (twice), John, Rom., 1 Cor., 2 Cor., Gal., Eph., Col., 1 Thess., 2 Tim., 1 Pet., 1 John). Of the Fathers St. Augustine five times (*Confessions* twice, *De Symbolo*, the *Letters* and *De Moribus Ecclesiæ* once each), St. Hilary, St. Basil, St. Gregory Nazianzen and St. John Chrysostom once each. St. Thomas Aquinas is quoted four times. There are two quotations from Horace (Ars Poetica and Odes III), and one each from Seneca and Quintilian. Tertullian appears twice, Silvio Antoniano, the Christian humanist, twice, Nicolo Tommaseo once, Manzoni once, and (with a fervent recommendation to study him) Taparelli once also. The Vatican Council is referred to once. Of his predecessors Pius XI quotes twice the encyclical *Quum non sine* of Pius IX and also the Syllabus, once the *Singulari Quadam* of Pius X, and in no fewer than fourteen citations he quotes from eleven of the encyclicals of Leo XIII. To such an extent does this so-called " diplomat pope " still affect the thought of Catholicism ! Finally, a most unusual feature, there is the reference to a judgment of the Supreme Court of the United States of America.

(ii) Marriage

The encyclical on marriage [1] is one of the longest of all the pope's messages. Like many another of Pius XI's pronouncements, it looks back to the teaching of that predecessor whom he quotes unceasingly, Leo XIII, recalls that teaching and renews it with such amplification as the needs of a later age call for.

Marriage is a thing that interests man universally, and in this letter the pope addresses himself to an explanation of what marriage really is, for the benefit not only of Catholics, but of all mankind.

The basic principle of this teaching is the truth that

---

[1] *Casti Connubii*, 31 December, 1930 ; translation *Christian Marriage*, 67 pp. Catholic Truth Society, London ; N.C.W.C., Washington, D.C.

marriage—all marriage, marriage as such—is a thing instituted by God. Man's will makes this or that particular marriage, but marriage itself, the institution, is of God's making and is a thing whose nature man is powerless to alter, as he is powerless to alter the conditions that are required to make a marriage, or the laws that the married must observe if their marriage is to function well and happily.

Taking as his text St. Augustine's celebrated summary of the threefold way in which marriage is a blessing to man —through the children it brings to birth, through the beauty of conjugal loyalty, and through its sacramental figuring of the union between Christ and the Church and its consequent indissolubility, Pius XI pronounces a splendid panegyric on matrimony, and on the high nobility of married life. " Amongst the blessings of matrimony, the child holds the first place . . . husband and wife receiving these children with joy and gratitude from the hand of God, will regard them as a talent committed to their charge by God . . . to be restored to God with interest on the day of reckoning. . . . Unity, chastity, charity, honourable noble obedience," these are " the elements which make up the blessing of conjugal faith, the benefits which accrue from the married state." Marriage carries with it a perpetual bond which no earthly power can break. The Church, by divine gift, has the power to declare dissolved " certain natural marriages between unbelievers or amongst Christians in the case of marriages which though valid have not been consummated," but " not even this power can ever affect for any cause whatsoever a Christian marriage which is valid and has been consummated."

In the second part of the encyclical the pope examines the modern criticism of Christian marriage and some of the dangers that menace its well-being.

There is first of all the universal tendency to make adultery—which is the treason of treasons where marriage is concerned—the subject-matter of men's recreation and amusement. A generation is growing up for which adultery—and divorce—are things devoid of moral significance, and very often, things whose practice is taken as proof of " emancipation " and a progressive, more noble spirit. Springing from the same root as this tendency, that is to say from the mistaken theory that marriage is a purely human institution, are the mischievous proposals of the would-be reformers of the current immorality, proposals for " temporary," " experimental " and " companionate " marriages.

Children, the crown of marriage, are often now regarded as its " disagreeable burden," and, it is urged, married people should avoid this burden " by frustrating the marriage act." Since to do this is to do something " intrinsically against nature " it is " a deed which is shameful and intrinsically vicious," and a horrible crime. " Any use whatsoever of matrimony exercised in such a way that the act is deliberately frustrated in its natural power to generate life is an offence against the law of God and of nature, and those who indulge in such are branded with the guilt of a grave sin."

So much for the modern plague called " birth-control." The pope next deals with the latest form of the sin of abortion, the destruction of the child's life before birth when this is called for by some " medical, social or eugenic indication," [1] a destruction which, in these circumstances, many are now beginning to urge should be allowed by the civil law. As to the " medical and therapeutic indication " the pope can only recall the traditional teaching, that there can never be a sufficient reason " for excusing in any way the direct killing of the innocent," and this is precisely what we are dealing with here. The lives of mother and child are equally sacred. This same principle also holds good in the case where " social and eugenic indications " are urged.

Last of all the question is dealt with of the marriage of

---

[1] " pergraves causæ, quas medicæ, socialis, eugenicæ *indicationis* nomine appellant."

those " who, even though naturally fit for marriage, they [1] [consider] according to the norms and conjectures of their investigations, would, through hereditary transmission, bring forth defective offspring." Whence proposals that the state should " deprive these of that natural faculty by medical action despite their unwillingness," and this not as punishment for a crime committed, nor as a preventive against future crimes. Although often these unfortunate individuals are to be dissuaded from marriage, they commit no crime if they do marry, with whatever safeguards are possible. As to the sterilisation proposals " public magistrates have no direct power over the bodies of their subjects : therefore, where no crime has taken place and there is no cause present for grave punishment, they can never directly harm, or tamper with the integrity of the body, neither for the sake of eugenics nor for any other reason."

It is not necessary to say that the pope condemns the whole movement to popularise divorce, but attention must be drawn to the masterly critique of it here, never bettered in so summary a form.

The letter ends with a long section of some twenty pages that deal with the remedies " whereby those most detestable abuses, which we have mentioned, may be removed and everywhere the reverence due to marriage be restored." [2]

(iii) *The Cinema*

The interest and concern of Pius XI in the life of all his children extends necessarily to every part of their life. It is not the soul merely that is the subject of his thought but man. This is evident throughout these great social encyclicals, *nil humani a me alienum puto*, and it is strikingly evident in the encyclical which considers, for the benefit and guidance of Catholics, the nature and the tendencies of

[1] *I.e.*, " Some who, over solicitous for the cause of eugenics, . . . put eugenics before aims of a higher order."

[2] The English translation (Catholic Truth Society) has " everywhere marriage may again be revealed : " the Latin text is " debita matrimonio reverentia ubique restituatur."

the greatest and most universal entertainment of the day, the cinema. [1]

The cinema is one of the arts and " the essential purpose of art, its *raison d'être*, is to assist in the perfection of the moral personality, which man is, and for this reason it must itself be moral " ; " moral, an influence for good morals, an educator " as the pope said in an address to the International Federation of the Motion Picture Press.

Everyone admits this and the directors of the industry, in March, 1930, publicly declared their resolve to safeguard the moral welfare of the patrons of the cinema—a promise not so well carried out, in the event, as it was hoped. " The parade of vice and crime continued on the screen." Then the American hierarchy organised the " League of Decency" and men of goodwill in every denomination joined to assist the good work. The crusade has been a great success, and ultimately a benefit to the cinema industry itself.

Pius XI proceeds to a simple and illuminating analysis of the power of the cinema. Recreation has become a necessity for people who work under the fatiguing conditions of modern industry, and " it admits of no discussion that the motion picture has achieved, in the last few years, a position of universal importance, as a means of diversion . . . the most popular form of diversion . . . with all classes of society."

" The power of the motion picture consists in this, that it speaks by means of vivid and concrete imagery which the mind takes in with enjoyment and without fatigue. Even the crudest and most primitive minds, which have neither the capacity nor the desire to make the efforts necessary for abstraction or deductive reasoning, are captivated by the cinema. In place of the effort which reading or listening demands, there is the continued pleasure of a succession of concrete and, so to speak, living pictures.

" This power is still greater in the talking picture for the

---

[1] *Vigilanti Cura*, 29 June, 1936, p. 22 ; translation *The Use and Misuse of Films*, published by Catholic Truth Society, London, and N.C.W.C., Washington, D.C.

reason that interpretation becomes even easier and the charm of music is added to the action of the drama. Dances and variety acts which are sometimes introduced between the films serve to increase the stimulation of the passions."

The cinema is also a sort of object lesson and, for good or for evil, it teaches the majority of men more effectively than abstract reasoning. Whence the pope's anxiety that it be brought into conformity with the aims of the Christian conscience and saved from depraving and demoralising effects.

There is no need to labour the point that the damage done by a picture which is bad is grave beyond all power of estimation. The surroundings in which the pictures are seen must also be borne in mind. They are productive of, or at least they assist very powerfully, a kind of collective exaltation, and this, as experience teaches us, may assume the most morbid forms. " The motion picture is viewed by people who are seated in a dark theatre, and whose faculties, mental and physical and often spiritual, are relaxed." The pope considers the whole detail of the influence, the " luxurious appointments, pleasing music, the vigour of realism, every form of whim and fancy." Never was there such a means, if badly directed, of corrupting innocence, and Pius XI quotes the grave words of Our Lord: " *Whoever shall scandalise one of these little ones who believe in Me, it were better for him that a mill stone be hanged about his neck and that he be drowned in the depths of the sea.*"

To keep the cinema morally wholesome, to see that it is no longer a school of corruption is one of the supreme necessities of our time.

The pope congratulates all those—governments and individual workers alike—who have already done so much in this good work. The production of good films is, however, not a work for uninstructed zeal, " they must make full use of the technical ability of experts, and not permit the waste of effort and of money by the employment of amateurs."

Bishops everywhere should use all their influence with

the Catholics who hold important positions in this industry. There are surely many of these—executive directors, authors, actors—and it is unfortunate that their influence has not always been in accordance with their Faith. Not only should bad films be denounced as such, but efforts should be made to persuade those who can see it done of the marvellous potentiality of the film for good.

The bishops should see that every year all Catholics pledge themselves not to see plays which are offensive to truth and to Christian morality. People should be plainly told which films are permitted to all, which are permitted with reservations, and which are harmful or positively bad. " This requires the prompt, regular, and frequent publication of classified lists of motion picture plays." Special notices should be put in the Catholic press. In each country there should be set up a permanent national reviewing office. All this will cost money, much money perhaps, says the pope, but it is a question of saving souls and " the effectiveness of our schools, of our Catholic associations, and even of our churches is lessened and endangered by the plague of evil and pernicious motion pictures."

Once again the care of Pius XI for the quality of the work done appears in his insistence that the censors shall be " persons who are familiar with the technique of the motion picture and who are, at the same time, well grounded in the principles of Catholic morality and doctrine."

Such is the pope's plan for a great international organisation to check a world-wide evil and turn the force that is the occasion of it into an occasion of universal good.

(iv) The Social Order

Pius XI once publicly thanked God for the grace that he lives in an age of critical change. The pope's whole temperament is, in fact, to speak philosophically, cast for the irascible emotions. Action and attack are in his blood. Fortitude, that stimulates in the presence of fear and that tempers impetuosity before attack, is his characteristic virtue. He can afford to look events in the face, and to know all the facts, for it is his nature to be happiest when he is facing them. If the policy of Pius XI with regard to the social and economic disorder and distress that is the great mark of human society in our time be studied, all these characteristics stand out very clearly. The pope pushes his analysis to the very last refinement, he describes what he finds in the baldest of terms, only anxious that the find shall be described for what it is, and with ruthless candour he points out the weak spots in the organism he proposes to heal—and first of all in the Catholic body. Not since the popes of the Counter-reformation has anyone from that chair spoken so frankly of Catholic failings, for not since the Counter-reformation has the Church faced a peril so serious as that which now threatens, universally, to tear her children from her, namely, Atheistic Communism whose breeding ground is the centuries old injustice of rich to poor and the all but total indifference to this sin on the part of only too many ecclesiastics. But let us hear the pope.

The first document of the pontificate which deals specifically with any part of what we call the " Social Question " is the reply of one of the Roman Congregations to a query sent from Lille. This document is an answer intended to settle a dispute between Catholic employers of that district and their Catholic workmen, and in its spirit and direct language alike it is, as it were, a forecast of the coming masterpiece *Quadragesimo Anno*. This letter to the Bishop of Lille[1] should be read for its ordered statements, arranged as answers to the several questions, and for the long extracts from the documents of previous pontificates, with which the Sacred Congregation of the Council each time supports its findings, as well as for the main decision itself.

One very brief extract will serve to exemplify its firm

[1] *Lettre à S. G. Mgr. Achille Liénart, Evèque de Lille, au sujet du conflit, existant entre les employeurs et les employés dans la région*, 5 June, 1929. Translation published by Catholic Social Guild, Oxford, *Trade Unions and Employers' Associations—The Catholic View.*

tone. "Passing now to what concerns the industrialists of the *Consortium*,[1] the Sacred Congregation has learnt with a real pleasure all that the *Consortium* has done to relieve the wretchedness of the workpeople and also of the magnificent works of charity that it has organised already, especially by the development of " Family Allowances," a work of great charity as well as of social justice.

" However, since it is speaking to Catholics, the Sacred Congregation cannot but ask them to reflect that if peace is to be maintained between employers and their workmen, it is not enough to appeal to ' professional solidarity,' nor to multiply charitable organisations inspired by purely human philanthropy. True harmony and real peace can only be attained by *everyone* adhering to the luminous principles of Christian morality."

The pronouncement which, in name at any rate, is the best known of all Pius XI's writings—the encyclical letter *Quadragesimo Anno*[2]—was written to commemorate the fortieth anniversary of Leo XIII's letter *Rerum Novarum*. It is dated 15 May, 1931. Leo XIII's teaching, the new encyclical begins, still holds all its value and keeps all its binding force for Catholics and, indeed, because it is reasonable, for men generally. But there were always points in it about whose meaning Catholics were not agreed, and again, in the forty years since it appeared, conditions had changed in more than one way. The new encyclical developing Leo XIII's charter[3] brings the Church's teaching and direction up to date. Pius XI also takes the opportunity this anniversary affords to criticise the present economic system and to examine contemporary Socialism. Finally he suggests the lines along which alone a solution of these problems will be found.

The new social encyclical, like the letter to Cardinal

---

[1] The association of employers who put the query to the Congregation.

[2] " *On reconstructing the Social Order and perfecting it conformably to the precepts of the Gospel.*" Translation published by Catholic Truth Society, London, pp. 59, and N.C.W.C., Washington, D.C.

[3] " Leo's encyclical has proved itself the *Magna Carta* on which all Christian activities in social matters ought to be based." *Quadragesimo Anno*, section 39.

Liénart just quoted, begins with a strong affirmation of the pope's right, and therefore duty, to deal authoritatively with social and economic problems : not indeed with what relates to their technical side [1] (for here the Church has neither the mission nor, as the Church, the equipment to deal with them), but in whatever falls under the moral law. The economic system and moral science are two separate things it is true, and each in its own sphere is guided by its own principles. But the two orders are not so dissociated that economic life is altogether independent of morals. To deny this would be erroneous. [2]

Pius XI next recalls the teaching of his predecessor on the meaning of ownership, the obligations that go with it, the state's duties in relation to it. He expounds once again Leo XIII's doctrine about the relation of capital and labour in the production of wealth, and states the principles for a just distribution of wealth.

Leo XIII's aim was " the emancipation of the proletariat." The proletariat must become owners. Alas " these salutary injunctions [of Leo XIII] have not infrequently been forgotten, deliberately ignored or deemed impracticable, though they were both feasible and imperative." They have, however, " lost none of their power or wisdom for our own age . . . and unless serious attempts be made, with all energy and without delay, to put these ideas into practice, let nobody persuade himself that public order and the peace and tranquillity of human society can be effectively defended against the forces of revolution."

If the proletariat are to become owners, the first measure is a just wage for the proletarian. " The wage paid to the working man must be sufficient for the support of himself and of his family. . . . Every effort must be made, that fathers of families receive a wage sufficient adequately [3] to

---

[1] " non iis quidem, quæ artis sunt, ad quæ neque mediis aptis est instructa nec officio prædita."

[2] " Nam, etsi œconomica res et moralis disciplina in suo quæque ambitu suis utuntur principiis, error tamen est œconomicum ordinem et moralem ita dissitos ac inter se alienos dicere, ut ex hoc ille nulla ratione pendeat."

[3] " convenienter subveniat."

meet normal domestic needs. If under present circumstances this is not always feasible, social justice demands that
reforms be introduced without delay, which will guarantee
such a wage to every adult working man."

The pope does not fail to see and to remark that the
state of trade and the common good of all must be taken
into account in this complicated business of determining
this just wage. But the guiding spirit here should be one
of mutual understanding and Christian harmony between
employers and workers.

When we come to the question of reforms, the first
institution to attract a critical eye is the state itself. The
pope proceeds to an extremely interesting criticism of the
development of the state in the nineteenth century, and of
the effect of this on the social situation. The action of the
state in the past has destroyed the associations, organically
linked with one another, in which men once combined for
different good purposes. Now, too often, there is on the
one hand the state and on the other the mass of individual
men—a bad state of things. "Social life has entirely lost
its organic form ; the State, encumbered to-day with all the
burdens once borne by those associations now destroyed,
has been submerged by an infinity of occupations. . . ."
Let the state restore to the groups the settlement of less
important affairs and for these encourage the formation of
professional societies, made up of all those who are engaged
(in no matter what capacity) in the same trade or profession.
These corporate, professional societies, groups, or guilds
should enjoy a certain self-government in the matters for
which they are formed. Within the groups the predominant
interest will be the welfare of the group and along with
this the special influence which each particular group can
contribute to the general good of the state.

In this way, among other real benefits, there will disappear that opposition of "classes" which makes the
labour market, so-called, a very arena where hostile forces
fight. In place of that opposition there will be a collaboration of the various groups, each contributing to the

national welfare what each alone can give, and within the group there will be again collaboration of employer and workman for the common good of the group.

What then should be the guiding principle of economic life ? It cannot be free competition, still less an economic dictatorship. One thing only will suffice, the noble principles of social justice and social charity.

The pope now summons before him the social order as it actually exists and Socialism its bitterest accuser. What is his judgment ?

The first thing to strike the observer who looks at the world of to-day and compares it with that of 1891 is that nowadys it is no longer wealth alone that is accumulated, but immense power and the means to ensure a despotic control of economic life. This power and these means have accumulated in the hands of a few, " who for the most part are not the owners, but only the trustees and directors of the invested funds which they administer at their own good pleasure."

" This domination is most powerfully exercised by those who, because they hold and control money, also govern credit and determine its allotment, for that reason supplying so to speak, the life-blood to the entire economic body, and grasping in their hands, as it were, the very soul of production, so that no one can breathe against their will.

" This accumulation of power, the characteristic note of the modern economic order, is a natural result of limitless free competition," in which often only those survive "who fight most relentlessly, who pay least heed to the dictates of conscience."

" This concentration of power has, in its turn, led to a threefold struggle. First, there is the struggle for economic supremacy itself ; then the fierce battle to acquire control of the state, so that its resources and authority may be abused in economic struggles ; finally the clash between states themselves. . . . Unbridled ambition to dominate has succeeded the desire for gain ; the whole economic *régime* has become hard, cruel and relentless to a ghastly degree.

. . . The State, moreover, which should be the supreme arbiter, ruling in kingly fashion far above all party fights, has become instead a slave, bound over to the service of human passion and greed." There is the serious menace of economic nationalism or even economic imperialism, and the " no less noxious and detestable internationalism or international imperialism in financial affairs, which holds that where a man's fortune is, there is his country."

Socialism to-day still retains its anti-Christian basis. One section of it has degenerated into Communism, and the other is slowly moving away from Socialism properly so-called. It has, for example, abandoned the class war and no longer attacks private property as such. But, even so, there is often no repudiation of the basic socialistic idea ; merely a mitigation of it in practice. Catholics cannot do likewise and meet such Socialists half way.

" Socialism, if it really remains Socialism, cannot be brought into harmony with the doctrines of the Catholic Church . . . for it conceives human society in a way utterly alien to Christian truth . . . a doctrine of human society peculiarly its own, which is opposed to true Christianity. . . . No one can be at the same time a sincere Catholic and a Socialist properly so-called."

There are Catholics who have deserted to Socialism, and their excuse, often, is that " those professing attachment to the Church favour the rich, and neglect the workers and have no care for them " ; they were obliged therefore in their own interests to join the Socialist ranks.

It is certainly lamentable, says the candid pope, " that there have been, and that there are even now, some who, while professing themselves to be Catholics, are well-nigh unmindful of that sublime law of justice and charity which binds us not only to give each man his due, but to succour our needy brethren as Christ our Lord Himself,[1] worse still, we must lament that there are those who, out of greed for gain, do not fear to oppress the workers. Indeed there are some who even abuse religion itself, trying to cloak their

---

[1] Jas. ii.

own unjust impositions under its name, that they may protect themselves against the manifestly just protests of their employees.   We shall never desist from gravely censuring such conduct.   Such men are the cause that the Church, without deserving it, may have had the appearance and might be accused of taking sides with the wealthy, and of being unmoved by the needs and the sufferings of the disinherited."

The root of the whole trouble, of course, is the moral disorder in individual souls.   The ungovernable thirst for riches which to-day, " owing to the conditions of the economic world," has more victims than ever.   " For the uncertainty of economic life, and especially of the economic *régime*, demands the keenest uninterrupted straining of energy on the part of those engaged therein ; and as a result some have become so hardened against the stings of conscience as to hold all means good which enable them to increase their profits, and to safeguard against sudden changes of fortune the wealth they have amassed by great and assiduous efforts.   The easy returns, which an un-regulated market offers indiscriminately, attract to the buying and selling of goods very many whose one aim is to make rapid profits with the least labour.   By their unchecked dealings, prices are raised and lowered out of mere greed for gain so frequently as to frustrate the most prudent calculations of manufacturers.   The laws enacted for joint-stock companies with limited liability have given occasion to abominable abuses.   For responsibility thus weakened makes little impression, as is evident, upon the conscience : very serious injustices and frauds are perpetrated beneath the shelter of the company's name ; boards of directors, unmindful of their trust, betray the rights of those whose savings they administer.   Finally, We must not omit to mention those crafty men who, absolutely indifferent as to whether their trade provides anything really useful, do not hesitate to stimulate human desires, and, when these have been aroused, make use of them for their own profit."   The state should here have interfered, and vigorously, but the fallacies of economic liberalism held it back.

Such is the realist view of the present situation with which Pius XI begins his new appeal for the realisation of the ideals of the gospel in public life—an appeal that has never changed in its nature or in its insistency since its first publication in the opening letter *Ubi Arcano Dei*. Catholics must practise their religion in the whole of their lives, and that they may do so it must be preached to them, the whole of it, in season and out of season. Here might perhaps be inserted a passage, which Pius XI has himself once quoted with great effect,[1] from the letter of Benedict XV to the Bishop of Bergamo (11 March, 1920). " Let no member of the clergy suppose that activity of this kind is something foreign to his priestly ministry because the field in which it is exercised is economic. It is precisely in this field that the eternal salvation of souls is imperilled. Therefore it is Our will that priests consider it as one of their duties to give as much of their life as possible, to social science and social action, by study, observation and work. . . . "

One particular aspect of the present crisis has moved Pius XI very deeply, the misery of the vast army of the unemployed. To this he devoted a special encyclical [2] only a few months after the publication of *Quadragesimo Anno*. The pope here pleads for the " Immense numbers of honest workers . . . reduced to compulsory idleness and therefore to extreme destitution, which involves also their families." With real pathos he reminds the Church of " the starving little children . . . the joyousness peculiar to their age is seen to fade away, and the natural sounds of mirth, in which their awakening soul seeks an outlet, grow weak and die upon their tender lips."

The pope calls upon the bishops to launch a crusade of love and pity, to relieve this distress, and a crusade of prayer that God will shorten its time.

---

[1] In the letter to Cardinal Liénart, *cit. sup.*
[2] *Nova Impendet*, 2 October, 1931; translation, *On the Economic Crisis, Unemployment and Increase of Armaments*, Catholic Truth Society, London.

Linked with this immense distress is the rivalry among the nations and "the enormous squandering of public moneys" due to the competition in armaments. "We exhort you, brethren,"—it is to the Catholic bishops of the world the pope is speaking—"to strive by every means in your power, in the pulpit and in the Press, to enlighten men's minds and to shape their hearts in conformity with the sane dictates of reason and Christian law."

Six months later Pius XI took up the matter of the sufferings of the unemployed once again.[1] Their number steadily increases, subversive elements make use of the terrible fact and the peril of terrorism and anarchy hangs over society ever more ominously. Not since the flood itself, the pope exclaims, has there been such universal misery as mankind is now experiencing. Even that tiny minority "who appear to have in their hands, together with enormous wealth, the destinies of the world, who with their speculations were and are, in great part, the cause of so much woe," are among the victims. "By what things a man sinneth," the pope quotes, "by the same also he is tormented."[2]

The roots of the trouble are not hard to discover. Human greed, and an exaggerated love of country whose chief sign is hatred of every other country, explain it all. For the wretches who lie awaiting the hour to put an end to civilisation all this is most welcome. Atheism, spreading rapidly through all classes, and by all manner of means, organised and militant atheism, is preparing the way for the destroyers. It releases man from every duty of self-control and points to religion as the cause or the condition of all his woes. "*For* God or *against God*, this once more is the alternative that shall decide the destinies of all mankind," and universally "in politics, in finance, in morals, in the sciences and arts, in the State, in civil and domestic society,

[1] Encyclical *Caritate Christi Compulsi*, 3 May, 1932; translation, *The Troubles Our Time*, Catholic Truth Society, London, pp. 24.
[2] *Wisdom* xi, 17.

in the East and in the West, everywhere this question confronts us as the deciding factor because of the consequences that flow from it."

There lies upon us all the necessity of ever more fervent prayer and of generous penance. "Jesus began to preach and to say ' Do Penance '"[1] It was with these words that the gospel began.

This same sombre problem is the subject of the latest of all the pope's messages[2] to the Church, and here he resumes and, so to speak, codifies all that he and his predecessors, for ninety years now, have said about Communism, its errors and its dangers, the menace it is to religion and to civilisation itself. This lengthy document is not any mere vigorous denunciation, but a skilful examination of the whole subject. It is not an attack on Russia, nor indeed on all Russians who are Communists. Pius XI is " well aware that not a few of them groan beneath the yoke imposed on them by men who, in very large part, are strangers to the real interests of their country." He " recognises that many others were deceived by fallacious hope. We blame only the system, with its authors and abettors. . . . " Again, realistically, the pope does not ignore the fact that " in Russia [Communism] has been a contributing factor in rousing men and national forces from the inertia of centuries."

But the social doctrine of Communism is false, deriving from the erroneous materialism of Marx. Its rapid spread is due to the promise it offers of a happier and a fuller life, to its proclaimed determination to end the abuses chargeable to the Liberal economic order, and to its programme of a more equitable distribution of the good things of this world. Its success is natural among a working class whom Liberalism had degraded and despoiled. Its propaganda is remarkably well organised and it has been very largely helped by the " conspiracy of silence on the part

[1] Matt. iv. 17.
[2] Encyclical Letter *Divini Redemptoris*, 19 March, 1937; translation, *On Atheistic Communism*, Catholic Truth Society, London, pp. 52, and N.C.W.C., Washington, D.C.

of a large section of the non-Catholic press of the world." [1]

Everywhere the story of the triumph of Communism is the same, murder, massacre, desolation, famine and a new slavery for the generality of the people, all in a spirit of hatred and barbarity one would not have believed possible in our own age. "No man of good sense nor any states-man conscious of his responsibility can fail to shudder at the thought that what is happening in Spain to-day may perhaps to-morrow be repeated in other civilised countries."

The pope sets out against all this the Catholic doctrine and ideal of human society, and then turns to suggest a constructive programme. It is the familiar reminder of the need for greater loyalty to duty in the life of every day. How far Catholics are from achieving that Catholic ideal ! "Even in Catholic countries [2] there are still too many who are Catholics hardly more than in name. There are too many who fulfil, more or less faithfully, the more essential obligations of the religion they boast is theirs, but who have no desire to know it better, to deepen their inward conviction . . . this is that empty pharisaic show that our divine Saviour so detested. . . . It is the Catholic of this type who exposes to ridicule the very name of Christian."

The rich must remember they are but stewards of their wealth. Hell awaits them if they misuse it. The poor should strive to remain poor in spirit, while they endeavour, legitimately, to better their actual condition.

Charity, the solution of much of the present misery, cannot function unless due regard is had to justice. "A 'charity' which deprives the working man of the wages due to him is not charity at all, but only its empty name

[1] "We say conspiracy," the pope continues, "because it is impossible otherwise to explain how a press usually so eager to exploit even the little daily incidents of life has been able to remain silent for so long about the horrors perpetrated in Russia, in Mexico and even in a great part of Spain ; and that it should have relatively so little to say about a world-organisation as vast as Russian com-munism."

[2] Cf. another striking instance of like pontifical candour : "That blot on the Catholic nations, namely, their ignorance of the divine religion." Motu Proprio Orbem Catholicum, 29 June, 1923.

and hollow semblance. The wage-earner is not to receive as alms what is his due in justice. Let no one attempt with trifling charitable donations to exempt himself from the great duties imposed by justice." These are stern words indeed, directed by anxiety for the salvation of those pious pharisees who will suffer everything for religion's sake but who boggle at the just demands of their servants and work-people. Pius XI is not ignorant of the infinity of harm which this particular scandal brings about, the disrepute into which religion falls, the ready argument for the Communist supplied by the spectacle of the Catholic employer, " a diligent partaker of all holy duties " at the week-end and a sweater during the rest of the week ; " externally faithful to the practice of their religion," says Pius XI of these, " yet in the field of labour and industry in the professions, trade and public offices they permit a deplorable cleavage in their conscience, and live a life too little in conformity with the clear principles of justice and Christian charity."

" It is unfortunately true," he says to the Catholic employer and industrialist, " that the manner of acting in certain Catholic circles has done much to shake the faith of the working classes in the religion of Jesus Christ. These groups have refused to understand that Christian charity demands the recognition of the working man's *rights* in certain matters." In the *Quadragesimo Anno* Pius XI recalled that Leo XIII's " noble and exalted teaching, quite novel to worldly ears, was looked upon with suspicion . . . even amongst Catholics." Eight years later he has to make the serious complaint, in his public letter, that his own message has been suppressed by some of his flock. " What is to be thought of those Catholic employers who in one place succeeded in preventing the reading of Our encyclical *Quadragesimo Anno* in their local churches ? Or of those Catholic industrialists who even to this day have shown themselves hostile to a labour movement that We ourselves have recommended ? Is it not deplorable that the right of private property defended by the Church should so often have been abused to defraud the working man of his wages and his social rights ? "

One of the most pressing needs, if the situation is to be saved, is for the reform of Catholic life in this respect and therefore, first of all, for the more frequent preaching of the Church's doctrine of social justice. To this " every other enterprise, however attractive and helpful, must yield." The priest must show himself the friend and the defender of the working masses, and live a life that is humble, poor and disinterested. Propaganda on a large scale must be the work of Catholic Action.

CHAPTER XIII

(i) France

THE relations of the Holy See with the French Republic at the election of Pius XI, might be counted among the more hopeful features of the world situation of the Catholic Church. After an interval of nearly sixteen years, there was once more a French ambassador at the Vatican and a papal nuncio at Paris. Also, although there was no movement to renew the concordat which the French government had years before repudiated, a plan was under consideration that would end the anomalous legal situation in which the Church in France had been placed by the Separation Law of 1905.

From the moment of that law the French government ceased to recognise or support any form of worship, and the whole property of the Church in France—which as a Church no longer existed in the eyes of the law—was considered henceforth as under the control of a network of committees known as *Associations Cultuelles*—societies for worship. All the Church's capital was to go to the state and the revenue from it would for the future be administered by these committees who would be the owners of all the buildings—churches, schools, seminaries, presbyteries—and other properties. There was no provision that the Church would have any say whatever in the constitution of the committees—in the eyes of the State the Church no longer existed. French Catholicism would henceforth have two sets of masters—the bishops ruling by divine right and the *Associations Cultuelles*, and these new committees would reign supreme, the civil power being, by law, the final arbiter of all differences between them and the ecclesiastical authorities. In two famous encyclical letters [1] the reigning pope, Pius X, condemned the Separation Law and the whole new system and forbade the Catholics of France to have anything to do with it. Rather than consent to a system which put the whole life of the Church at the absolute discretion of a fanatically hostile anti-religious government, the Catholics of France gave up everything—churches, schools, seminaries, the priests' houses, a property worth in all something like £3,000,000 a year of present value. From January 1907 Catholic worship in the parish churches of France continued on a basis of mere toleration and without any legal title.

Was there no means by which the system of *Associations* could be made acceptable? One only, recognition in the system of the divinely founded authority of the Catholic bishop over his own diocese. But to ask this, at the time, was tantamount to asking for the repeal of the law. Compromises which fell short of this essential were discussed, and at length, but the pope held firm. There must be explicit recognition of the Catholic system, for in such recognition alone could security for the future be found.

The years went by. The Catholics of France performed prodigies of generosity and self-sacrifice to make good the losses of 1906. Then came the war, and with it a new unity in France that lessened the power of the masonic bloc. Too many priests lost their lives in battle, too many exiled monks and friars returned to share in the nation's agony for the legend of " Clericalism our great enemy " to survive. By the time that Benedict XV canonised Jeanne D'Arc in 1920 the spirit in which France was being ruled was very different from that which had prevailed for the twenty years before the war. The renewal of diplomatic relations was one sign of this, and the appearance of a really workable scheme of *Associations* was a second—a scheme that would satisfy the Church's rights no less than the principle of separation to which the French government still clung.

[1] *Vehementer*, 11 February, 1906; *Gravissimo*, 10 August, 1906.

It was characteristic of Pius XI's sense of responsibility, his patience and his unwavering perseverance before the prospect of immense personal drudgery, that although when his predecessor died the scheme was ready for signature, he set himself, before approving it, to study the whole vast problem from its very beginnings. It was the nuncio to Poland all over again. The scheme as finally determined is set forth in an annex to the encyclical *Maximam Gravissimamque* [1] which explains the principles on which it is based and the relation of what is now approved and recommended to what, in 1906, Pius X had been obliged to condemn.

The Holy See has not changed its views about the iniquity of the Separation Law, nor modified the language in which it describes it. Pius XI recalls, approves, and makes his own the principles upon which Pius X had condemned the *Associations Cultuelles*—they constituted a denial in practice of the divine constitution of the Church and the unchangeable rights of the Holy See and the bishops. The magnificent work of French Catholicism during the intervening years is praised as it merited to be praised. The new spirit which, since 1914, has animated the French nation is gratefully acknowledged. The lack of any legal status or stability from which Catholicism in France suffers is, none the less, a most serious hindrance, and now that public opinion is so much more favourable, and the circumstances of the time as well as the relations between the Holy See and the Republic so profoundly changed, it seems possible to consider—not whether the *Associations* once condemned can now be acceptable, but whether a new kind of *Association* altogether will not work. The new *Associations—Associations Diocesaines* is their title—offer guarantees that are legal and secure in the sense demanded by Pius X. They have the unanimous approval of the highest legal authority in France in such matters, the Conseil d'Etat. The pope therefore allows Catholics to make use of them, and without formally commending their adoption, appeals very strongly for it.

[1] 18 January, 1924.

The statutes of the new *Associations Diocesaines* only need to be read for the difference between them and what Pius X condemned to be evident. The president of each *Association* is the bishop of the diocese. Its executive committee of four is elected by the Council of the *Association* from a list of eight names proposed by the bishop, and of the four one must be a vicar-general, and another a canon of the Cathedral Chapter. Furthermore, it is distinctly provided that the functions of the *Association* shall be strictly confined to temporal administration. The spiritual side of Catholic life—church-services, sermons, nominations of clergy—they in no way touch. The Church in France is once more acknowledged by the state to be mistress in her own domain. It seems a small thing to ask, and an elementary condition of normal life, but until twenty years ago it was an altogether exceptional state of affairs, and this throughout the world. The liberation of Catholic life from the dead hand of the Catholic state—or more truly from the hand of the long dead Catholic absolutist states—has been one of the greatest achievements of Pius XI's pontificate. It is an achievement whose blessing has touched France too.

The date of the encyclical *Maximam* is January 1924. Within a couple of years there began in France, within the Catholic body itself, a disturbance that was to continue, violently, for five or six years. This was the reaction of the partisans of the *Action Française* to the papal condemnation of certain features of that movement and of the writings of its leader, Charles Maurras. It is a long story, easy to find for those who are interested,[1] too long to tell here even in summary, but of which something must be said since it illustrates the unity of Pius XI's action in the Universal Church, his initial patience in all he undertakes, his final firmness.

L'Action Française is the name of a movement whose aim is the restoration of the monarchy in France in the person

[1] *Cf.*, for a very readable account, DENIS GWYNN, *The Condemnation of the Action Française*.

of the head of the House of Orleans. It is also the name of the daily newspaper which is the movement's best-known organ of propaganda. Charles Maurras, the prophet of the movement, is one of the most powerful writers of contemporary France. To this movement very many Catholics, laymen, priests and even bishops had belonged. It seemed to promise the creation of a new France, and a national reorganisation, of which Catholics, or the Catholic Church as organised in France, would be the soul. The anomalous feature of this otherwise happy state of things was that Charles Maurras was not a Catholic. He was a professed infidel, and his writings—like the writings of more than one of his collaborators—were not merely deserving of censure, but a real danger, by Catholic standards, to the moral life of his readers. It was a queer leadership for the coming Catholic renaissance, and yet so violent and powerful a critic was Maurras of the republican anti-clericalism, so strong a defender—on natural grounds—of Catholic orthodoxy against Modernism, and of the policies of the Holy See, that his Catholic followers bore with his moral aberrations, treating them as individual aberrations merely, that did not spoil the good he wrought, for which he was not so answerable as a Catholic would have been, and meanwhile they prayed for his conversion.

Pius XI has condemned the *Action Française*, forbidden Catholics to belong to it, to read the works of its leaders or its daily newspaper. His action produced such a storm of opposition, of violent denunciation of himself and of his right to intervene in the matter, and such a display of cunning subterfuge to evade the prohibitions, as to reveal how serious indeed the matter was and how far the mischief had gone with a great number of Catholics in France, and of French ecclesiastics not least.

Why did Pius XI condemn the *Action Française* ? How did the condemnation come about ? [1] The handiest summary answer to the first of these questions is the Pastoral

---

[1] *Cf.* FONTENELLE, *Pie XI*, pp. 185–202, for a lucid, candid, dispassionate account, with quotations from the principal documents.

Letter of the late Bishop of Nice, Mgr. Ricard. "Why has the pope condemned the *Action Française* ?" he asks, and replies, "Because the *Action Française* is a school whose creator, teacher and leader, M. Charles Maurras, aims at a reconstruction of the state—of the organism that is to say which sets up and keeps in being the social order—on principles contrary to Christian principles. He has never set out these principles in a systematic treatise. They are to be found scattered through his various works, not expressed in the form of definite theses, but in language that is poetic, highly imaginative and, occasionally, lit up by phrases that flash like lightning. When linked together in their logical relation these principles form a veritable ' system of religion, morality, and social order ' that is definitely anti-Christian.

"Because, masked by the ambiguous description of ' school of politics ' in which his followers can perhaps see no more than a party that aims at the restoration of the monarchy, the leader's object is, in reality, to fashion after his own mind and train in his own methods disciples who, grouped in leagues, will diffuse, defend and give concrete form to a political scheme far wider than this, a scheme which in its main lines, and its details too, derives from his own naturalistic—materialist—conception of man, of society, of religion, of the state.

"Because the teacher of this school, in order to fire the minds of his partisans and to give force to their certainty, sets forth his theories anew in a popular newspaper, insinuating them in the articles in which, day by day, he is occupied with a critical or philosophical commentary on the events of the political world. So he manages to distil them into the midst of those young people, of both sexes, who attracted by the conclusions of monarchist or patriotic theories of politics, are without means to resist the philosophical spirit in which these conclusions have their being.

"Because these disciples, these partisans, these readers and sympathisers are, in large measure, recruited from amongst Catholics and ecclesiastics, and to these the pope has the right and the duty of pointing out to what ultimate goal their leader, an unbeliever and an atheist, is leading them now he has drugged them with his own spirit and worked on them with his sophistry.

"Because, in the state as Charles Maurras would refashion it, the Church, while it might be free to lay down the rules of individual conduct, would find itself stripped of any right to control the social order. This last, it is claimed, is ruled by laws that are fixed, laws collected and defined in a kind of ' moral physics.' Thus the Church of which the *Action Française* dreams is a Church from which the Gospel has been emptied out, and Maurras, if his desires were realised, would have succeeded in ' dechristianising Catholicism '."

The pope has not condemned the political movement that looks for a restoration of the monarchy as the salvation of France. That question he has left aside. "La-dessus, l'Eglise laisse à chacun la juste liberté," he wrote to the Archbishop of Bordeaux in the very first letter in which he dealt with the matter.[1] But to follow blindly the directions of the chiefs of the *Action Française* in matters of faith and morals is quite another thing.

The history of the condemnation of the *Action Française* begins with the reign of Pius X (1903–1914). Its leaders had, even then, many opponents and critics in the episcopate who divined the ultimate tendency of the movement and, finally, delated the matter to the Holy Office. The theological experts of this congregation, on 15 January, 1914, unanimously voted for the condemnation, as really bad books, of four works by Maurras. Eleven days later the cardinals of the Holy Office condemned the books and the *Action Française* too (it was at that time a review). They left to the pope the decision when to publish the decree. Pius X, on whom pressure had been brought to bear—as he told the cardinals when giving them leave to proceed— in order that the matter might go no further, confirmed the condemnation and, although he did not order its immediate

[1] Letter to Cardinal Andrieu *Nous avons lu* of 5 September, 1926.

publication, ordered that when published it should bear the date 29 January, 1914.

Pius X died seven months later, before publishing the decree. When the matter came before his successor, Benedict XV, in January 1915, he considered that to publish the condemnation of so prominent a Frenchman, an ultra-patriot, in those early months of the war, would be to court certain misunderstanding and to invite only mis-representation. The papers were once more laid aside.

When Pius XI succeeded Pope Benedict, the question was brought up once again whether or not the chiefs of the *Action Française* should be condemned. Since the last discussion in 1915 a reorganisation of the Roman Curia had incorporated the Congregation of the Index with that of the Holy Office. There had been a great transfer of archives and—this was no doubt the cause—all the docu-ments relating to Pius X's condemnation had disappeared. Pius XI set himself to study the question anew. By the autumn of 1926 his decision was taken, and in the letter to the Archbishop of Bordeaux from which we have quoted,[1] he gave his first, firm, clear, but kindly-worded warning about this " new religious, moral and social system " that had something different to say about " God, the Incarna-tion, the Church and Catholic dogma and morals generally, especially in their relation to politics. . . . " The pope noted " the traces of a renaissance of paganism, to which indeed the naturalism that these writers have drunk in— unconsciously We believe—is attached ; a naturalism," he adds, " that like many of their contemporaries, they have absorbed from the public teaching of that poisonous modern ‘ lay ’ school that they have themselves often fought so vigorously."

All through the autumn of 1926 the fury continued in France. The pope made a memorable speech to the French seminarists in Rome and a last appeal in the Consistorial Allocution of 20 December. In January 1927 the formal condemnation was published. By a happy coincidence, on

[1] *Nous avons lu*, 5 September, 1926.

the eve almost of this condemnation the missing documents were found, and Pius XI was able to rout once and for all the disloyal Catholics who claimed the patronage of Pius X for their endeavour to be at the same time followers of Maurras and good Catholics too. " Nous avons fini," Pius XI was able to say, " là où Pie X a commencé." [1]

(ii) Mexico

With Russia and Spain this American republic forms what Pius XI has called " the terrible triangle " of his reign, the three states where a definite attempt has been made to root out Catholicism in the interests of an atheistic philosophy of life.

Mexico is a land where, for the best part of a century, the work of the Catholic Church has been restricted in every sense and the exercise of religion harassed by a world of vexatious regulations. In all that time the country has been the victim of one rascally set of politicians after another and behind the various politicians there have been, in more recent times, the wealthy foreign commercial corporations anxious for monopolies in the exploitation of the natural wealth of these vast territories.

The Constitution of 1857 stripped the Church of all its property and exactly sixty years later the Constitution of Queretaro beggared it once again. It was this last Constitution of 1917 that also provided that any ecclesiastic who violated the new anti-religious laws should be tried without a jury. There were years of real persecution following the revolution of 1914, when churches were destroyed, priests murdered, and nuns outraged. Then in 1924 the Nero of the Mexican Church was elected president, Plutarco Elias Calles, and with the aid of a group of likeminded masonic fanatics he inaugurated a renewal of the persecution.

Pius XI's first reference to Mexico is in the Allocution of 14 December, 1925. He has been speaking of the separation of Church and State in Chili, which, though he

---

[1] Letter to Cardinal Andrieu *C'est de tout cœur*, 5 January, 1927.

cannot but condemn the principles which have produced it, has yet been carried out in so friendly a spirit that it has produced " a friendly union rather than a separation." In Mexico, however, things are much worse and are really a source of anxiety. Despite the remarkable patience and fortitude of the bishops, the clergy, and the faithful generally, there seems no hope of better times unless through some special act of God's mercy.

Two months later [1] appeared the letter *Paterna Sane Sollicitudo* to the bishops of Mexico. After a silence of two years—a deliberate silence lest he seem to invite further trouble—the pope protests against the treacherous expulsion of the Delegate Apostolic. He protests too, that the Mexican government is doing all in its power to assist the schismatic " national church " while penalising Catholicism, and he praises highly the magnificent loyalty to the faith of the great mass of the population. In the matter of practical advice and direction the pope is very definite. He calls for a great increase of Catholic Action, but not in political matters. The bishops, the clergy and all Catholic organisations must steer clear of party politics of any kind, and this especially lest they give the enemy any pretext to identify Catholicism with particular factions.

There must then be no attempt to organise a Catholic political party, and though Catholics are by no means forbidden to use their rights as citizens and take what part they think good in political life, the clergy must continue in their present praiseworthy abstinence from all intervention in political matters. They must ceaselessly endeavour, by word and by example, to make good loyal citizens of their people, and assist the welfare of Mexico by organised effort in what relates to the religious, moral, intellectual and economic life of the country.

Calles' instrument was the infamous Constitution of 1917. By its provisions the Church was deprived of all civil rights, and even in what related to worship and ecclesiastical discipline it was subjected to state regulation. Privileges

[1] 2 February, 1926.

for the clerical status there were, of course, none. All priests had to be Mexican by birth, the number of priests per state was strictly limited and, upon ordination, they lost all civil and political rights. Nor could they enter on their functions without sanction of the local magistrate. Vows of religion and religious orders were strictly forbidden. Mass could only be said in public churches and even then it was under the surveillance of the police. Churches, schools, seminaries, the residences of the clergy were all of them confiscated. Priests could not inherit except from their nearest kin, nor could any priests or religious teach in any school. Religious instruction was forbidden even in the infant schools.

Calles, by the new law of July 1926, heaped additional penalties and burdens on the Church, and a skilful propaganda of anti-religious calumny, by means of subsidised lectures and the press, warned the Catholics of new troubles yet to come. All non-Mexican priests were now banished. Every school in which religious instruction was given, or where so much as a statue or religious picture showed, was closed. The number of authorised priests was cut down ruthlessly, to a total of about 4,000 (and this for a population of something like 17,000,000 Catholics, spread over an area fifteen times that of England and Wales).[1] Even these few priests only officiated at the goodwill of the local government officials. Impossible and ridiculous conditions were sometimes attached to the permit, e.g., that the priest should be civilly married, that he should only baptise with running water. In some of the states only one bishop was allowed for the whole state. All the teachers of Mexico were summoned to declare explicitly that they were heart and soul with the government in this campaign. Those who refused lost their places. Everywhere Catholics stood firm and everywhere the prisons began to fill with these real confessors for the faith. " Whole chapters of canons, old men amongst them who had to be transported in their beds, were haled to prison. Priests and laymen,

---

[1] The number of priests in England and Wales (1937) is something over 5,000.

too, were pitilessly slain, at the cross-roads, in the public squares, before their very churches." [1]

And thanks to " a conspiracy of silence " [2] in the leading newspapers of the world all these iniquities were hushed up and hidden away.

It was partly to break through this silence, and to proclaim to the whole Church throughout the world the heroism of these faithful Mexican Catholics that Pius XI wrote the great letter *On the most bitter state of the Catholic Church in Mexico*.[1] It is a remarkably concise and moderately worded account of the whole persecution, and the pope is careful nowhere to give the tyrannical power the shadow of an excuse, in the language he uses, further to afflict the unfortunate Mexican Catholics. For the Catholics themselves he cannot find words sufficient to praise their patient heroism, and the thought of all those young people who have cheerfully gone to their death, rosaries in hand, to cry " Long live Christ the King " [3] as the rifles went off, moves him to tears.

At the December Consistory that same year, 1926, the pope denounced to the indignation of civilised humanity everywhere the craft, treachery and black savagery of these inhuman devils who held Mexico in their grip, who murdered the youth who stood firmly to Christ and raping the girls in the prisons published what had been done to terrorise the rest.

Slowly, in the next two years, the fury of the persecution slackened, and died down, and a " Modus Vivendi " was patched together. The " peace " did not last. The state renewed the old tactics of reducing the number of " authorised " priests until presently there was allowed in Michoacan one priest only for every 45,000 Catholics, the same in Chiapas, and in Vera Cruz one for every 100,000. And once again the persecution took up in all its old rigour.

[1] Encyclical Letter *Iniquis Afflictisque*, 18 November, 1926.
[2] The words of Pius XI, *cf.* p. 280, note 1, *sup.*
[3] *Cf.* for the story of one of the best known of these martyrs, *God's Jester*, by Mrs. George Norman, or an admirable sketch, *Fr. Miguel Pro, S.J.*, by John Rimmer, S.J., Catholic Truth Society, London, pp. 40.

Once again Pius XI intervened with a public letter, to advertise to Catholics everywhere the sufferings of their fellows in Mexico, and to obtain prayers for them, to denounce to the world this latest evidence, of the cruelty of militant atheism and to advise the Catholics of Mexico on the important matter of their own attitude to the persecution. Not a few Mexicans would have liked to see a Holy War initiated, to have risen in arms in an attempt to overthrow the *régime*, to have attempted a "Catholic revolution." To determine this last grave matter was one of Pius XI's chief anxieties in the letter *Acerba Nimis*.[1]

The laws are, undoubtedly, wicked laws, that letter declares, but it is not co-operation in wickedness, if as the laws require, permission to administer the sacraments is sought from the government's agents. Catholics are not bound in conscience to refrain from asking such a permission. No one can interpret their asking as a formal approval of the law on the part of the Church, considering the constant protests of the Holy See against the law. Priests must use every means available to them to administer the sacraments, and the bishops must see that such explanations are given to the faithful as will prevent the scandal that in this matter, ignorance can so easily cause. Catholics must here allow the Holy See to be judge of what is lawful and loyally follow its decision.

The reign of Calles came to an end in 1934. Under his successor, Cardenas, the persecution has changed its form. It is less violent. But the confiscation of Church property continues and the policy of restricting the number of authorised priests has been pushed to the point that in March 1936 there were but 293 allowed in all Mexico. By December last this had dropped to 197. Meanwhile a new education law, of 6 January, 1934, has instituted in all the schools a course of lessons in atheism together with a particularly repulsive system of sexual instruction.

The latest action of the pope is the letter of Easter

[1] 29 September, 1932.

Sunday last to the Mexican bishops, *Nos es Muy*.[1] The letter is taken up with detailed, constructive advice. Pius XI, looking to the future of Catholicism in Mexico, makes a special application to its particular case of the general principles that are the burden of all his teaching. He asks, first, for a greater holiness of life in the clergy, and recommends the closest study of his own encyclical *Ad Catholici Sacerdotii*. The aid of the laity is hardly less necessary, " it would be very difficult to reconquer for Christ so many misguided souls without the providential assistance which the laity give by means of Catholic Action. . . . It is true that not all understand fully the necessity of this holy apostolate of the laity . . . " but " wisdom and care in their formation " are only second in importance to care for the clergy themselves. There is an immense task before Catholic Action, but the bishops must not " be preoccupied more with the numbers than with the quality of the collaborators. . . . " They " should care first of all for the supernatural formation of leaders and propagandists " and not be grieved because at the beginning they are but a " little flock." [2]

As to the means " Publicity and the method of the circus have no place in it. It looks upon noisy methods as an enemy." Four classes of men need especially all the aid that Catholicism can give, namely, the labourers, the millions of Indians, the Mexican emigrants (especially those in the United States), and the students. For these last the pope insists that " to the practice of the Christian religion, to the formation of character and the Christian conscience, which are fundamental elements for all the faithful, you must associate a special and correct education and intellectual preparation, supported by Christian philosophy—that is, that philosophy which was truthfully called *philosophia perennis*."

With regard to the wicked laws that oppress Catholics

---

[1] 28 March, 1937 ; *On the Religious Situation in Mexico* ; translation published by the N.C.W.C., Washington, D.C.

[2] Luke xii. 32.

and to the means of remedying them, Pius XI pleads for an increasing interest in all that belongs to the national life, the training of every Catholic to be an informed and enthusiastic citizen. As to any protest in arms the pope repeats the general principles which have always determined the morality of such action. Insurrection is a means, not an end. As a means there must never be about it what makes it intrinsically evil. Again, there must be proportion between the means and the end it is hoped to attain. The damage done must not be greater than the damage it is hoped to repair. Such methods, however lawful they may be in certain conditions, can never form part of Catholic Action, nor be the task of the clergy. Why? Because although Catholic Action and the clergy may train Catholics to know what their rights and duties are and to make a just use of their rights, for the common good, the actual use of the rights brings in problems of a material and technical nature.

Finally, the pope appeals most strongly for an ever greater loyalty of Catholics to their bishops. " We conjure the good Mexican Catholics to hold Obedience and Discipline dear," and he quotes as the rule for their conduct the words of St. Paul " which ought to be the fundamental norm of all those who work in Catholic Action "—" I, therefore, a prisoner in the Lord, beseech you that you walk worthy . . . with all humility and mildness, with patience, supporting one another in charity, careful to keep the unity of the Spirit in the bond of peace, one body and one Spirit." [1]

(iii) Germany

The present crisis in the affairs of the Catholic Church in Germany goes back a little more than four years. Already, before Hitler's appointment as Chancellor—30 January, 1933—there were Catholics who viewed with misgiving the theories and the methods of the movement he led. Pastoral letters from different bishops had already criticised both and condemned them. At the general election of

[1] Eph. iv. 1–4.

February 1933 the Nazi party won 322 seats " and from this point all pretence of respect for legality and constitutional form vanished. Jews, Social Democrats and Communists were, in effect, outlawed. Large numbers of them were driven from their homes, confined in concentration camps or subjected to great physical brutality." [1]

With regard to Catholicism—and to German Protestantism also—the Führer had already declared that he saw in these religions great national assets, bulwarks of the nation's moral life, and, more particularly, that good relations with the Holy See were a necessity for the Reich. Nevertheless, the different Catholic associations did not escape the brutal pressure of the now all-powerful Nazi clubs, the Catholic Trades Unions were " absorbed " into the Nazi unions, the Centre Party made its submission, here and there priests were arrested, maltreated. And Catholic anxiety grew as to the compatibility with Catholicism of the totalitarian doctrine, now advertised more and more as the touchstone of loyalty and patriotism.

It was in these circumstances that the concordat with the Reich was signed on 19 July, 1933. The details of that agreement have been summarised already. Did the Nazi government but keep to its pledged word, Catholicism in Germany would have little to fear from the future. The Hitler press, however, soon betrayed the spirit in which its leaders had negotiated. The concordat, it was explained, was a capitulation to Germany on the part of the Holy See, a victory for the Nazi. A bitter controversy began in the *Osservatore Romano*, and a new anxiety among Catholics as to the spirit in which the concordat would be applied. Pius XI speaking to a great pilgrimage of German Youth, did not hide his anxiety, " We are by temperament and by choice optimist," he said, " the future is in the hands of God ; We must then hope, but our hope cannot hide the danger from us."

Meanwhile, there began to spread in a quasi-official, and even in an official way, those theories as to the purity of

[1] CARR, p. 197.

blood as the basis of German racial superiority, and the theories that nothing is of any real good to German humanity that is not itself wholly German. Whence a purge of all the inhabitants of " mixed " blood, the sterilisa-tion law, and the open advocacy of a restoration of German paganism as the national religion, the attempt to " Ger-manise " Protestantism and the wholesale attacks on the Hebrew elements in Christianity. With what courage the clergy, Protestant and Catholic, are resisting, and have replied to, this lunacy is well known, and well known, too, the price of that resistance. In the Christmas Allocution of December 1934, Pius XI spoke of the folly of recent attempts to make Law and Justice depend on particular types of national or racial law. He contrasted this con-ception with the superhuman creation of Christian Law,[1] and he referred with anxiety to the new moral, social and even state paganism now in process of construction before the eyes of the world.

The attack on Christians continued. There was an attempt to murder the Archbishop of Munich, clergy were arrested on all manner of pretexts, Catholic societies were broken up, magazines suppressed and Catholic Action declared to be incompatible with National Socialism. Everywhere pressure was brought to bear on Catholics to surrender their schools, and in Bavaria the Catholic Training Colleges were suppressed.

Hitler's chief adviser in matters educational—Alfred Rosenberg—set out the new gospel of race and blood and the duty of total subjection to the state ; and his book was put on the Index, with a detailed statement of the errors it contained. When on Whit-Sunday, 1934, the pope canonised the German Franciscan, Conrad of Parzham, he spoke of the tragic hour in which God had chosen to illuminate this great personage, an hour when we could see homage paid to thoughts, ideas and practices that were not Christian nor

[1] This very year had seen in Rome, under the pope's patronage, a great inter-national congress of lawyers to celebrate the fourteenth centenary of Justinian's great reform of the Civil Law and the seventh centenary of the publication of the Decretals of Gregory IX which are the foundation of the Canon Law.

even human, and an exaltation of race which could only produce a monstrous pride, the very antithesis of the Christian spirit, and even of the spirit of humanity itself.

The most serious measure of all—more harmful than the much advertised trials of priests and religious for transferring their property to safer lodging abroad, or for alleged immoralities—was the law of 1 December, 1936, by which the state takes possession of all young people to form them for the service of the state. "All German young people," runs the text of article 2 of the law, " shall be educated—apart from [education in] the family and the school—in the Hitler Youth, educated physically, spiritually and morally, in the spirit of National Socialism, for the service of the people and the commonwealth." At the head of this Hitler Youth is one of the leaders of the neo-pagan renaissance, Baldur von Schirach.

The German bishops have protested in a joint pastoral against these many breaches of the concordat, and have protested too against the attacks on Catholicism, and indeed on religion generally, made so continuously by responsible ministers of the government. "After Bolshevism, public enemy No. 1, it will be the turn of Catholicism, public enemy No. 2," was one such declaration.

The latest papal action is the encyclical of Passion Sunday last,[1] a letter written in German first, and addressed not only to the German bishops but to the Catholic episcopate throughout the world. This letter—which by the concordat the pope was free to send and the priests to read to their people—had to be smuggled into Germany. It was not actually delivered to the priests until the early morning of the day on which it had to be read.

"Mit brennender Sorge—With deep anxiety and increasing dismay We have for some time past beheld the sufferings of the Church " in Germany. The story of the concordat is told and how the pope " in spite of serious

---

[1] Mit brennender Sorge, 14 March, 1937 ; translation, On the Condition of the Church in Germany, pp. 36, published by Catholic Truth Society, London ; and N.C.W.C., Washington, D.C.

misgivings at the time" consented to negotiate. The events of the years since then "make it clear where the responsibility lies" for the present conflict, and "disclose machinations that from the beginning had no other aim than a war of extermination." Every trick, every artifice has been used to evade the concordat, to empty it of all meaning.

The object of this letter is not to denounce the treachery of the Nazi *régime*, but to instruct and comfort the Catholics who are suffering under its oppression. Pius XI deals, point by point, with the different Nazi aberrations in the field of doctrine, and warns his people against them, the pantheistic idea that equates God with the universe, the substitution of a weird impersonal fate for a personal God, the exaltation of race, the people and the state, or the ruler, to be the standard by which everything else—religion too —must be valued, the use of God's name as a meaningless label for a more or less capricious form of human yearning. God is God and to His law the highest of mankind is as subject as the lowest. "Only superficial minds can . . . make the mad attempt to confine within the boundaries of a single people, within the narrow blood stream of a single race, God the Creator of the world, the King and the Lawgiver of all peoples before whose greatness all people 'are as a drop of a bucket'" (Isa. xl. 15).

There is like timely correction of the fashionable errors about Jesus Christ, an exposition of the nature of the Catholic Church and of its divine mission. There is, as so often in the letters of Pius XI, an insistence that "It is not enough to be counted a member of the Church of Christ. One must be also a living member of this Church—in spirit and in truth. And only they are such, who are in the grace of the Lord and ever walk in His presence—in innocence or in sincere and efficacious penance." So must all Catholics, in the present hour, be careful to show themselves. As for the reforms of which, now as in every age, Catholic life stands in need, "In the final analysis every true and lasting reform has proceeded from the sanctuary, from men who were inflamed and driven by love of God and their neighbour."

There can be no lasting belief in God if it is not supported by belief in Christ, no lasting belief in Christ if it is not supported by belief in the Church, and "belief in the Church will not be kept pure and genuine if it is not supported by belief in the primacy of the Bishop of Rome."

The Bishop of Rome then proceeds to a simple warning against those who keep the old theological terminology but give it a new meaning; emptying of their meaning such terms as " revelation," " faith," " immortality," " original sin," " the Cross of Christ," " humility," and " grace." It is on true doctrine alone that moral conduct ultimately rests. "Every attempt to dislodge moral teaching and moral conduct from the rock of faith, and to build them on the shifting sands of human regulations, sooner or later leads the individual and the community to moral destruction." And, with unwonted emphatic brevity, Pius XI says " the number of such fools, who to-day attempt to separate morality and religion, is legion."

As there is need for this recognition of God and His Church, so there must also be acknowledged that Natural Law " written by the finger of the Creator on the tables of men's hearts, which can be read there by sound reason, when sin and passion do not darken it." This is the law by which the morality of all man-made laws must be judged.

The concluding sections of this beautifully worded letter are addressed to Youth, to priests and religious, and to the faithful laity.

To Youth, Pius XI, " as the vicegerent of Him Who said to the young man of the gospel, ' If thou wilt enter into life keep the commandments '," says " By a thousand tongues to-day a gospel is preached in your ears that is not revealed by your Heavenly Father. A thousand pens write in the service of a sham Christianity." He praises the firm stand that endures despite bitter misunderstanding, suspicion, contempt and manifold injury in professional and social life. "Many an unknown soldier of Christ stands in your ranks who with heavy heart but head erect bears his lot and finds comfort solely in the thought of suffering reproach for the name of Jesus." As to the Hitler Youth—or State Youth as it is now called—in which all must be enrolled, Catholics have the obvious, inalienable right to demand that this obligatory organisation should be purged of all manifestations of a spirit hostile to Christianity and to the Church. These manifestations place Catholic parents in hopeless conflicts of conscience " since they cannot give to the State what is demanded in the name of the State, without robbing God of what belongs to God." The pope here touches the heart of the matter : " What We object to, and what We must object to, is the intentional systematically fomented opposition which is set up between these educational purposes and those of religion."

To the priests and religious Pius XI urges prayer for an increase of charity, charity which will enable them to forgive, if not to forget, the many undeserved offences against them, charity towards the erring and even towards the contemptuous.

To the faithful laity and to parents especially and to the members of the Catholic associations most of all, the pope sends words of praise and of encouragement. The future of the children's souls is the all-important matter. "Do not forget this : from the bond of responsibility established by God that binds you to your children, no earthly power can loose you." None of the present oppressors who pretend to free parents from their duty in this will be able to answer for the parents to the Eternal Judge. In words that leave no room for even a shadow of doubt the pope describes the issue. " When the attempt is made to desecrate the tabernacle of a child's soul, sanctified in baptism, by an education that is hostile to Christ ; when from this living temple of God the eternal lamp of belief in Christ is cast out and in its place is brought the false light of a substitute faith that has nothing in common with the faith of the Cross, then the time of spiritual profanation of the temple is at hand, then it is the duty of every professing Christian to separate clearly his responsibility from that of the other side, to keep his conscience clear of any culpable co-operation in such dreadful work and corruption."

Above all, the letter concludes, Catholics in Germany must not despair. If they are ready for love of Christ to suffer and confess the faith, the physical violence of the persecutor will fail. The hour of triumph and the *Te deum* will surely come. God's arm is not shortened. "And for the persecutor and the oppressors too We pray, that the Father of all light and all mercy grant them an hour of enlightenment, such as was vouchsafed to Paul on the road to Damascus, for themselves and for all those who with them have erred and err."

(iv) Spain

As in Germany, so in Spain, the troubles of Catholicism belong to the last few years of the pontificate. But while in Germany the Church's oppressor is the sworn foe of Communism, in Spain, as in Russia and in Mexico, Communism is the chief inspiration of the oppressor.

Pius XI's first personal contact with Spain was the ceremonial visit of Alphonso XIII to the Vatican in November 1923. Standing before the pope, who received him surrounded by the College of Cardinals, with a ceremonial more magnificent than even the Vatican had known for generations, the young king—he was then but thirty-six—made a most eloquent dedication of his kingdom to the cause of Christ. He recalled all the ancient glories of Spain, the long centuries of warfare against Islam, the fight against the Reformation, Lepanto, the conversion of central and southern America. He spoke of the great Spanish saints, the mystics like St. Teresa and St. John of the Cross " who have taught our native tongue to speak the language of the angels." He reminded the pope that he had himself consecrated his people to the Sacred Heart of Jesus. Spain to-day remained at the service of the Church in any new crusade against the enemies of Christ.

Spain at that moment was in the first months of the "dictatorship" of Primo de Rivero, that lasted for seven years, the most prosperous and most peaceful years the country had known for more than a generation. How they ended, with a mysterious financial collapse engineered through the exchanges by forces outside Spain and—not unconnected with Primo de Rivero's suppression of seventy masonic lodges—how the "dictator" retired, how in April of the next year (1931) the king left Spain when it seemed that only at the cost of war could he keep his throne, and how a republic was set up, all this is well known. From the beginning that republic was a prey to intrigue and corruption. Like many another reform administration it owed its initial success to the votes of honest men seeking a millenium and confident that "liberals," "democrats" and "republicans," if they do but so style themselves, must be honest, disinterested and worthy of trust. And, like the French movement of 1789,[1] the Spanish Republic of 1931 owed much to the votes of the parish clergy.

Within a matter of months the anti-religious forces were at work and convents and churches were burnt down by the score. In December 1931, the new Constitution was adopted and it was seen at once that the new state, far from being indifferent to religion, was mightily concerned with its suppression. Henceforward Spain as a nation was to have no religion. Church and State were separated and the state would not recognise the existence of the Church as such. All the Church's legal rights disappeared. All its property was confiscated—the property painfully collected and built up in the last hundred years, for the last of the Church's mediæval wealth was confiscated as long ago as the great spoliation of 1831. Schools, colleges, hospitals, convents and monasteries, their furnishings, the very church plate, all this was confiscated. Restrictions were imposed on the teaching of religion in the schools, and the religious services in the churches were fettered by new regulations. The churches would indeed continue to be

---

[1] *Cf.* Louis Madelin, *La Révolution*, ch. i.

used " for divine service," although they were now " national property," but henceforth they would be taxed like other buildings.

Nor was the Church to acquire property for the future. Her rights in this respect were so limited that they ceased to be rights at all. Property could only be acquired " for the purpose of fulfilling religious duties " and it was left to the state to decide, in each case, how far this condition was fulfilled. Along with the property, the government confiscated the miserable doles on which the clergy lived, doles dignified by the name of salary and paid, as was expressly stated in the public documents that instituted the system, in part compensation for the wealth taken from the Church in former days.

The religious orders were to be subjected to a tyrannical *régime* of inspection and reports. Their members were specially taxed, forbidden to teach or to work in any way and, their property now all taken from them, they were deprived of all means of living. The Jesuits were expelled the country. The destruction of the religious orders—for that is what was accomplished—meant the end of what education the poor received and of the greatest part of the charitable assistance that came their way. " If the religious orders are distrusted," writes Professor Allison Peers, surely an authority on modern Spain, and not a Catholic, " it is not by the poor, the sick, the hungry."

An encyclical letter of 3 June, 1933, reviewed the whole situation and condemned the new laws.[1]

Meanwhile Spain was passing through " *El Triste Bienio* "—the two tragic years of 1932–1933, when successful jerrymandering tactics kept a minority of " intellectuals " in control. The general election of November 1933 saw them displaced and the Socialists, despite a campaign of terrorism, gained barely 50 seats out of the total 475. The Radicals numbered about 100 and the Coalition of the right something more than 100. All through 1934 political life staggered from one parliamentary crisis to another under a

[1] *Dilectissima Nobis*, A.A.S., XXV, 10 ; pp. 261–274.

succession of joint governments which all had in common the one feature that they never included any members of the Right. Finally, in October 1934, a coalition of Radicals and the Right was formed. Within a few weeks the revolution, threatened so frequently by the extreme Socialists, had broken out, and in the province of Asturias was soon master. Of the horrible cruelties that everywhere marked the success of the revolution this is not the place to say anything in detail. Besides, they are matter of history.

The incipient revolution was suppressed, but after the General Election of 1936 its partisans came into supreme power—thanks to a successful combination of violence during the elections and trickery after them. This, too, is matter of history.

What happened in the next five months—16 February to 18 July—was the releasing of all the prisoners from the gaols, a general distribution of arms to the mob of the cities, and a general orgy of arson, loot and murder of which Catholic Churches and convents, the clergy and the nuns were the principal (but not the only) victims. In that period, it was stated in the Cortes, 160 churches were destroyed and another 251 sacked, 269 people were murdered, another 1,278 wounded. Everywhere the police looked on passively, forbidden to interfere.

To those familiar with the history of similar things elsewhere it was not difficult to guess what all this portended. These events were the preparation for the institution of a Communist state on the classic Russian model. It was determined to forestall the Communists, and on 18 July a military revolt broke out, headed by a General Franco. Since that date civil war has held Spain in its grip and has come near to causing another general war in Europe.

With the fortunes of the wars in Spain as such, this book is not concerned, any more than it is concerned with the purely political issues between the different parties in Spain. We must yet say a word at least about the effect on Catholicism in Spain, the position taken up officially by the leaders of Spanish Catholicism, and, the sole feature that brings this matter into the book, the action of Pope Pius XI.

The first two points are dealt with at great length, soberly, judicially and with an unearthly calm, in the joint letter of the Spanish bishops to all the bishops of the Catholic world. From this letter some facts and statements may be usefully quoted—the more usefully in that the issue of the letter has been most carefully hushed up in the general press of this country [1]—for it shows how closely the local ecclesiastical authorities in Spain have carried out the policies of Pius XI throughout these critical years, the policy that Catholics as such do not form political parties and that the bishops and clergy carefully abstain from any political action at all.

The Spanish bishops estimate the number of Catholics who have lost their lives—not in battle but by execution or murder—for religious reasons, as 6,000 secular priests alone and 300,000 laity. More than 22,000 persons were murdered in Madrid alone during the first three months. Twenty thousand churches in all have been destroyed and plundered. They state emphatically that the Church " neither wished for this war nor provoked it. . . . She was vexed and persecuted before it broke out ; she has been the chief victim of the fury of one of the litigant parties ; and she has not ceased to work with her prayers, with her exhortations and her influence, in order to lessen its damages and to cut short the days of trial."

The Church remained loyal to the Republic despite the continual offences to the persons, property and rights of the Church. In the war " it appears clear from its beginnings that one of the belligerent parties was aiming directly

---

[1] The letter is dated 1 July, 1937, and was published, if not in full, with generous extracts running in some cases to two full pages of close type, in *The Catholic Herald*, *The Universe*, *The Catholic Times* and *The Tablet*, week ending 14 August, 1937. The first-named paper—20 August, 1937—listed the following papers which had never so much as referred to the letter : *The Times*, the *Daily Telegraph*, the *Daily Express* and the *Morning Post*. A translation of the whole letter has since been published by the Catholic Truth Society, London : *Joint Letter of the Spanish Bishops to the Bishops of the Whole World Concerning the War in Spain*, pp. 32.

at the abolition of the Catholic religion in Spain. . . . "
Nevertheless the bishops are not partisans. " We have not
tied ourselves to anybody—persons, powers or institutions
—even though we thank for their protection those who
have been able to preserve us from the enemy who wished
to ruin us."

What brought on the war ? " The war has been
occasioned by the rashness, the mistakes, and may be the
malice and the cowardice, of those who could have avoided
it by governing the nation with justice. . . . " Too often
was public authority, in the last few years, seen to succumb
to the strength of hidden powers which controlled its
functions."

The government, after the elections of 1936, formed a
political machine that was in conflict with the will of the
majority of the nation. Russian propaganda, meanwhile,
was allowed a free hand in the cinema, the theatre, the press.
Spain, all Spain, was rapidly sliding into that dreadful state
of anarchy which still obtains wherever the government
has maintained its hold.

The military revolt of July 1936 merely anticipated a
Communist transformation of the country. The bishops
quote " a leading anarchist " to this effect, who, broad-
casting in January 1937, stated : " The truth is none other
than that the military have stolen a march on us to prevent
our unchaining the revolution." Spain had to face the
alternative, either to perish in the definite assault of
destructive Communism, already prepared and decreed, or
to attempt a titanic effort of resistance.

The bishops state the common teaching as to the conditions required before a rebellion can be lawfully begun,
they cite all the facts and they justify the act of insurrection.
" The civic-military revolt was in its origin a national
movement of defence of the fundamental principles of every
civilised society." In the triumph of this movement lies
Spain's only hope of survival.

The atrocities are summarily described, the murders, the
outrages on women, the violation of the very tombs, the

wanton destruction of libraries and works of art. It is pointed out that " Long Live Russia " was the cry to which this was done, and that " mural inscriptions " told the same tale of Russian influence. Above all the revolution is an anti-Christian thing.

Even so the bishops decline to be political partisans, or to give an unqualified sanction to the Nationalist movement in whatever it proposes to do or shall in the future turn to doing. " The Church . . . feels herself now protected by a power which until now has guaranteed the fundamental principles of all society, without any consideration of political tendency. As regards the future we cannot tell what will happen. Nevertheless, we affirm that the war has not been undertaken in order to build up an autocratic state on a humiliated nation. . . . We would be the first to regret that the irresponsible autocracy of a parliament should be replaced by the yet more terrible power of a dictatorship, without roots in the nation. . . . It would be a mistake to interrupt the spiritual orientation of the country, and it is not probable that the mistake will be made."

I make no apology for the length of these extracts, even in a book that has already grown beyond the limits to which a book of this simple sort should go. The letter of the Spanish bishops coming so late in the pontificate of Pius XI is magnificent testimony to the acceptance of the policies first preached in *Ubi Arcano Dei* and preached unceasingly ever since. It is wonderful evidence how the spirit of this pope is working through the Church, evidence of the fruits it must bring if only Catholics everywhere will make it their own.

On 14 September, 1936, Pius XI received in audience some 500 refugees from Spain, bishops, priests, nuns and layfolk. He spoke [1] in moving terms of the admiration the whole Catholic world feels for the heroism of these thousands of modern martyrs and confessors, and of the readiness of all of them to offer what they had suffered in

[1] *The Pope on the Spanish Terror*, pp. 20, Catholic Truth Society, London.

reparation for the crimes and the blasphemies of their tormentors. Once again the pope turned to the first source of all this wickedness, " the absurd and disastrous ideologies " of Atheistic Communism and described the terrible scene in Spain as " a school in which the most serious lessons are being taught to Europe and the whole world." It is, yet once again, made evident to all who have minds to think, that the one real obstacle to the success of Communism is " Christian teaching, and the consistent practice of Christian living as these are enjoined by the Catholic Religion and the Catholic Church." What the world stands most in need of is full freedom for the Church to pursue its divine mission, and what the Church most needs is a generation of Catholics who live the Catholic ideal to the full in all the activities of their life, in their public life and career as in their private life. " There will always be, of course, the fearful possibilities of negligence, of inertia, of resistance, of opposition, to all of which free will exposes man," says the pope, touching here—in the fact of man's wrong use of his free will—on one of the main sources of what failures mark the long history of the Catholic Church. But the Church is in no way to blame for failures that arise in this way. " How many sad happenings find here their explanation and their source, not only without any fault on the part of the Church and the Catholic Religion, but rather in full and constant opposition to, and contradiction of, all that the Church teaches and tries, by all the means in her power, to have worked out in practice, that is in lives lived in Christian fashion."

The pope then blesses all those who are striving to defend " the rights and honour of God and of Religion, which is to say the rights and dignity of conscience, the primary condition and the most solid of all foundations for human and civic welfare." This defence is no easy task, for defence is a thing that has to be kept within certain defined limits or it ceases to be a just defence. " Also intentions less pure, selfish interests and mere party feeling may just as easily enter into, cloud and change the morality of what is being done and the responsibility for it." Pius XI is grateful to all those who have undertaken this difficult work.

Finally he has a message for the Catholics who are now leagued with God's enemies. They are still his children, and the pope, since his love for them and his compassion cannot otherwise reach them, prays that God will change their hearts.

CONCLUSION

WHAT will be the place of Pius XI in history ? Not for another generation and more can that question be answered in any detail. One of the great tests of a long-lived pope is the history of his successors, for it is from his chosen assistants, the counsellors whom he has made cardinals, that some of these will come. It is certainly safe to say that his pontificate will stand out as amongst the most important of the last three hundred years. There is not about the action of Pius XI that classic brilliance which distinguished Leo XIII, but as ruler of the universal Church Leo alone, of all the popes since Innocent XI,[1] is in the same category with him. The reign of Pius XI has been filled with events, and charged with papal initiative. Not since the days when the monastic popes of the Hildebrandine Reformation toured Europe to make their policies known and to secure their execution, has the ordinary Catholic of the rank and file been in such close continuous contact with the mind of the reigning pope. Pius XI has taken the whole Church into his confidence. He has spoken to it month by month, thought aloud for its benefit, one may say, and through nearly sixteen years he has displayed an interest in all that touches the life of every one of his children that is new in its obvious warmheartedness. When we consider the initiative, the courageous readiness to experiment, the immense activity and the vigorous personal action manifested in the whole life of the Church and remember that all this is, in the main, a constructional activity, we run little risk in suggesting that the verdict of history will place Pius XI among the very greatest of his predecessors, the peer of those whom he has himself styled " the glorious popes of the Counter-Reformation." His reign will mark

[1] 1676–1689.

a definite turning point in the development of Catholicism, and the main reason for the change will be his throwing open to the laity all that field of activity to which their vocation as Catholics entitles, and indeed obliges, them.

All this immense activity has its roots in prayer and contemplation. Not a letter, not a direction, has come from Pius XI that fails to stress the truth that the first care of the Catholic, and his last, must be prayer, union with God, the cultivation of his spiritual life. There are no better words with which to close this study of his life, no words which more truly express the heart of it all, than his own to the monks of the various Charterhouses : " We ourselves bear the Carthusian monks no less good will [than Our predecessors] nor are We less desirous that so valuable an institution should spread and increase. For if ever it was needful that there should be anchorites of that sort in the Church of God it is most especially expedient nowadays . . . they who assiduously fulfil the duty of prayer and penance contribute much more to the increase of the Church and the welfare of mankind than those who labour in tilling the Master's field." [1]

[1] Apostolic Constitution *Umbratilem*, 8 July, 1924 ; translation *The Power of Contemplation*, published by Burns, Oates and Washbourne, London, 1933 ; *cf.* also the Apostolic Letter, *Monachorum Vita*, 26 January, 1925, to the Reformed Cistercian Order.

OFFICIAL PONTIFICAL DOCUMENTS
USED AND REFERRED TO IN THE TEXT.[1]

[1] The list is arranged according to the alphabetical order of the titles. The capital letter indicates the class to which the document belongs: Apostolic Constitution (A.C.); Apostolic Letter (A.L.); Autograph Letter (Au.); Decretal Letter (D.); Encyclical Letter (E.); Letter (L.); and Motu Proprio (M.P.).